Ancient Thought:
Plato and Aristotle

ARISTOTLE

PLATO

Ancient Thought

PLATO &
ARISTOTLE

MONUMENTS OF WESTERN THOUGHT

Edited by **Norman F. Cantor** and **Peter L. Klein,** Brandeis University

BLAISDELL PUBLISHING COMPANY
A Division of Ginn and Company

Waltham, Massachusetts | Toronto | London

FOREWORD

The basis of a university education is an understanding of the great
writings that have shaped Western civilization. The aim of this twelve-
volume series is to make these doctrines of Western thought available
to the student in the most convenient and readily comprehensible form.
Each volume presents carefully selected texts by the two major thinkers
of a particular historical period. In choosing the texts, the entire works
of each thinker have been drawn upon, and passages from both familiar
and unfamiliar writings are presented to bring the reader to an
understanding of the central thought of the author. Following the
selections are commentaries by leading modern scholars on the works
studied. Many of these statements are drawn from books which are
available only in the very best libraries. Again, these modern commentaries are carefully edited to present the main points as succinctly as
possible. The first two chapters of each volume delineate the relevant
historical context and biographical information and suggest the main
outlines of the two thinkers' arguments, thus providing a framework
for the student's own analysis of the texts. The source texts are followed
by study guide questions which challenge the student's understanding
of the arguments he has been reading and force him to go back and
analyze the texts again. These study guides will also serve as a basis
for class discussion. The modern commentaries are similarly followed
by study guides, requiring the student to consider the merits of the
authors' critiques.

We believe that the richness of the material selected and the peda-
gogical principles that have determined the organization of each volume
will enable the student to carry away from his study a sophisticated
understanding of the imperishable ideas the two great thinkers have
propounded. The student who studies all twelve volumes will have
an excellent basis for comprehending the fundamental thought of
Western civilization.

N. F. C.
P. L. K.

CONTENTS

Ancient Thought:
Plato and Aristotle

1
THE HISTORICAL CONTEXT

Primitive, violent, and unstable, civilization emerged in the Near East, chiefly in Egypt, Mesopotamia, and South Asia. Then, it spread West to the islands of the Aegean Sea and settled in the Balkan Peninsula. Living under marginal conditions, each generation of ancient man was, as Homer said, "like the generation of leaves." Yet, civilization outlived man's poverty and death. And, periodically, independent but analogous cultural traditions flourished—first in Egypt and Babylonia in the third millennium B.C.; in Egypt, Asia Minor, and part of Greece in the second millennium; in Assyria, Babylonia, and Persia between the eighth and sixth centuries B.C.; and finally in Greece from the sixth to the fourth century B.C.

In Greece, however, Near Eastern civilization underwent a unique and rapid transformation. Not only did the Greeks fashion new forms of intellectual and artistic expression—tragedy, history, and philosophy —but they provided an entirely new set of intellectual categories through which the world could be viewed and judged. And, unlike previous civilization, Greek civilization was imitated and reproduced throughout the Mediterranean and perpetuated in Western civilization. Thus, Western philosophy, originating in Greece before the fifth century B.C. and perfected by Plato and Aristotle less than two centuries later, represents to the present day a fairly continuous and an essentially unaltered tradition.

Modern scholarship has long sought to solve the question of why Western philosophy and Western civilization should have emerged in Greece. Two interpretations, although by and large unsatisfactory, prevail. On the one hand, historians educated in Victorian and post-Victorian England explain this development in terms of the "Greek rational genius." Attracted by the literary and artistic achievements of Athens and traduced by her rational and urbane philosophy, they fail to notice the violence and irrationality also characteristic of Greece. H. D. F. Kitto (*The Greeks*), for instance, explains the origin of Greek art and philosophy by attributing an innate tidiness to the Greek mind.

1

On the other hand, beginning in the 1920's, a new group of historians, conditioned to violence and irrationality, began to minimize the Greek rational genius and to emphasize the Oriental origin of Western civilization. Thus, historians of philosophy such as C. M. Cornford (*Principium Sapientiae*) dwell on the irrational in Greek thought, rather than the rational, tracing the origin of Greek philosophy from the Oriental seer-prophets.

Contemporary historians, dissatisfied with both interpretations, are again evaluating the Greek experience. Although no new theory has yet emerged, the work of two scholars, Claude Levi-Strauss (*The Savage Mind*) and Marshall McLuhan (*Guttenburg Galaxy*), both writing in fields far removed from Greek civilization, might be helpful in formulating one. Levi-Strauss, an anthropologist, maintains that different types of society can be most meaningfully distinguished by the kind of classification system each uses. A classification system comprises the intellectual categories by which a society attempts to explain or make sense of the world in which it lives. McLuhan, a communication theorist, maintains that the media through which a society communicates shape the society's patterns of thought and life. Thus, a change in media results in a fundamental change in life and thought.

Using the theories of Levi-Strauss and McLuhan, we might speculate that Greek philosophy originated in the following way: In an attempt to come to terms with the categories and patterns of thought created by the introduction and use of a written, phonetic language, the Greeks gave a new form and, consequently, a new nature to the older classification system. The Greeks did not invent philosophy or reason. Numerous other peoples in the Near East had tried to make sense of the world, but the Greeks invented the tradition of explaining the world in terms of the problems and patterns of thought associated with the use of a written, phonetic language. Greek philosophy, in contrast to other forms of Near Eastern speculation, recognized a plurality of individual interpretations, employed a system of representation—for example, the way the word "chair" represents its object—which facilitated the development of deductive logic and geometry, and expressed its conclusions in terms of the concepts "being" and "cause." Not only can each of these characteristics be explained by the use of a written, phonetic language, but the Greeks themselves observed the intimate relationship between language and philosophy. A fundamental principle of Greek philosophy is that language mirrors reality. Thus, Plato explains the notion of "form" or "essence" as a definition; and Aristotle asserts that being or substance is that which can never be predicated of another subject.

Language alone, however, cannot account for the philosophy of Plato and Aristotle. If it is true that language played a primary role in the formation of Greek philosophy, its adaptation and use can be understood only in terms of the unique characteristics of Greek society— the mode of social and political organization called a "*polis*," the system of individual and regional economic exploitation, and the ethical ideals and standards, which developed along with it.

The origin of the *polis* is obscured by meager evidence and unreliable myths. Some historians have attributed its origin to the narrow valleys and formidable mountains of the Peloponnese; but this is, no doubt, a simplification. Surely, provincialism, and the *polis*, also originated from the primitive methods of land communication, the general impotence of rival *poleis*—and the relative balance of power among them—and the generally chaotic and unstable texture of life.

Three distinct types of *polis*, the aristocratic, the oligarchic, and the democratic, each distinguished by a particular hierarchy of power and standard of life, emerged in Greece as a modification of the society described in the Homeric poems, the *Iliad* and the *Odyssey*. Although composed between the tenth and eighth centuries B.C. and containing several anachronisms, the poems faithfully describe a twelfth-century society. The fundamental condition of this society was warfare—a condition which shaped the institutions and ideals of the people. Political power resided exclusively in the aristocratic warriors, one of whom was king and presided in war and peace. Beneath the aristocracy came the general population, divided from one another by occupation, place of residence, and social position. Finally, there were slaves, typical of this bellicose society. In addition to political power, virtue (*arete*) resided exclusively in the aristocratic warrior class and entailed wise counsel and courageous conduct. This emphasis on individual excellence was unique in the Mediterranean and Near Eastern world and must be considered a fundamental factor in the development of Greek civilization.

Changing conditions of life in the Mediterranean altered the character of Homeric society; the oligarchic *polis* first emerged in the Eastern Greek settlements of Asia Minor, primarily as a function of increased prosperity. Beginning at the end of the second millennium and continuing periodically, large waves of immigrants left the Greek peninsula. Initially driven out by vast folk migrations from the North and later by economic and political discontent on the mainland, they settled first on the islands of the Aegean and then on the coast of Asia Minor. By the eighth century B.C., Eastern Greece was involved in the growing trade and commerce stimulated by the vast and prosperous Persian empire. As a consequence of prosperity, new cities replaced rural villages as focal points of life; and a new aristocracy, based on wealth, grew up beside the old warrior-class. Seeking a more meaningful system of values, the new aristocracy opposed the older tradition of *arete* with a new ethic based on the principles of justice and law. This ethic initially found favor among the oligarchs because they were incompetent as warriors, and it applied only to the wealthy few; yet the creation of an urban community governed by law and sanctioned by justice provided the context for the first philosophical disputes. In the single surviving fragment of Anaximander, who is reputed to be the first speculator on nature to write in prose, the concept of "justice" plays a primary role. Similarly, Heraclitus, another Ionian thinker, inaugurated the tradition of solving problems by reference to laws of nature.

The three foundations of the democratic *polis* were extensive economic exploitation, a system of law and justice which protected individual rights, and a government of direct participation and selection by lot. The development of the democratic *polis* from the oligarchic, however, was neither inevitable nor direct. On the mainland, the *polis* developed in two distinct ways: in a democratic way in Athens, and in an aristocratic way (similar to the old Homeric society) in Sparta. Sparta's *polis* limited the king's power—as it increased the power of the aristocratic families, consolidated government into a single center, and fashioned a remarkable constitution, it was organized along strict military lines and idealized the Homeric *arete*. Similarly, the increased interest in law did not lead directly to a wider application of law. For example, in the sixth century, when the small landowners of Athens, suffering under severe economic exploitation, sought protection under the law, their cause went unaided except when aid proved profitable for some powerful party. Under the guise of reform, the rival aristocrats and oligarchs sought to solidify their power. Indirectly, these reforms, by breaking down the old clan structure, contributed to the development of democracy.

Athenian democracy had its origin in the sea; it required the threat of foreign invasion by Persia, beginning in 492 B.C., and the subsequent formation of the Delian League, to precipitate incorporation of lower classes into the Athenian power structure. When the Athenians decided to resist the Persian invasion by concentrating their resources in the navy, the urban poor enjoyed for the first time a position of power. An anonymous fifth-century pamphleteer, the "Old Oligarch," said, "It is the 'people' which drives the boats and gives the state its power." As a consequence of the changing conditions, politicians, foremost among them Pericles, courted the favor of the city poor and formed a new power base by enfranchising them and including them within the officers of the community. Yet, full democratic participation among the male citizens, who actually numbered less than 20 per cent of the population, could not develop unless an extensive system of economic exploitation also developed, for the economic demands of an urban democracy far exceeded the economic resources of Athens. The formation of the Delian League after the second Persian invasion (ostensibly to rid the Aegean of the enemy), and its transformation into a regional system of economic exploitation, provided sufficient resources for Athens to be able to afford democracy. By charging smaller *poleis* for naval protection, Athens acquired a profitable source of income.

Within this urban, democratic *polis* of Athens, unique and rapid cultural transformation took place. Yet, political and social discontent kept pace with the cultural advances shown in the tragedies of Aeschylus, Sophocles, and Euripides, the comedies of Aristophanes, and the sculptures of Phidias. Economic instability and greed for power led to internal factions and external wars. The strained atmosphere of the Peloponnesian War, which lasted from 431 to 404 B.C., fostered a breakdown of morals and encouraged a reactionary movement which tried to preserve the ancient customs at all costs. The ethical standards which had first been forwarded by the oligarchs were derived from the notions of law and justice and grounded in the *polis*. When the *polis*, as a way of life, crumbled, the standards went with it.

"The Owl of Minerva spreads its wings only with the falling of dusk," observed the philosopher Hegel; and nowhere is his dictum more applicable than in the present case. While Greek civilization burned on the pyre of the Peloponnesian War, the classical age of philosophy rose from its ashes. The first significant Athenian philosopher was Socrates who, confronted with the demonstrable instability of the *polis* system, replaced custom with knowledge as the ultimate criterion of conduct. Official Athens, however, could not tolerate his eccentric behavior and constant criticism. Socrates was brought before the courts and accused of corrupting the youth and subverting the state religion. The charges were arbitrary and ill-founded: but his death was inevitable. Socrates had become the scapegoat for a frustrated and war-weary Athens. Plato, Socrates' disciple, perpetuated his master's faith in the virtue of knowledge and the value of the *polis;* but having witnessed Socrates' trial and execution, he did not share his teacher's confidence in democracy. Aristotle followed within a generation after Plato. His ideal society remained the *polis*. Man is, he said, a *polis*-being, but his analysis was dry and detached. Life had already passed from the *polis*.

Although the history of Greek philosophy before Socrates can be traced for nearly 150 years, the details and significance of its events are difficult to comprehend. In the field of pre-Socratic philosophy more secondary material has been written about less primary material than in almost any other field. In spite of their effort, contemporary historians have not improved upon Aristotle's interpretation—that philosophy began with Thales, a shrewd scientist and business man, who tried to explain the cosmos in terms of one material principle, water; and that after Thales, men began to uncover other principles. One modern interpretation by J. Burnet (*Early Greek Philosophy*) preserves the major lines of this approach. On the other hand, the only other significant modern interpretation, the one by Cornford, has a very Platonic flavor.

The influence of Plato and Aristotle on contemporary historiography is not accidental: it is the central issue in the history of pre-Socratic philosophy. There are actually two problems involved: the date of composition of the early records and the validity of these records as historical documents. Practically everything we know about early Greek philosophy was preserved either by Aristotle, by a student of Aristotle, or by a commentator using the information of Aristotle but writing between two and nine centuries after his death. Whatever else we know about the subject comes from Plato or a disciple of Plato. Thus, on the one hand, the time between the actual composition of pre-Socratic philosophy and the record we have of its existence varies between 100 and 1,000 years; on the other hand, all of this information has been filtered through Platonic and Aristotelian categories, and both Plato and Aristotle approached their predecessors as philosophers, not as historians. Aristotle recorded the statements of earlier philosophers for a methodological reason; he began his inquiry into a problem by listing what those who preceded him had to say about the problem. Plato had a similar but less clearly defined interest in his predecessors. In either case, the unique characteristics of the earlier philosophy was obscured by later developments.

Without trying to isolate the exact course of pre-Socratic thought, it is possible to distinguish four distinct approaches to the problems of philosophy. First, the Pythagoreans believed that philosophy was a way of life in which knowledge of the secret properties of numbers brought one into harmony with the universe. Second, Parmenides believed that the nature of the cosmos was one and unchanging. Third, Heraclitus and the materialists, Democrates and Empedocles, believed that the world was changing and diverse. Fourth, Protagoras and the Sophists were relativists and remained skeptical about the possibility of any kind of knowledge.

Viewed in this way, the philosophy of Plato was an attempt to reconcile the philosophies of Parmenides and Heraclitus, restricting the former to intelligible things and the latter to sensible things, and to make use of the Pythagorean mathematics to express the unchanging character of being. Aristotle, on the other hand, tried to reconcile the doctrines of Plato with those of the materialists.

2

AN INTRODUCTION TO THE LIFE AND WORK OF PLATO AND ARISTOTLE

An Introduction to Plato

Immediately after the death of Socrates, Plato fled Athens; however, within several months, he returned home and renewed his career in philosophy. Along with a desire to eulogize Socrates, to carry forward, to explicate, and to expand his master's work, foremost in Plato's mind was the ambition to provide a new rational foundation for human conduct and the organization of society. Although Plato's course of action was inspired by the death of Socrates, its origin lay in his frustrated dreams of social reform. Like other young aristocrats of the day, Plato planned to enter politics as soon as he came of age. In the last decade of the fifth century, when the Athenian democracy was overthrown by an oligarchy partially composed of Plato's family and friends, his opportunity materialized. However, after he viewed at first hand the sordid and vicious practices of Athenian politics, his youthful idealism quickly soured; and when the oligarchy fell and democracy was restored, Plato considered the event merely as an opportunity for those in power to perpetrate new forms of abuse and aggrandizement. Socrates' death at the hands of the democracy confirmed and intensified his feelings. Thus, Plato abandoned direct political and social reform and devoted his attention to the theoretical construction of an ideal state. As Plato himself explains:

> Now as I considered these matters, as well as the sort of men who were active in politics, and the laws and the customs, the more I examined them and the more I advanced in years, the harder it appeared to me to administer the government correctly. For one thing, nothing could be done without friends and loyal companions, and such men were not easy to find ready at hand, since our city was no longer administered according to the standards and practices of our fathers. Neither could such men be created afresh with any facility. Furthermore the written law and the customs were being corrupted at an astounding rate. The result was that I, who had at first been full of eagerness for a public career, as I gazed upon

the whirlpool of public life and saw the incessant movement of shifting currents, at last felt dizzy, and, while I did not cease to consider means of improving this particular situation and indeed of reforming the whole constitution, yet, in regard to action, I kept waiting for favorable moments, and finally saw clearly in regard to all states now existing that without exception their system of government is bad. Their constitutions are almost beyond redemption except through some miraculous plan accompanied by good luck. Hence I was forced to say in praise of the correct philosophy that it affords a vantage point from which we can discern in all cases what is just for communities and for individuals, and that accordingly the human race will not see better days until either the stock of those who rightly and genuinely follow philosophy acquire political authority, or else the class who have political control be led by some dispensation of providence to become real philosophers.

Plato founded a school of philosophy called the Academy in 388 B.C., and, until his death in 348 B.C., he remained director of its researches. From this vantage point, he attempted to reform society indirectly by writing a series of entertaining and educational dialogues. Serving the dual function of pedagogy and propaganda, these works re-created the Socratic method of questioning and answering in the form of written, dramatic dialogues which advertised the Academy and its methods while exposing the poverty of contemporary thought and practice. In addition to the Socratic dialogues, Plato also wrote a number of other works which, although still written in dialogue form, possessed neither the artistic nor the propaganda value of the earlier works. Generally, these dialogues pursued questions and explored methods which fell beyond the limits of Socratic philosophy. The former, the Socratic-Platonic dialogues, functioned as catalysts, exposing philosophical difficulties and stimulating discussions; they delineated the road to truth but did not presuppose a fully formulated doctrine of the truth. The latter, the doctrinal-critical dialogues, began with the presupposition of a systematic and fully developed philosophy and tried to clarify its dogmas through self-criticism and to expand its scope of comprehension through examination of topics not previously covered. Collectively the dialogues of Plato represent his extant works; nowhere in his written work is there a systematic account of his philosophy.

Besides writing dialogues, Plato annually delivered lecture courses at the Academy, and it was in these lectures that he developed his fundamental doctrines. The contents of these lectures, however, were closely guarded secrets and never organized for public presentation. Mystery was a fundamental characteristic of Plato's school and expressed the influence on his thought by the Pythagoreans, who viewed philosophy as a way of life in which the philosopher participated in the harmony of the cosmos. In spite of this veil of secrecy, we do have an account of Plato's lectures from Aristotle, who was a dropout of the Academy after being Plato's student for twenty years. According to

Aristotle, Plato's lectures primarily dealt with his doctrine of being and the doctrines of his predecessors. Two fundamental characteristics of this doctrine were its reliance on the concepts of geometry and its insistence on the priority of dualistic principles, the One and the Many.

The metaphysical propositions of all philosophers are conditioned and limited by the experience of their age. Since each age differs in its experience, it is difficult for succeeding generations to appreciate the conclusions of an earlier age; however, the methodology and style of thought of a philosopher usually have a more direct and enduring influence. Plato remains relevant to the modern age because he originated a methodology and a style of thought which became the fountainhead for Western mysticism and rationalism.

The Socratic-Platonic dialogues are those in which Plato delivers his eulogy of Socrates, elucidates his master's method and teaching, and provides the solution for the central Socratic problem, "How should one best live the life that is his?" In general, it is easy to distinguish the philosophy of Socrates from that of Plato. The former was exclusively concerned with man and ethical knowledge and remained agnostic about all other knowledge; the latter considered man and ethical knowledge in their cosmic context and made a definite commitment to metaphysical knowledge. However, it is impossible to isolate passages which are either exclusively Platonic or exclusively Socratic. The reason for this is that Socrates left no written account of his own thought. Thus, the *Apology*, *Crito*, and *Phaedo*, which ostensibly describe the trial and death of Socrates, must also be considered sources of Platonic thought.

In general, the Socratic-Platonic works are characterized by their dialogue form, their orientation towards ethical problems, and their goal of ethical knowledge. Platonic dialogue is both a literary form and a philosophical method. As a philosophical method, dialogue entails an interchange between two protagonists who seek to resolve a question by ascertaining the definition or essential nature of fundamental concepts. As a literary form, dialogue is a dramatic work concerning a philosophical problem. The philosophical starting point of the Socratic-Platonic dialogue is the examination of man; the end, the resolution of the primary question, is seldom achieved within the dramatic context of the dialogue. And the object of the Socratic-Platonic dialogue is both dramatic and philosophic, varying from dialogue to dialogue.

Although not among the earliest written dialogues, the *Meno* provides a good starting point for the study of Plato and is an excellent example of a Socratic-Platonic work. Dramatically, it concerns the confrontation of Socrates with two political types, the aristocrat and the demagogue, both of whom try to come to grips with Socrates over the question, "Is virtue teachable?" Both of these political types were characters who would have been easily recognized by any Athenian who heard the dialogue; thus, the conclusion of this dialogue, like most Socratic-Platonic works, is ironical. Meno, who is an aristocrat and an infamous embezzler, cannot understand what virtue is; and Anytus, an amoral politician, defends contemporary virtue. Philosophically, the dialogue also exhibits several typical Socratic-Platonic characteristics. First, there is the claim that it is necessary to know what a thing is before it can be determined whether that thing possesses a particular property. In other words, the universal is more intelligible and is prior to the individual. Second, Plato defends the Socratic position that virtue is knowledge with the famous slave-boy demonstration, which proves that it is possible to come to know something. Third, in order to account for the slave boy's knowledge, Plato introduces a theory of knowledge called "reminiscence" or "recollection." This theory postulates that we possess innate ideas which are implanted in our minds before birth and that we acquire knowledge by recalling these ideas. And, fourth, the existence of innate ideas demands a theory of the immortality of the soul.

The *Republic* is the dividing line between the Socratic-Platonic dialogues and the critical-doctrinal dialogues. On the one hand, it is the culmination of the Socratic approach which sought a new foundation for virtue and a new rationale for the structure of society. Just as in the Socratic-Platonic dialogues, the analysis of the *Republic* centers on an ethical question, "What is justice?" and begins by examining the nature of man. On the other hand, the solution to this problem demands a new methodology and a more comprehensive commitment. To see justice in the individual, Plato draws a parallel between the individual and the state: "the state is the individual writ large." The ideal state, a three-tiered hierarchy based on the worth and desires of three distinct classes, is delineated and justice is found to reside in the condition of each class doing its proper job. Similarly, the right order of the soul is the hierarchy of reason, appetite, and passion; and justice in the individual is the condition of each performing its proper function. The possibility of the existence of the just state or the just man depends on the condition that the philosopher will be king in the state and that reason will reign in the soul. The philosopher and reason provide the new foundation for society and man because they reflect the image of reality. In fact, the ultimate condition of morality and the new foundation for the *polis* are one and the same. Behind the philosopher and behind reason stands unchanging reality and knowledge; knowledge and reality can only be reached through an intensive system of education culminating in the study of dialectic. In the *Republic*, dialectic is no longer simply equated with philosophical dialogue; rather, it is a method designed to isolate the ultimate constituents of a concept and to elucidate the totality of its implications.

The *Republic* provides the bridge to the doctrinal and critical works of Plato; all of these are devoted to the explication of the theory of reality presented in the *Republic* and of the problems associated with it. The fundamental feature of this theory is the following: the universe is a hierarchy of being, value, and knowledge—ranging from the objects of art, the most corrupt, intransient, and unknowable things, to the objects of philosophy, which possess truth, beauty, and knowledge—which can only be understood and appreciated in terms of forms or essences. The forms, universal and independent of experience, are the objects of philosophy and can only be reached through the method of dialectic.

Platonism has remained a living philosophy to the present day. Alfred North Whitehead, one of the most significant philosophers of this century, considered himself a Platonist and regarded the entire history of Western philosophy merely as a footnote to the writings of Plato. Whitehead's view is not pure fantasy, for the history of Platonism, like the history of all ideas, is characterized by a sequence of differing interpretations. Each of these interpretations might have had a legitimate claim to Plato, but not all of them could live together comfortably. Thus, mystics and rationalists and scientists and poets have all found intellectual inspiration in Plato. Augustine, Dante, Descartes, Rousseau, Hegel, and Nietzsche, to name a few, were all profoundly influenced by Plato and perpetuated his ideas. Perhaps the most important Platonist was Aristotle, for practically every significant Western philosopher who did not find inspiration in Plato followed the guidance of Aristotle.

An Introduction to Aristotle

Far from urban Athens, in the town of Stagira on the peninsula of Chalcidice, Aristotle grew up—as the son of a court physician to Amyntas II, King of Macedon. In later life both Aristotle's medical background and Macedonian connections proved significant, the former providing early training in empirical investigation and biological science, the latter leading to his appointment as tutor to Alexander the Great and causing his ultimate expulsion from Athens. In 368 B.C., at the age of 17, Aristotle was first sent to Athens, where he joined the Academy and remained Plato's student for 20 years until the master's death. Between 348 and 335 he spent several years in Asia Minor, collecting biological specimens and serving as Alexander's tutor. When Aristotle returned to Athens, he founded his own school, the Lyceum, and within the extraordinarily short period of twelve years he completed his entire philosophical corpus. When Alexander died in 323, the intense anti-Macedonian feeling in Athens exposed Aristotle to the fate of Socrates. He fled Athens, as he said, so that the Athenians would not sin twice against philosophy; and he died within a year.

Three fundamental characteristics distinguish Plato and Aristotle. First, each wrote for a different purpose and in a different style. Plato's dialogues were often propaganda pieces or short discourses on selected topics, indicating a correct method or a fallacious argument, but seldom did he systematically treat an entire problem. Aristotle, on the other hand, wrote as a man who, having studied and mastered the extant knowledge of the world, was trying to provide the principles and organization necessary for studying it systematically. And, unlike the elegant and witty dialogues of Plato, Aristotle's works are stark and humorless. Second, each began his inquiry from a different point. Plato banished particulars to a world of unintelligibility, while Aristotle asserted the primacy of the particular. Third, their positions on the crucial question of "being" were significantly different. Plato ascribed "being" (and "truth" and "beauty") to the world of universal and intelligible forms, that is, to the world of thought. Aristotle depicted thought and matter as two aspects united in the concrete particular, which was "being" in a primary sense.

In general, Aristotle's works are written either about a mode of thought or a form of science. Those about thought are collectively called the *Organon* and are concerned with two problems: the techniques of proof and the principles of proof. The first of these, the *Categories*, is concerned with simple terms considered under the ten most universal forms of speech. The second, *On Interpretation*, is concerned with pairs of terms combined in propositions which express truths and falsities. The *Prior Analytics* is concerned with inference, a series of syllogisms, which entails the combination of at least three terms to form an argument. The conditions relevant to the selection of true first principles which lead to scientific knowledge are treated in the *Posterior Analytics*; the condition relevant to the selection of principles which express opinions, in the *Topics*; and, lastly, the analysis of fallacious, but generally accepted, arguments based on opinion, in *On Sophistical Refutations*. Those works which deal with a science are distinguished into three kinds according to subject matter: physics, mathematics, and metaphysics. Since all three pursue knowledge, they are collectively called "theoretical sciences." There are also practical sciences and productive sciences—the former directed to action and conduct, the latter to the making of artificial things.

All of these works are bound together by a complex and systematic pattern of thought; each part amplifies every other part. This character of Aristotle's thought presents formidable problems for the introductory student unless he is aware of some of the principles which bind the works together. Therefore, we will consider three of the unifying concepts: "equivocals," "causation," and "substance."

Aristotle has been frequently criticized for being needlessly obscure in discussing his central concepts. The problem, however, does not lie in obscurity or in uncertainty, but, as Joseph Owens (*The Doctrine of Being in the Aristotelian Metaphysics*) pointed out, it lies in Aristotle's doctrine of equivocals. The opening lines of the *Categories* define "equivocal" as follows:

> Things are said to be named "equivocally" when, though they have a common name, the definition corresponding with the name differs for each. Thus, a real man and a figure in a picture can both lay claim to the name "animal"; yet these are equivocally so named, for, though they have a common name, the definition corresponding with the name differs for each. For should anyone define in what sense each is an animal, his definition in the one case will be appropriate to that case only.

Thus, equivocals are things which have one name in common, but different definitions insofar as they are denoted by that name. A model airplane and a real plane are related equivocally; so are "box" and "box" (when the former refers to a sport and the latter to a container) and a medical book and a medical nurse. In general, as Owens points out, there are three primary kinds of equivocation: by chance, by reference, and by analogy. "Box" and "box" are equivocals by chance, the airplanes by analogy, and the medical book and nurse by reference. Of the three, equivocals by reference are the most difficult and the most important. It must be noticed that the concepts of "cause" and "substance" which we will treat next are both equivocals by reference.

It is typical of Aristotle's method that he introduces a problem by indicating what his predecessors had to say on the subject. Thus, he views his contribution as the synthesis and resolution of all previous considerations of the subject. In the case of "cause," Aristotle felt that his predecessors, from Thales to Democrates, had tried to explain things in terms of their material elements or constituents. This he called the material cause. Others, from the Pythagoreans to Plato, tried to explain things in terms of their intelligible properties. This he called the formal cause. To these two, he added the efficient cause and the final cause; and he defined them all as follows:

> In one sense, then, that out of which a thing comes to be and which persists, is called "cause", e.g. the bronze statue, the silver of the bowl, and the genera of which the bronze and the silver are species.
> In another sense, the form or the archetype, i.e. the statement of the

essence, and its genera, are called "causes" (e.g. of the octave, the relation of 2:1, and generally number), and the parts in the definition.

Again, the primary source of the change or coming to rest; e.g. the man who gave advice is a cause, the father is cause of the child, and generally what makes of what is made and what causes change of what is changed.

Again, in the sense of end or "that for the sake of which" a thing is done, e.g. health is the cause of walking about. Why is he walking about? we say. To be healthy, and, having said that, we think we have assigned the cause. The same is true also of all the intermediate steps which are brought about through the action of something else as means towards the end, e.g. reproduction of the flesh, purging, drugs, or surgical instruments are means towards health. All these things are "for the sake of" the end, though they differ from one another in that some are activities, others instruments.

Ideally, the four causes are used by Aristotle to explain any thing or situation, although, in some cases, only some are accessible to investigation; in other cases, some are identical. Not only do the four causes provide a unity of explanation throughout all the treatises; they are themselves unified, in that "cause" is equivocal by reference to the primary notion of formal cause; and, further, within each general cause is a cluster of equivocal causes—for example, the essence and the genera in formal cause.

Like the notions of "cause" and "equivocation," the concept of "substance" underlies all of the Aristotelian treatises. And, as in the case of "cause," Aristotle views the problem in terms of what he considers its historical origin. In this case the controversy is between Democrates, who views all substance and being as if it could be explained by its material components, and Plato, who views all substance and being as if it could be explained in terms of universal forms or definitions. The unique character of Aristotle's solution is the manner in which he treats "substance" in different ways, in equivocal ways, depending upon which kind of treatise he is writing. Only in the *Metaphysics*, which alone has as its proper subject being or substance, does Aristotle delineate all of its senses. In the *Categories*, Aristotle provides the logical definition of substance as that of which all else is predicated, but which itself is not predicated of anything else. In the *Physics*, Aristotle gives the theory of the individual as a composite of form and matter. This theory is set forth in order to explain the possibility of change, the primary subject of physics. The three principles of change delineated are "substratum," "form," and "privation." In this context, however, form refers to both affections—for example, quantities, qualities, and so forth—and the substantial forms. When the form gained or lost is only an affection, the change is only qualified change or alteration; when the form gained or lost is a substantial form the change is unqualified, coming-to-be or passing-away. The importance of this distinction lies in sense in which "predication" is used. When Aristotle turns red from embarrassment, redness is predicated of Aristotle, whereas it was not before. When I die, humanness is no longer predicated of the heap of flesh and bones, whereas it was before. Since flesh and bones can pass away again, decompose, they too must be analyzed in terms of form and matter. If we follow this analysis, it points to the hierarchy which starts with prime matter, which underlies all form, and proceeds through the elements of fire, water, earth, and air; and of compounds of these, tissues, living things, and so forth—up to the superlunary elements. Since at each level of the hierarchy the kinds of entities we encounter are a composite of form and matter, with the form being predicated of the matter, it would follow that the ultimate subject of predication is matter, not individuals, and that matter is the primary instance of substance.

Viewed in another way, Aristotle does not seem ultimately to be providing a materialistic solution. In *On Generation and Corruption*, which deals with unqualified change, he maintains that there is a sharp difference between qualified and unqualified change, between modifications in things and generation or destruction, and that the difference resides in the fact that the forms involved in unqualified change indicate a "this"; that is, by virtue of these forms things are individual things which we can designate as "this" and can refer to as subjects of predication and discourse. In the *Metaphysics*, he asserts the converse of this point: matter by itself is not cut up into things; a particular heap of matter only becomes a thing by possessing a certain form. A substance then, for Aristotle, in the primary sense, is a unity of material components, these components being what they are only as part of the unity.

If Platonism is the foundation of all purely intellectual and mystical traditions in Western thought, Aristotelianism is the beginning of empiricism and what we would call scientific inquiry. For Aristotle, sense experience is not nonsense; sense data—the products of observation and experimentation—provide the raw material upon which the mind operates to derive general propositions about the nature of man, society, and the universe. For Plato, the way to truth is analysis of general concepts; for Aristotle, knowledge of reality is gained by examining sense experience so as to derive general propositions from this data. Systematic thought—logic—is necessary in this work; but we begin by observation and by collecting the data provided by our senses.

3
SELECTIONS FROM PLATO'S WORK

Meno

Meno begins with the question, How is virtue acquired? But, as in all Platonic dialogues, this initial question merely provides the occasion for raising more fundamental issues. Primarily, the Meno *is a comparison of methodologies: the first part of the dialogue examines the method of dialectic while the second employs the method of mathematics. The former leads to a discussion of "definition," "knowledge," and "soul"; the latter leads to a critique of Athenian society. The following selection presents the entire first part of the dialogue.*

MENO Can you tell me, Socrates, whether virtue is acquired by teaching or by practice; or if neither by teaching nor by practice, then whether it comes to man by nature, or in what other way?

SOCRATES O Meno, there was a time when the Thessalians were famous among the other Hellenes only for their riches and their riding; but now, if I am not mistaken, they are equally famous for their wisdom, especially at Larisa, which is the native city of your friend Aristippus. And this is Gorgias' doing; for when he came there, the flower of the Aleuadae, among them your admirer Aristippus, and the other chiefs of the Thessalians, fell in love with his wisdom. And he has taught you the habit of answering questions in a grand and bold style, which becomes those who know, and is the style in which he himself answers all comers; and any Hellene who likes may ask him anything. How different is our lot! my dear Meno. Here at Athens there is a dearth of the commodity, and all wisdom seems to have emigrated from us to you. I am certain that if you were to ask any Athenian whether virtue was natural or acquired, he would laugh in your face, and say: "Stranger, you have far too good an opinion of me, if you think that I can answer your question. For I literally do not know what virtue is, and much less whether it is acquired by teaching or not." And I myself, Meno, living

SOURCE: *The Dialogues of Plato,* translated by B. Jowett (3rd ed., Oxford: Clarendon Press, 1892), *2,* pp. 27–48.

as I do in this region of poverty, am as poor as the rest of the world; and I confess with shame that I know literally nothing about virtue; and when I do not know the "quid" of anything how can I know the "quale"? How, if I knew nothing at all of Meno, could I tell if he was fair, or the opposite of fair; rich and noble, or the reverse of rich and noble? Do you think that I could?

MEN. No, indeed. But are you in earnest, Socrates, in saying that you do not know what virtue is? And am I to carry back this report of you to Thessaly?

SOC. Not only that, my dear boy, but you may say further that I have never known of any one else who did, in my judgment.

MEN. Then you have never met Gorgias when he was at Athens?

SOC. Yes, I have.

MEN. And did you not think that he knew?

SOC. I have not a good memory, Meno, and therefore I cannot now tell what I thought of him at the time. And I dare say that he did know, and that you know what he said: please, therefore, to remind me of what he said; or, if you would rather, tell me your own view; for I suspect that you and he think much alike.

MEN. Very true.

SOC. Then as he is not here, never mind him, and do you tell me: By the gods, Meno, be generous, and tell me what you say that virtue is; for I shall be truly delighted to find that I have been mistaken, and that you and Gorgias do really have this knowledge; although I have been just saying that I have never found anybody who had.

MEN. There will be no difficulty, Socrates, in answering your question. Let us take first the virtue of a man—he should know how to administer the state, and in the administration of it to benefit his friends and harm his enemies; and he must also be careful not to suffer harm himself. A woman's virtue, if you wish to know about that, may also be easily described: her duty is to order her house, and keep what is indoors, and obey her husband. Every age, every condition of life, young or old, male or female, bond or free, has a different virtue: there are virtues numberless, and no lack of definitions of them; for virtue is relative to the actions and ages of each of us in all that we do. And the same may be said of vice, Socrates.

SOC. How fortunate I am, Meno! When I ask you for one virtue, you present me with a swarm of them, which are in your keeping. Suppose that I carry on the figure of the swarm, and ask of you, What is the nature of the bee? and you answer that there are many kinds of bees, and I reply: But do bees differ as bees, because there are many and different kinds of them; or are they not rather to be distinguished by some other quality, as for example beauty, size, or shape? How would you answer me?

MEN. I should answer that bees do not differ from one another, as bees.

SOC.   And if I went on to say: That is what I desire to know, Meno; tell me what is the quality in which they do not differ, but are all alike;—would you be able to answer?

MEN.   I should.

SOC.   And so of the virtues, however many and different they may be, they have all a common nature which makes them virtues; and on this he who would answer the question, "What is virtue?" would do well to have his eye fixed: Do you understand?

MEN.   I am beginning to understand; but I do not as yet take hold of the question as I could wish.

SOC.   When you say, Meno, that there is one virtue of a man, another of a woman, another of a child, and so on, does this apply only to virtue, or would you say the same of health, and size, and strength? Or, is the nature of health always the same, whether in man or woman?

MEN.   I should say that health is the same, both in man and woman.

SOC.   And is not this true of size and strength? If a woman is strong, she will be strong by reason of the same form and of the same strength subsisting in her which there is in the man. I mean to say that strength, as strength, whether of man or woman, is the same. Is there any difference?

MEN.   I think not.

SOC.   And will not virtue, as virtue, be the same, whether in a child or in a grown-up person, in a woman or in a man?

MEN.   I cannot help feeling, Socrates, that this case is different from the others.

SOC.   But why? Were you not saying that the virtue of a man was to order a state, and the virtue of a woman was to order a house?

MEN.   I did say so.

SOC.   And can either house or state or anything be well ordered without temperance and without justice?

MEN.   Certainly not.

SOC.   Then they who order a state or a house temperately or justly order them with temperance and justice?

MEN.   Certainly.

SOC.   Then both men and women, if they are to be good men and women, must have the same virtues of temperance and justice?

MEN.   True.

SOC.   And can either a young man or an elder one be good, if they are intemperate and unjust?

MEN.   They cannot.

SOC.   They must be temperate and just?

MEN.   Yes.

SOC.   Then all men are good in the same way, and by participation in the same virtues?

MEN.   Such is the inference.

SOC. And they surely would not have been good in the same way, unless their virtue had been the same?

MEN. They would not.

SOC. Then now that the sameness of all virtue has been proven, try and remember what you and Gorgias say that virtue is.

MEN. Will you have one definition of them all?

SOC. That is what I am seeking.

MEN. If you want to have one definition of them all, I know not what to say, but that virtue is the power of governing mankind.

SOC. And does this definition of virtue include all virtue? Is virtue the same in a child and in a slave, Meno? Can the child govern his father, or the slave his master; and would he who governed be any longer a slave?

MEN. I think not, Socrates.

SOC. No, indeed; there would be small reason in that. Yet once more, fair friend; according to you, virtue is "the power of governing;" but do you not add "justly and not unjustly"?

MEN. Yes, Socrates; I agree there; for justice is virtue.

SOC. Would you say "virtue," Meno, or "a virtue"?

MEN. What do you mean?

SOC. I mean as I might say about anything; that a round, for example, is "a figure" and not simply "figure," and I should adopt this mode of speaking, because there are other figures.

MEN. Quite right; and that is just what I am saying about virtue—that there are other virtues as well as justice.

SOC. What are they? tell me the names of them, as I would tell you the names of the other figures if you asked me.

MEN. Courage and temperance and wisdom and magnanimity are virtues; and there are many others.

SOC. Yes, Meno; and again we are in the same case: in searching after one virtue we have found many, though not in the same way as before; but we have been unable to find the common virtue which runs through them all.

MEN. Why, Socrates, even now I am not able to follow you in the attempt to get at one common notion of virtue as of other things.

SOC. No wonder; but I will try to get nearer if I can, for you know that all things have a common notion. Suppose now that some one asked you the question which I asked before: Meno, he would say, what is figure? And if you answered "roundness," he would reply to you, in my way of speaking, by asking whether you would say that roundness is "figure" or "a figure;" and you would answer "a figure."

MEN. Certainly.

SOC. And for this reason—that there are other figures?

MEN. Yes.

SOC.   And if he proceeded to ask, What other figures are there? you would have told him.

MEN.   I should.

SOC.   And if he similarly asked what colour is, and you answered whiteness, and the questioner rejoined, Would you say that whiteness is colour or a colour? you would reply, A colour, because there are other colours as well.

MEN.   I should.

SOC.   And if he had said, Tell me what they are?—you would have told him of other colours which are colours just as much as whiteness.

MEN.   Yes.

SOC.   And suppose that he were to pursue the matter in my way, he would say: Ever and anon we are landed in particulars, but this is not what I want; tell me then, since you call them by a common name, and say that they are all figures, even when opposed to one another, what is that common nature which you designate as figure—which contains straight as well as round, and is no more one than the other—that would be your mode of speaking?

MEN.   Yes.

SOC.   And in speaking thus, you do not mean to say that the round is round any more than straight, or the straight any more straight than round?

MEN.   Certainly not.

SOC.   You only assert that the round figure is not more a figure than the straight, or the straight than the round?

MEN.   Very true.

SOC.   To what then do we give the name of figure? Try and answer. Suppose that when a person asked you this question either about figure or colour, you were to reply, Man, I do not understand what you want, or know what you are saying; he would look rather astonished and say: Do you not understand that I am looking for the 'simile in multis'? And then he might put the question in another form: Meno, he might say, what is that 'simile in multis' which you call figure, and which includes not only round and straight figures, but all? Could you not answer that question, Meno? I wish that you would try; the attempt will be good practice with a view to the answer about virtue.

MEN.   I would rather that you should answer, Socrates.

SOC.   Shall I indulge you?

MEN.   By all means.

SOC.   And then you will tell me about virtue?

MEN.   I will.

SOC.   Then I must do my best, for there is a prize to be won.

MEN.   Certainly.

SOC.   Well, I will try and explain to you what figure is. What do you say to this answer?—Figure is the only thing which always follows colour.

Will you be satisfied with it, as I am sure that I should be, if you would let me have a similar definition of virtue?

MEN. But, Socrates, it is such a simple answer.

SOC. Why simple?

MEN. Because, according to you, figure is that which always follows colour.

SOC. Granted.

MEN. But if a person were to say that he does not know what colour is, any more than what figure is—what sort of answer would you have given him?

SOC. I should have told him the truth. And if he were a philosopher of the eristic and antagonistic sort, I should say to him: You have my answer, and if I am wrong, your business is to take up the argument and refute me. But if we were friends, and were talking as you and I are now, I should reply in a milder strain and more in the dialectician's vein; that is to say, I should not only speak the truth, but I should make use of premisses which the person interrogated would be willing to admit. And this is the way in which I shall endeavour to approach you. You will acknowledge, will you not; that there is such a thing as an end, or termination, or extremity?—all which words I use in the same sense, although I am aware that Prodicus might draw distinctions about them: but still you, I am sure, would speak of a thing as ended or terminated—that is all which I am saying—not anything very difficult.

MEN. Yes, I should; and I believe that I understand your meaning.

SOC. And you would speak of a surface and also of a solid, as for example in geometry.

MEN. Yes.

SOC. Well then, you are now in a condition to understand my definition of figure. I define figure to be that in which the solid ends; or, more concisely, the limit of solid.

MEN. And now, Socrates, what is colour?

SOC. You are outrageous, Meno, in thus plaguing a poor old man to give you an answer, when you will not take the trouble of remembering what is Gorgias' definition of virtue.

MEN. When you have told me what I ask, I will tell you, Socrates.

SOC. A man who was blindfolded has only to hear you talking, and he would know that you are a fair creature and have still many lovers.

MEN. Why do you think so?

SOC. Why, because you always speak in imperatives: like all beauties when they are in their prime, you are tyrannical; and also, as I suspect, you have found out that I have a weakness for the fair, and therefore to humour you I must answer.

MEN. Please do.

SOC. Would you like me to answer you after the manner of Gorgias, which is familiar to you?

MEN.   I should like nothing better.

SOC.   Do not he and you and Empedocles say that there are certain effluences of existence?

MEN.   Certainly.

SOC.   And passages into which and through which the effluences pass?

MEN.   Exactly.

SOC.   And some of the effluences fit into the passages, and some of them are too small or too large?

MEN.   True.

SOC.   And there is such a thing as sight?

MEN.   Yes.

SOC.   And now, as Pindar says, "read my meaning:"—colour is an effluence of form, commensurate with sight, and palpable to sense.

MEN.   That, Socrates, appears to me to be an admirable answer.

SOC.   Why, yes, because it happens to be one which you have been in the habit of hearing: and your wit will have discovered, I suspect, that you may explain in the same way the nature of sound and smell, and of many other similar phenomena.

MEN.   Quite true.

SOC.   The answer, Meno, was in the orthodox solemn vein, and therefore was more acceptable to you than the other answer about figure.

MEN.   Yes.

SOC.   And yet, O son of Alexidemus, I cannot help thinking that the other was the better; and I am sure that you would be of the same opinion, if you would only stay and be initiated, and were not compelled, as you said yesterday, to go away before the mysteries.

MEN.   But I will say, Socrates, if you will give me many such answers.

SOC.   Well then, for my own sake as well as for yours, I will do my very best; but I am afraid that I shall not be able to give you very many as good: and now, in your turn, you are to fulfil your promise, and tell me what virtue is in the universal; and do not make a singular into a plural, as the facetious say of those who break a thing, but deliver virtue to me whole and sound, and not broken into a number of pieces: I have given you the pattern.

MEN.   Well then, Socrates, virtue, as I take it, is when he, who desires the honourable, is able to provide it for himself; so the poet says, and I say too—

    Virtue is the desire of things honourable and the power of attaining them.

SOC.   And does he who desires the honourable also desire the good?

MEN.   Certainly.

SOC.   Then are there some who desire the evil and others who desire the good? Do not all men, my dear sir, desire good?

MEN.   I think not.

SOC.   There are some who desire evil?

MEN. Yes.

SOC. Do you mean that they think the evils which they desire, to be good; or do they know that they are evil and yet desire them?

MEN. Both, I think.

SOC. And do you really imagine, Meno, that a man knows evils to be evils and desires them notwithstanding?

MEN. Certainly I do.

SOC. And desire is of possession?

MEN. Yes, of possession.

SOC. And does he think that the evils will do good to him who possesses them, or does he know that they will do him harm?

MEN. There are some who think that the evils will do them good, and others who know that they will do them harm.

SOC. And, in your opinion, do those who think that they will do them good know that they are evils?

MEN. Certainly not.

SOC. Is it not obvious that those who are ignorant of their nature do not desire them; but they desire what they suppose to be goods although they are really evils; and if they are mistaken and suppose the evils to be goods they really desire goods?

MEN. Yes, in that case.

SOC. Well, and do those who, as you say, desire evils, and think that evils are hurtful to the possessor of them, know that they will be hurt by them?

MEN. They must know it.

SOC. And must they not suppose that those who are hurt are miserable in proportion to the hurt which is inflicted upon them?

MEN. How can it be otherwise?

SOC. But are not the miserable ill-fated?

MEN. Yes, indeed.

SOC. And does any one desire to be miserable and ill-fated?

MEN. I should say not, Socrates.

SOC. But if there is no one who desires to be miserable, there is no one, Meno, who desires evil; for what is misery but the desire and possession of evil?

MEN. That appears to be the truth, Socrates, and I admit that nobody desires evil.

SOC. And yet, were you not saying just now that virtue is the desire and power of attaining good?

MEN. Yes, I did say so.

SOC. But if this be affirmed; then the desire of good is common to all, and one man is no better than another in that respect?

MEN. True.

SOC. And if one man is not better than another in desiring good, he must be better in the power of attaining it?

MEN. Exactly.

SOC.   Then, according to your definition, virtue would appear to be the power of attaining good?

MEN.   I entirely approve, Socrates, of the manner in which you now view this matter.

SOC.   Then let us see whether what you say is true from another point of view; for very likely you may be right:—You affirm virtue to be the power of attaining goods?

MEN.   Yes.

SOC.   And the goods which you mean are such as health and wealth and the possession of gold and silver, and having office and honour in the state— those are what you would call goods?

MEN.   Yes, I should include all those.

SOC.   Then, according to Meno, who is the hereditary friend of the great king, virtue is the power of getting silver and gold; and would you add that they must be gained piously, justly, or do you deem this to be of no consequence? And is any mode of acquisition, even if unjust or dishonest, equally to be deemed virtue?

MEN.   Not virtue, Socrates, but vice.

SOC.   Then justice or temperance or holiness, or some other part of virtue, as would appear, must accompany the acquisition, and without them the mere acquisition of good will not be virtue.

MEN.   Why, how can there be virtue without these?

SOC.   And the non-acquisition of gold and silver in a dishonest manner for oneself or another, or in other words the want of them, may be equally virtue?

MEN.   True.

SOC.   Then the acquisition of such goods is no more virtue than the non-acquisition and want of them, but whatever is accompanied by justice or honesty is virtue, and whatever is devoid of justice is vice.

MEN.   It cannot be otherwise, in my judgment.

SOC.   And were we not saying just now that justice, temperance, and the like, were each of them a part of virtue?

MEN.   Yes.

SOC.   And so, Meno, this is the way in which you mock me.

MEN.   Why do you say that, Socrates?

SOC.   Why, because I asked you to deliver virtue into my hands whole and unbroken, and I gave you a pattern according to which you were to frame your answer; and you have forgotten already, and tell me that virtue is the power of attaining good justly, or with justice; and justice you acknowledge to be a part of virtue.

MEN.   Yes.

SOC.   Then it follows from your own admissions, that virtue is doing what you do with a part of virtue; for justice and the like are said by you to be parts of virtue.

MEN.   What of that?

SOC.   What of that! Why, did not I ask you to tell me the nature of virtue as
a whole? And you are very far from telling me this; but declare every
action to be virtue which is done with a part of virtue; as though you
had told me and I must already know the whole of virtue, and this too
when frittered away into little pieces. And, therefore, my dear Meno,
I fear that I must begin again and repeat the same question: What is
virtue? for otherwise, I can only say, that every action done with a part
of virtue is virtue; what else is the meaning of saying that every action
done with justice is virtue? Ought I not to ask the question over again;
for can any one who does not know virtue know a part of virtue?

MEN.   No; I do not say that he can.

SOC.   Do you remember how, in the example of figure, we rejected any
answer given in terms which were as yet unexplained or unadmitted?

MEN.   Yes, Socrates; and we were quite right in doing so.

SOC.   But then, my friend, do not suppose that we can explain to any one the
nature of virtue as a whole through some unexplained portion of virtue,
or anything at all in that fashion; we should only have to ask over again
the old question, What is virtue? Am I not right?

MEN.   I believe that you are.

SOC.   Then begin again, and answer me, What, according to you and your
friend Gorgias, is the definition of virtue?

MEN.   O Socrates, I used to be told, before I knew you, that you were always
doubting yourself and making others doubt; and now you are casting
your spells over me, and I am simply getting bewitched and enchanted,
and am at my wits' end. And if I may venture to make a jest upon you,
you seem to me both in your appearance and in your power over others
to be very like the flat torpedo fish, who torpifies those who come near
him and touch him, as you have now torpified me, I think. For my
soul and my tongue are really torpid, and I do not know how to answer
you; and though I have been delivered of an infinite variety of speeches
about virtue before now, and to many persons—and very good ones
they were, as I thought—at this moment I cannot even say what virtue
is. And I think that you are very wise in not voyaging and going
away from home, for if you did in other places as you do in Athens, you
would be cast into prison as a magician.

SOC.   You are a rogue, Meno, and had all but caught me.

MEN.   What do you mean, Socrates?

SOC.   I can tell why you made a simile about me.

MEN.   Why?

SOC.   In order that I might make another simile about you. For I know
that all pretty young gentlemen like to have pretty similes made about
them—as well they may but I shall not return the compliment. As to
my being a torpedo, if the torpedo is torpid as well as the cause of

torpidity in others, then indeed I am a torpedo, but not otherwise; for I perplex others, not because I am clear, but because I am utterly perplexed myself. And now I know not what virtue is, and you seem to be in the same case, although you did once perhaps know before you touched me. However, I have no objection to join with you in the enquiry.

MEN.   And how will you enquire, Socrates, into that which you do not know? What will you put forth as the subject of enquiry? And if you find what you want, how will you ever know that this is the thing which you did not know?

SOC.   I know, Meno, what you mean; but just see what a tiresome dispute you are introducing. You argue that a man cannot enquire either about that which he knows, or about that which he does not know; for if he knows, he has no need to enquire; and if not, he cannot; for he does not know the very subject about which he is to enquire.

MEN.   Well, Socrates, and is not the argument sound?

SOC.   I think not.

MEN.   Why not?

SOC.   I will tell you why: I have heard from certain wise men and woman who spoke of things divine that—

MEN.   What did they say?

SOC.   They spoke of a glorious truth, as I conceive.

MEN.   What was it? and who were they?

SOC.   Some of them were priests and priestesses, who had studied how they might be able to give a reason of their profession: there have been poets also, who spoke of these things by inspiration, like Pindar, and many others who were inspired. And they say—mark, now, and see whether their words are true—they say that the soul of man is immortal, and at one time has an end, which is termed dying, and at another time is born again, but is never destroyed. And the moral is, that a man ought to live always in perfect holiness. *"For in the ninth year Persephone sends the souls of those from whom she has received the penalty of ancient crime back again from beneath into the light of the sun above, and these are they who become noble kings and mighty men and great in wisdom and are called saintly heroes in after ages."* The soul, then, as being immortal, and having been born again many times, and having seen all things that exist, whether in this world or in the world below, has knowledge of them all; and it is no wonder that she should be able to call to remembrance all that she ever knew about virtue, and about everything; for as all nature is akin, and the soul has learned all things, there is no difficulty in her eliciting or as men say learning, out of a single recollection all the rest, if a man is strenuous and does not faint; for all enquiry and all learning is but recollection. And therefore we ought not to listen to this sophistical argument about the impossibility of enquiry: for it will make us idle, and is sweet only to the sluggard; but the other saying will make us active and inquisitive. In that confiding, I will gladly enquire with you into the nature of virtue.

MEN. Yes, Socrates; but what do you mean by saying that we do not learn, and that what we call learning is only a process of recollection? Can you teach me how this is?

SOC. I told you, Meno, just now that you were a rogue, and now you ask whether I can teach you, when I am saying that there is no teaching, but only recollection; and thus you imagine that you will involve me in a contradiction.

MEN. Indeed, Socrates, I protest that I had no such intention. I only asked the question from habit; but if you can prove to me that what you say is true, I wish that you would.

SOC. It will be no easy matter, but I will try to please you to the utmost of my power. Suppose that you call one of your numerous attendants, that I may demonstrate on him.

MEN. Certainly. Come hither, boy.

SOC. He is Greek, and speaks Greek, does he not?

MEN. Yes, indeed; he was born in the house.

SOC. Attend now to the questions which I ask him, and observe whether he learns of me or only remembers.

MEN. I will.

SOC. Tell me, boy, do you know that a figure like this is a square?

BOY I do.

SOC. And you know that a square figure has these four lines equal?

BOY Certainly.

SOC. And these lines which I have drawn through the middle of the square are also equal?

BOY Yes.

SOC. A square may be of any size?

BOY Certainly.

SOC. And if one side of the figure be of two feet, and the other side be of two feet, how much will the whole be? Let me explain: if in one direction the space was of two feet, and in the other direction of one foot, the whole would be of two feet taken once?

BOY Yes.

SOC. But since this side is also of two feet, there are twice two feet?

BOY There are.

SOC. Then the square is of twice two feet?

BOY Yes.

SOC. And how many are twice two feet? count and tell me.

BOY Four, Socrates.

SOC. And might there not be another square twice as large as this, and having like this the lines equal?

BOY   Yes.

SOC.   And of how many feet will that be?

BOY   Of eight feet.

SOC.   And now try and tell me the length of the line which forms the side of that double square: this is two feet—what will that be?

BOY   Clearly, Socrates, it will be double.

SOC.   Do you observe, Meno, that I am not teaching the boy anything, but only asking him questions; and now he fancies that he knows how long a line is necessary in order to produce a figure of eight square feet; does he not?

MEN.   Yes.

SOC.   And does he really know?

MEN.   Certainly not.

SOC.   He only guesses that because the square is double, the line is double.

MEN.   True.

SOC.   Observe him while he recalls the steps in regular order. (*To the Boy.*) Tell me, boy, do you assert that a double space comes from a double line? Remember that I am not speaking of an oblong, but of a figure equal every way, and twice the size of this—that is to say of eight feet; and I want to know whether you still say that a double square comes from a double line?

BOY   Yes.

SOC.   But does not this line become doubled if we add another such line here?

BOY   Certainly.

SOC.   And four such lines will make a space containing eight feet?

BOY   Yes.

SOC.   Let us describe such a figure: Would you not say that this is the figure of eight feet?

BOY   Yes.

SOC.   And are there not these four divisions in the figure, each of which is equal to the figure of four feet?

BOY   True.

SOC.   And is not that four times four?

BOY   Certainly.

SOC.   And four times is not double?

BOY   No, indeed.

SOC.   But how much?

BOY   Four times as much.

SOC.   Therefore the double line, boy, has given a space, not twice, but four times as much.

BOY   True.

SOC.   Four times four are sixteen—are they not?

BOY   Yes.

SOC.   What line would give you a space of eight feet, as this gives one of sixteen feet;—do you see?

BOY	Yes.
SOC.	And the space of four feet is made from this half line?
BOY	Yes.
SOC.	Good; and is not a space of eight feet twice the size of this, and half the size of the other?
BOY	Certainly.
SOC.	Such a space, then, will be made out of a line greater than this one, and less than that one?
BOY	Yes; I think so.
SOC.	Very good; I like to hear you say what you think. And now tell me, is not this a line of two feet and that of four?
BOY	Yes.
SOC.	Then the line which forms the side of eight feet ought to be more than this line of two feet, and less than the other of four feet?
BOY	It ought.
SOC.	Try and see if you can tell me how much it will be.
BOY	Three feet.
SOC.	Then if we add a half to this line of two, that will be the line of three. Here are two and there is one; and on the other side, here are two also and there is one: and that makes the figure of which you speak?
BOY	Yes.
SOC.	But if there are three feet this way and three feet that way, the whole space will be three times three feet?
BOY	That is evident.
SOC.	And how much are three times three feet?
BOY	Nine.
SOC.	And how much is the double of four?
BOY	Eight.
SOC.	Then the figure of eight is not made out of a line of three?
BOY	No.
SOC.	But from what line?—tell me exactly; and if you would rather not reckon, try and show me the line.
BOY	Indeed, Socrates, I do not know.
SOC.	Do you see, Meno, what advances he has made in his power of recollection? He did not know at first, and he does not know now, what is the side of a figure of eight feet: but then he thought that he knew, and answered confidently as if he knew, and had no difficulty; now he has a difficulty, and neither knows nor fancies that he knows.
MEN.	True.
SOC.	Is he not better off in knowing his ignorance?
MEN.	I think that he is.
SOC.	If we have made him doubt, and given him the "torpedo's shock," have we done him any harm?
MEN.	I think not.
SOC.	We have certainly, as would seem, assisted him in some degree to the

discovery of the truth; and now he will wish to remedy his ignorance, but then he would have been ready to tell all the world again and again that the double space should have a double side.

MEN.   True.

SOC.   But do you suppose that he would ever have enquired into or learned what he fancied that he knew, though he was really ignorant of it, until he had fallen into perplexity under the idea that he did not know, and had desired to know?

MEN.   I think not, Socrates.

SOC.   Then he was the better for the torpedo's touch?

MEN.   I think so.

SOC.   Mark now the farther development. I shall only ask him, and not teach him, and he shall share the enquiry with me: and do you watch and see if you find me telling or explaining anything to him, instead of eliciting his opinion. Tell me, boy, is not this a square of four feet which I have drawn?

BOY   Yes.

SOC.   And now I add another square equal to the former one?

BOY   Yes.

SOC.   And a third, which is equal to either of them?

BOY   Yes.

SOC.   Suppose that we fill up the vacant corner?

BOY   Very good.

SOC.   Here, then, there are four equal spaces?

BOY   Yes.

SOC.   And how many times larger is this space than this other?

BOY   Four times.

SOC.   But it ought to have been twice only, as you will remember.

BOY   True.

SOC.   And does not this line, reaching from corner to corner, bisect each of these spaces?

BOY   Yes.

SOC.   And are there not here four equal lines which contain this space?

BOY   There are.

SOC.   Look and see how much this space is.

BOY   I do not understand.

SOC.   Has not each interior line cut off half of the four spaces?

BOY   Yes.

SOC.   And how many such spaces are there in this section?

BOY   Four.

SOC.   And how many in this?

BOY   Two.

SOC.   And four is how many times two?

BOY   Twice.

SOC.	And this space is of how many feet?
BOY	Of eight feet.
SOC.	And from what line do you get this figure?
BOY	From this.
SOC.	That is, from the line which extends from corner to corner of the figure of four feet?
BOY	Yes.
SOC.	And that is the line which the learned call the diagonal. And if this is the proper name, then you, Meno's slave, are prepared to affirm that the double space is the square of the diagonal?
BOY	Certainly, Socrates.
SOC.	What do you say of him, Meno? Were not all these answers given out of his own head?
MEN.	Yes, they were all his own.
SOC.	And yet, as we were just now saying, he did not know?
MEN.	True.
SOC.	But still he had in him those notions of his—had he not?
MEN.	Yes.
SOC.	Then he who does not know may still have true notions of that which he does not know?
MEN.	He has.
SOC.	And at present these notions have just been stirred up in him, as in a dream; but if he were frequently asked the same questions, in different forms, he would know as well as any one at last?
MEN.	I dare say.
SOC.	Without any one teaching him he will recover his knowledge for himself, if he is only asked questions?
MEN.	Yes.
SOC.	And this spontaneous recovery of knowledge in him is recollection?
MEN.	True.
SOC.	And this knowledge which he now has must he not either have acquired or always possessed?
MEN.	Yes.
SOC.	But if he always possessed this knowledge he would always have known; or if he has acquired the knowledge he could not have acquired it in this life, unless he has been taught geometry; for he may be made to do the same with all geometry and every other branch of knowledge. Now, has any one ever taught him all this? You must know about him, if, as you say, he was born and bred in your house.
MEN.	And I am certain that no one ever did teach him.
SOC.	And yet he has the knowledge?
MEN.	The fact, Socrates, is undeniable.
SOC.	But if he did not acquire the knowledge in this life, then he must have had and learned it at some other time?

MEN. Clearly he must.

SOC. Which must have been the time when he was not a man?

MEN. Yes.

SOC. And if there have been always true thoughts in him, both at the time when he was and was not a man, which only need to be awakened into knowledge by putting questions to him, his soul must have always possessed this knowledge, for he always either was or was not a man?

MEN. Obviously.

SOC. And if the truth of all things always existed in the soul, then the soul is immortal. Wherefore be of good cheer, and try to recollect what you do not know, or rather what you do not remember.

MEN. I feel, somehow, that I like what you are saying.

SOC. And I, Meno, like what I am saying. Some things I have said of which I am not altogether confident. But that we shall be better and braver and less helpless if we think that we ought to enquire, than we should have been if we indulged in the idle fancy that there was no knowing and no use in seeking to know what we do not know;—that is a theme upon which I am ready to fight, in word and deed, to the utmost of my power.

MEN. There again, Socrates, your words seem to me excellent.

SOC. Then, as we are agreed that a man should enquire about that which he does not know, shall you and I make an effort to enquire together into the nature of virtue?

MEN. By all means, Socrates. And yet I would much rather return to my original question, Whether in seeking to acquire virtue we should regard it as a thing to be taught, or as a gift of nature, or as coming to men in some other way?

SOC. Had I the command of you as well as of myself, Meno, I would not have enquired whether virtue is given by instruction or not, until we had first ascertained "what it is." But as you think only of controlling me who am your slave, and never of controlling yourself,—such being your notion of freedom, I must yield to you, for you are irresistible. And therefore I have now to enquire into the qualities of a thing of which I do not as yet know the nature.

Apology

The Apology, Crito, *and* Phaedo *comprise a trilogy devoted to the
teachings and martyrdom of Socrates and are among Plato's
earliest writings. The* Apology *recounts Socrates' trial; and the
following selection, beginning after he has been sentenced, presents
Socrates' final statements to the jury. His thoughts dwell on death.
Plato is usually studied only for his historical value, but the
following statement could be relevant to the present age.*

It is for the sake of but a short span, O Athenians, that you have incurred the imputation, from those who wish to speak evil against the
city, of having put to death Socrates, a wise man (for those who are
inclined to reproach you, will say that I am wise even if I am not).
Had you waited a short time, the thing would have happened without
your agency; for you see my years; I am far advanced in life, and near
to death. I address this not to all of you, but to those who have voted
for the capital sentence. And this too I say to the same persons: Perhaps you think that I have been condemned from want of skill in such
modes of working upon your minds, as I might have employed with
success if I had thought it right to employ all means in order to escape
from condemnation. Far from it. I have been condemned, not for
want of things to say, but for want of daring and shamelessness; because
I did not choose to say to you the things which would have been
pleasantest to you to hear, weeping and lamenting, and doing and
saying other things which I affirm to be unworthy of me; as you are
accustomed to see others do. But neither did I then think fit, because
of my danger, to do anything unworthy of a freeman; nor do I now
repent of having thus defended myself; I would far rather have made
the one defence and die, than have made the other and live. Neither
in a court of justice, nor in war, ought we to make it our object, that,
whatever happens, we may escape death. In battle, it is often evident
that a man may save his life by throwing away his arms, and imploring
mercy of his pursuers; and in all other dangers, there are many contrivances by which a person may get off with life, if he dare do or say
everything. The difficulty, O Athenians, is not to escape from death,
but from guilt; for guilt is swifter than death, and runs faster. And now
I, being old, and slow of foot, have been overtaken by death, the slower
of the two; but my accusers, who are brisk and vehement, by wickedness, the swifter. We quit this place, I having been sentenced by you
to death, but they, having sentence passed upon them by Truth, of
guilt and injustice. I submit to my punishment, and they to theirs.
These things, perhaps, are as they should be, and for the best.

SOURCE: "Four Dialogues of Plato," translated by J. S. Mill, *Monthly Repository*
(1834–35).

But I wish, O men who have condemned me, to prophesy to you what is next to come; for I am in the position in which men are most wont to prophesy, being at the point of death. I say, then, O you who have slain me—that immediately after my death there will come upon you a far severer punishment than that which you have inflicted upon me. For you have done this, thinking by it to escape from being called to account for your lives. But I affirm that the very reverse will happen to you. There will be many to call you to account, whom I have hitherto restrained, and whom you saw not: and being younger they will give you more annoyance, and you will be still more provoked. For if you think, by putting men to death, to deter others from reproaching you with living amiss, you think ill. That mode of protecting yourselves is neither very possible, nor very noble: the noblest and the easiest too, is not to cut off other people, but so to order yourselves, as to obtain the greatest excellence. Having prophesied thus to those who have condemned me, I leave them.

With those who voted for my acquittal, I would gladly, while the officers are busy, and I am not yet going to the place where I am to be put to death, converse a little about this which has happened. Stay with me, my friends, until then; for I would explain to you, as my well wishers, the meaning of what has now happened to me. There has occurred to me, O judges (for you I may rightly call by that name), something surprising. My accustomed daemonic warning has, in all former times, been very frequent, and given on small occasions, if I was about to do any thing not for my good. But now, as you see, those things have happened to me, which are generally esteemed the worst of evils; yet the divine monitor did not warn me, neither when I left my home in the morning, nor when I came up hither to the judgment-seat, nor at any time when I was speaking; though on other occasions I have often, while speaking, experienced the warning, and been checked in what I was about to say. But in neither word nor deed connected with this business, have I been checked by the sign. What do I suppose to be the cause? I will tell you. This which has happened is most likely a good; and those of us who think death an evil are probably in the wrong. For the accustomed warning would certainly have been given to me, if what I was about to do had not been for my good.

We may also, from the following considerations, conclude that there is much hope of its being a good. For death must be one of two things: either the dead are incapable of feeling or perceiving anything; or death is, as we are told, a change of abode, a passage of the soul from this to some other place. Now, if after death there be no sensation, but it be like a sleep in which there are no dreams, death is a mighty gain. For if any one were to choose from his life, a night in which he had slept without dreaming, and comparing with this all the other nights and

days of his life, were required to say in how many of them he had lived
better and more pleasantly than in that night, I imagine that not a
private man merely, but the Great King, would find that such days
and nights were soon counted. If then this be death, it is a gain: since
all eternity would not thus appear longer than one night. But if death
be to quit this place for another, and if it be true as is affirmed, that in
that other place is the abode of all the dead; what greater good can
there be, O judges, than this? If, arriving in the other world, and leaving these people who call themselves judges, we shall see the real
judges, who are said to judge there, Minos and Rhadamanthus and
Aeacus and Triptolemus, and all other demigods who lived justly
while they were alive, would it not be a noble journey? What would not
any of you give to converse with Orpheus, and Musaeus, and Hesiod,
and Homer? I would gladly die many times if this be true; since to me
it would be a delightful residence when I had met with Palamedes,
and the Telamonian Ajax, and any other of the ancients who perished
in consequence of an unjust judgment. To compare my own fate with
theirs, would not, I think, be disagreeable: and best of all, to live examining and interrogating the people there, as I have done here, to discover who among them are wise, and who think themselves so, but are
not. How much would not one give, O judges, for an opportunity of
examining him who led the great expedition to Troy; or Ulysses, or
Sisyphus, or ten thousand others whom one could mention, both men
and women; with whom to converse and associate there, and to examine
them, would be the height of happiness. They do not, there, put one to
death for such things; for the people there are happier than the people
here, both in other things, and in this, that when once there they are
immortal; if what we are told is true.

It behoves you, O judges, to be of good cheer concerning death;
and to fix this truth in your minds, that to a good man, whether he
die or live, nothing is evil, nor are his affairs neglected by the gods;
neither did what has happened to me occur spontaneously, but it is
evident to me that to die, and come to an end now, was most for my
good. For this reason was it that the sign did not interpose to check me;
and I do not much complain of my accusers, nor of those who condemned me. Though they, indeed, accused and condemned me not
with any such intention, but purposing to do me harm; and for this it
is fit to blame them.

Thus much, however, I beg of them: When my sons grow up, punish
them, O Athenians, by tormenting them as I tormented you, if they
shall seem to study riches, or any other ends, in preference to virtue.
And if they are thought to be something, being really nothing, reproach them as I have reproached you, for not attending to what they
ought, and fancying themselves something when they are good for

nothing. And if you do this, both I and my sons shall have received what is just at your hands.

It is now time that we depart, I to die, you to live; but which has the better destiny is unknown to all, except the gods.

Phaedo

Dramatically set in a prison cell, the Phaedo *is Socrates' last conversation with his friends and disciples. Confident and cheerful to the end, Socrates thanks the guard who reluctantly hands him the cup of poison and drinks a toast to the health and happiness which await him. The following excerpt once again concerns death; this time the subject is approached from a speculative point of view and leads to a consideration of the nature of philosophy, the theory of forms, and the immortality of the soul.*

Never mind him, he [Socrates] replied. But I wish now to explain to you, my judges, why it seems to me that a man who has really spent his life in philosophy has reason to be of good cheer when he is about to die, and may well hope after death to gain in the other world the greatest good. I will try to show you, Simmias and Cebes, how this may be.

The world, perhaps, does not see that those who rightly engage in philosophy, study only dying and death. And, if this be true, it would be surely strange for a man all through his life to desire only death, and then, when death comes to him, to be vexed at it, when it has been his study and his desire for so long.

Simmias laughed, and said: Indeed, Socrates, you make me laugh, though I am scarcely in a laughing humour now. If the multitude heard that, I fancy they would think that what you say of philosophers is quite true; and my countrymen would entirely agree with you that philosophers are indeed eager to die, and they would say that they know full well that philosophers deserve to be put to death.

And they would be right, Simmias, except in saying that they know it. They do not know in what sense the true philosopher is eager to die, or what kind of death he deserves, or in what sense he deserves it. Let us dismiss them from our thoughts, and converse by ourselves. Do we believe death to be anything?

We do, replied Simmias.

And do we not believe it to be the separation of the soul from the body? Does not death mean that the body comes to exist by itself, separated from the soul, and that the soul exists by herself, separated from the body? What is death but that?

SOURCE: *The Trial and Death of Socrates,* translated by F. J. Church (London: Macmillan and Co., 1887), pp. 115–127.

It is that, he said.

Now consider, my good friend, if you and I are agreed on another point which I think will help us to understand the question better. Do you think that a philosopher will care very much about what are called pleasures, such as the pleasures of eating and drinking?

Certainly not, Socrates, said Simmias.

Or about the pleasures of sexual passion?

Indeed, no.

And, do you think that he holds the remaining cares of the body in high esteem? Will he think much of getting fine clothes, and sandals, and other bodily adornments, or will he despise them, except so far as he is absolutely forced to meddle with them?

The real philosopher, I think, will despise them, he replied.

In short, said he, you think that his studies are not concerned with the body? He stands aloof from it, as far as he can, and turns towards the soul?

I do.

Well then, in these matters, first, it is clear that the philosopher releases his soul from communion with the body, so far as he can, beyond all other men?

It is.

And does not the world think, Simmias, that if a man has no pleasure in such things, and does not take his share in them, his life is not worth living? Do not they hold that he who thinks nothing of bodily pleasures is almost as good as dead?

Indeed you are right.

But what about the actual acquisition of wisdom? If the body is taken as a companion in the search for wisdom, is it a hindrance or not? For example, do sight and hearing convey any real truth to men? Are not the very poets forever telling us that we neither hear nor see anything accurately? But if these senses of the body are not accurate or clear, the others will hardly be so, for they are all less perfect than these, are they not?

Yes, I think so, certainly, he said.

Then when does the soul attain truth? he asked. We see that, as often as she seeks to investigate anything in company with the body, the body leads her astray.

True.

Is it not by reasoning, if at all, that any real truth becomes manifest to her?

Yes.

And she reasons best, I suppose, when none of the senses, whether hearing, or sight, or pain, or pleasure, harasses her: when she has dismissed the body, and released herself as far as she can from all intercourse or contact with it, and so, coming to be as much alone with herself as is possible, strives after real truth.

That is so.

And here too the soul of the philosopher very greatly despises the body, and flies from it, and seeks to be alone by herself, does she not?

Clearly.

And what do you say to the next point, Simmias? Do we say that there is such a thing as absolute justice, or not?

Indeed we do.

And absolute beauty, and absolute good?

Of course.

Have you ever seen any of them with your eyes?

Indeed, I have not, he replied.

Did you ever grasp them with any bodily sense? I am speaking of all absolutes, whether size, or health, or strength; in a word of the essence or real being of everything. Is the very truth of things contemplated by the body? Is it not rather the case that the man, who prepares himself most carefully to apprehend by his intellect the essence of each thing which he examines, will come nearest to the knowledge of it?

Certainly.

And will not a man attain to this pure thought most completely, if he goes to each thing, as far as he can, with his mind alone, taking neither sight, nor any other sense along with his reason in the process of thought, to be an encumbrance? In every case he will pursue pure and absolute being, with his pure intellect alone. He will be set free as far as possible from the eye, and the ear, and, in short, from the whole body, because intercourse with the body troubles the soul, and hinders her from gaining truth and wisdom. Is it not he who will attain the knowledge of real being, if any man will?

Your words are admirably true, Socrates, said Simmias.

And, he said, must not all this cause real philosophers to reflect, and make them say to each other, It seems that there is a narrow path which will bring us safely to our journey's end, with reason as our guide. As long as we have this body, and an evil of that sort is mingled with our souls, we shall never fully gain what we desire; and that is truth. For the body is for ever taking up our time with the care which it needs: and, besides, whenever diseases attack it, they hinder us in our pursuit of real being. It fills us with passions, and desires, and fears, and all manner of phantoms, and much foolishness: and so, as the saying goes, in very truth we can never think at all for it. It alone, and its desires, cause wars and factions and battles: for the origin of all wars is the pursuit of wealth, and we are forced to pursue wealth because we live in slavery to the cares of the body. And therefore, for all these reasons, we have no leisure for philosophy. And last of all, if we ever are free from the body for a time, and then turn to examine some matter, it falls in our way at every step of the inquiry, and causes confusion and trouble and panic, so that we cannot see the truth for it. Verily we have learnt that if we are to have any pure knowledge at all, we must be freed from the body; the soul by herself must behold things as they are. Then, it seems, after we are dead, we shall gain the wisdom which we desire, and for which we say we have a passion, but not while we are alive, as the argument shows. For if it be not possible to have pure knowledge while the body is with us, one of two things must be true: either we cannot gain knowledge at all, or we can gain it only after death. For then, and not till then, will the soul exist by herself, separate from the body. And while we live, we shall come nearest to knowledge, if we have no communion or intercourse with the body beyond what is absolutely necessary, and if we are not defiled with its nature. We must live pure from it until God himself releases us. And when we are thus pure and released from its follies, we shall dwell, I suppose, with others who are pure like ourselves, and we shall of ourselves know all that is pure; and that may be the truth. For I think that the impure is not allowed to attain to the pure. Such, Simmias, I fancy must needs be the language and the reflections of the true lovers of knowledge. Do you not agree with me?

Most assuredly I do, Socrates.

And, my friend, said Socrates, if this be true, I have good hope that, when I reach the place whither I am going, I shall there, if anywhere, gain fully that which we have sought so earnestly in the past. And so I shall set forth cheerfully on the journey that is appointed me to-day, and so may every man who thinks that his mind is prepared and purified.

That is quite true, said Simmias.

And does not the purification consist, as we have said, in separating the soul from the body, as far as is possible, and in accustoming her to collect and rally herself together from the body on every side, and to dwell alone by herself as much as she can both now and hereafter, released from the bondage of the body?

Yes, certainly, he said.

Is not what we call death a release and separation of the soul from the body?

Undoubtedly, he replied.

And the true philosopher, we hold, is alone in his constant desire to set his soul free? His study is simply the release and separation of the soul from the body, is it not?

Clearly.

Would it not be absurd then, as I began by saying, for a man to complain at death coming to him, when in his life he has been preparing himself to live as nearly in a state of death as he could? Would not that be absurd?

Yes, indeed.

In truth, then, Simmias, he said, the true philosopher studies to die, and to him of all men is death least terrible. Now look at the matter in this way. In everything he is at enmity with his body, and he longs to possess his soul alone. Would it not then be most unreasonable, if he were to fear and complain when he has his desire, instead of rejoicing to go to the place where he hopes to gain the wisdom that he has passionately longed for all his life, and to be released from the company of his enemy? Many a man has willingly gone to the other world, when a human love, or wife or son has died, in the hope of seeing there those whom he longed for, and of being with them: and will a man who has a real passion for wisdom, and a firm hope of really finding wisdom in the other world and nowhere else, grieve at death, and not depart rejoicing? Nay, my friend, you ought not to think that, if he be truly a philosopher. He will be firmly convinced that there and nowhere else will he meet with wisdom in its purity. And if this be so, would it not, I repeat, be very unreasonable for such a man to fear death?

Yes, indeed, he replied, it would.

Does not this show clearly, he said, that any man whom you see grieving at the approach of death, is after all no lover of wisdom, but a lover of his body? He is also, most likely, a lover either of wealth, or of honour, or, it may be, of both.

Yes, he said, it is as you say.

Well then, Simmias, he went on, does not what is called courage belong especially to the philosopher?

Certainly I think so, he replied.

And does not temperance, the quality which even the world calls temperance, and which means to despise and control and govern the passions—does not temperance belong only to such men as most despise the body, and pass their lives in philosophy?

Of necessity, he replied.

For if you will consider the courage and the temperance of other men, said he, you will find that they are strange things.

How so, Socrates?

You know, he replied, that all other men regard death as one of the great evils to which mankind are subject?

Indeed they do, he said.

And when the brave men of them submit to death, do not they do so from a fear of still greater evils?

Yes.

Then all men but the philosopher are brave from fear and because they are afraid. Yet it is rather a strange thing for a man to be brave out of fear and cowardice.

Indeed it is.

And are not the orderly men of them in exactly the same case? Are not they temperate from a kind of intemperance? We should say that this cannot be: but in them this state of foolish temperance comes to that. They desire certain pleasures, and fear to lose them; and so they abstain from other pleasures because they are mastered by these. Intemperance is defined to mean being under the dominion of pleasure: yet they only master certain pleasures because they are mastered by others. But that is exactly what I said just now, that, in a way, they are made temperate from intemperance.

It seems to be so.

My dear Simmias, I fear that virtue is not really to be bought in this way, by bartering pleasure for pleasure, and pain for pain, and fear for fear, and the greater for the less, like coins. There is only one sterling coin for which all these things ought to be exchanged, and that is wisdom. All that is bought and sold for this and with this, whether courage, or temperance, or justice, is real: in one word true virtue cannot be without wisdom, and it matters nothing whether pleasure, and fear, and all other such things, are present or absent. But I think that the virtue which is composed of pleasures and fears bartered with one another, and severed from wisdom, is only a shadow of true virtue, and that it has no freedom, nor health, nor truth. True virtue in reality is a kind of purifying from all these things: and temperance, and justice, and courage, and wisdom itself, are the purification. And I fancy that the men who established our mysteries had a very real meaning: in truth they have been telling us in parables all the time that whosoever comes to Hades uninitiated and profane, will lie in the mire; while he that has been purified and initiated shall dwell with the gods. For "the thyrsus-bearers are many," as they say in the mysteries, "but the inspired few." And by these last, I believe, are meant only the true philosophers. And I in my life have striven as hard as I was able, and have left nothing undone that I might become one of them. Whether I have striven in the right way, and whether I have succeeded or not, I suppose that I shall learn in a little while, when I reach the other world, if it be the will of God.

That is my defence, Simmias and Cebes, to show that I have reason for not being angry or grieved at leaving you and my masters here. I believe that in the next world, no less than in this, I shall meet with good masters and friends, though the multitude are incredulous of it. And if I have been more successful with you in my defence than I was with my Athenian judges, it is well.

Republic

The Republic *begins by raising two questions: What is justice?
and Is the just man also the happiest man?—and proceeds
inductively until Plato uncovers the ultimate principles of reality.
Having reached this pinnacle Plato descends deductively until he
establishes that the just man is truly the happiest man. Both of the
following selections are from the upward journey: the first presents
the definition of justice in the individual and in the state, and the
second, the education of the ruling element in the state and in the
soul. The latter, marking the zenith of the upward journey, is
presented in the form of a myth.*

"But do you also take note of this?" "Of what?" "That what we now
think about the spirited element is just the opposite of our recent surmise. For then we supposed it to be a part of the appetitive, but now,
far from that, we say that, in the factions of the soul, it much rather
marshals itself on the side of the reason." "By all means," he said. "Is
it then distinct from this too, or is it a form of the rational, so that there
are not three but two kinds in the soul, the rational and the appetitive,
or just as in the city there were three existing kinds that composed its
structure, the money-makers, the helpers, the counsellors, so also in the
soul there exists a third kind, this principle of high spirit, which is the
helper of reason by nature unless it is corrupted by evil nurture?" "We
have to assume it as a third," he said. "Yes," said I, "provided it shall
have been shown to be something different from the rational, as it has
been shown to be other than the appetitive." "That is not hard to be
shown," he said; "for that much one can see in children, that they are
from their very birth chock-full of rage and high spirit, but as for reason,
some of them, to my thinking, never participate in it, and the majority
quite late." "Yes, by heaven, excellently said," I replied; "and further,
one could see in animals that what you say is true. And to these instances we may add the testimony of Homer quoted above:

He smote his breast and chided thus his heart.

For there Homer has clearly represented that in us which has reflected
about the better and the worse as rebuking that which feels unreason-
ing anger as if it were a distinct and different thing." "You are entirely
right," he said.

XVI. "Through these waters, then," said I, "we have with difficulty
made our way and we are fairly agreed that the same kinds equal in

---

SOURCE: Plato, *The Republic*, translated by Paul Shorey (Cambridge, Mass.: Harvard
University Press, 1963), *1*, pp. 402–417, and *2*, pp. 119–143. Reprinted with permission of the publishers.

number are to be found in the state and in the soul of each one of us."
"That is so." "Then does not the necessity of our former postulate immediately follow, that as and whereby the state was wise so and thereby
is the individual wise?" "Surely." "And so whereby and as the individual is brave, thereby and so is the state brave, and that both should have
all the other constituents of virtue in the same way?" "Necessarily."
"Just too, then, Glaucon, I presume we shall say a man is in the same
way in which a city was just." "That too is quite inevitable." "But we
surely cannot have forgotten this, that the state was just by reason of each
of the three classes found in it fulfilling its own function." "I don't think
we have forgotten," he said. "We must remember, then, that each of us
also in whom the several parts within him perform each their own
task—he will be a just man and one who minds his own affair." "We
must indeed remember," he said. "Does it not belong to the rational
part to rule, being wise and exercising forethought in behalf of the entire
soul, and to the principle of high spirit to be subject to this and its ally?"
"Assuredly." "Then is it not, as we said, the blending of music and
gymnastics that will render them concordant, intensifying and fostering
the one with fair words and teachings and relaxing and soothing and
making gentle the other by harmony and rhythm?" "Quite so," said
he. "And these two thus reared and having learned and been educated
to do their own work in the true sense of the phrase, will preside over
the appetitive part which is the mass of the soul in each of us and the
most insatiate by nature of wealth. They will keep watch upon it,
lest, by being filled and infected with the so-called pleasures associated
with the body and so waxing big and strong, it may not keep to its
own work but may undertake to enslave and rule over the classes
which it is not fitting that it should, and so overturn the entire life of
all." "By all means," he said. "Would not these two, then, best keep
guard against enemies from without also in behalf of the entire soul
and body, the one taking counsel, the other giving battle, attending
upon the ruler, and by its courage executing the ruler's designs?"
"That is so." "Brave, too, then, I take it, we call each individual by
virtue of this part in him, when, namely, his high spirit preserves in
the midst of pains and pleasures the rule handed down by the reason
as to what is or is not to be feared." "Right," he said. "But wise by
that small part that ruled in him and handed down these commands,
by its possession in turn within it of the knowledge of what is beneficial
for each and for the whole, the community composed of the three."
"By all means." "And again, was he not sober by reason of the friendship and concord of these same parts, when, namely, the ruling principle and its two subjects are at one in the belief that the reason ought
to rule, and do not raise faction against it?" "The virtue of soberness

certainly," said he, "is nothing else than this, whether in a city or an individual." "But surely, now, a man is just by that which and in the way we have so often described." "That is altogether necessary." "Well then," said I, "has our idea of justice in any way lost the edge of its contour so as to look like anything else than precisely what it showed itself to be in the state?" "I think not," he said. "We might," I said, "completely confirm your reply and our own conviction thus, if anything in our minds still disputes our definition—by applying commonplace and vulgar tests to it." "What are these?" "For example, if an answer were demanded to the question concerning that city and the man whose birth and breeding was in harmony with it, whether we believe that such a man, entrusted with a deposit of gold or silver, would withhold it and embezzle it, who do you suppose would think that he would be more likely so to act than men of a different kind?" "No one would," he said. "And would not he be far removed from sacrilege and theft and betrayal of comrades in private life or of the state in public?" "He would." "And, moreover, he would not be in any way faithless either in the keeping of his oaths or in other agreements." "How could he?" "Adultery, surely, and neglect of parents and of the due service of the gods would pertain to anyone rather than to such a man." "To anyone indeed," he said. "And is not the cause of this to be found in the fact that each of the principles within him does its own work in the matter of ruling and being ruled?" "Yes, that and nothing else." "Do you still, then, look for justice to be anything else than this potency which provides men and cities of this sort?" "No, by heaven," he said, "I do not."

XVII. "Finished, then, is our dream and perfected—the surmise we spoke of, that, by some Providence, at the very beginning of our foundation of the state, we chanced to hit upon the original principle and a sort of type of justice." "Most assuredly." "It really was, it seems, Glaucon, which is why it helps, a sort of adumbration of justice, this principle that it is right for the cobbler by nature to cobble and occupy himself with nothing else, and the carpenter to practise carpentry, and similarly all others. But the truth of the matter was, as it seems, that justice is indeed something of this kind, yet not in regard to the doing of one's own business externally, but with regard to that which is within and in the true sense concerns one's self, and the things of one's self—it means that a man must not suffer the principles in his soul to do each the work of some other and interfere and meddle with one another, but that he should dispose well of what in the true sense of the word is properly his own, and having first attained to self-mastery and beautiful order within himself, and having harmonized these three principles, the notes or intervals of three terms quite literally the lowest, the highest, and the mean, and all others there may be between them, and having linked and bound all three together and made of himself a unit, one man instead of many, self-controlled and in unison, he should then and then only turn to practice if he find aught to do either in the getting of wealth or the tendance of the body or it may be in political action or private business, in all such doings believing and naming the just and honourable action to be that which preserves and helps to produce this condition of soul, and wisdom the science that presides over such conduct; and believing and naming the unjust action to be that which ever tends to overthrow this spiritual constitution, and brutish ignorance, to be the opinion that in turn presides over this."

. . . .

I. "Next," said I, "compare our nature in respect of education and its lack to such an experience as this. Picture men dwelling in a sort of subterranean cavern with a long entrance open to the light on its entire width. Conceive them as having their legs and necks fettered from childhood, so that they remain in the same spot, able to look forward only, and prevented by the fetters from turning their heads. Picture further the light from a fire burning higher up and at a distance behind them, and between the fire and the prisoners and above them a road along which a low wall has been built, as the exhibitors of puppet-shows have partitions before the men themselves, above which they show the puppets." "All that I see," he said. "See also, then, men carrying past the wall implements of all kinds that rise above the wall, and human images and shapes of animals as well, wrought in stone and wood and every material, some of these bearers presumably speaking and others silent." "A strange image you speak of," he said, "and strange prisoners." "Like to us," I said; "for, to begin with, tell me do you think that these men would have seen anything of themselves or of one another except the shadows cast from the fire on the wall of the cave that fronted them?" "How could they," he said, "if they were compelled to hold their heads unmoved through life?" "And again, would not the same be true of the objects carried past them?" "Surely." "If then they were able to talk to one another, do you not think that they would suppose that in naming the things that they saw they were naming the passing objects?" "Necessarily." "And if their prison had an echo from the wall opposite them, when one of the passersby uttered a sound, do you think that they would suppose anything else than the passing shadow to be the speaker?" "By Zeus, I do not," said he. "Then in every way such prisoners would deem reality to be nothing else than the shadows of the artificial objects." "Quite inevitably," he said. "Consider, then, what would be the manner of the release and healing from these bonds and this folly if in the course of nature something of this sort should happen to them:

When one was freed from his fetters and compelled to stand up suddenly and turn his head around and walk and to lift up his eyes to the light, and in doing all this felt pain and, because of the dazzle and glitter of the light, was unable to discern the objects whose shadows he formerly saw, what do you suppose would be his answer if someone told him that what he had seen before was all a cheat and an illusion, but that now, being nearer to reality and turned toward more real things, he saw more truly? And if also one should point out to him each of the passing objects and constrain him by questions to say what it is, do you not think that he would be at a loss and that he would regard what he formerly saw as more real than the things now pointed out to him?" "Far more real," he said.

II. "And if he were compelled to look at the light itself, would not that pain his eyes, and would he not turn away and flee to those things which he is able to discern and regard them as in very deed more clear and exact than the objects pointed out?" "It is so," he said. "And if," said I, "someone should drag him thence by force up the ascent which is rough and steep, and not let him go before he had drawn him out into the light of the sun, do you not think that he would find it painful to be so haled along, and would chafe at it, and when he came out into the light, that his eyes would be filled with its beams so that he would not be able to see even one of the things that we call real?" "Why, no, not immediately," he said. "Then there would be need of habituation, I take it, to enable him to see the things higher up. And at first he would most easily discern the shadows and, after that, the likenesses or reflections in water of men and other things, and later, the things themselves, and from these he would go on to contemplate the appearances in the heavens and heaven itself, more easily by night, looking at the light of the stars and the moon, than by day the sun and the sun's light." "Of course." "And so, finally, I suppose, he would be able to look upon the sun itself and see its true nature, not by reflections in water or phantasms of it in an alien setting, but in and by itself in its own place." "Necessarily," he said. "And at this point he would infer and conclude that this it is that provides the seasons and the courses of the year and presides over all things in the visible region, and is in some sort the cause of all these things that they had seen." "Obviously," he said, "that would be the next step." "Well then, if he recalled to mind his first habitation and what passed for wisdom there, and his fellow-bondsmen, do you not think that he would count himself happy in the change and pity them?" "He would indeed." "And if there had been honours and commendations among them which they bestowed on one another and prizes for the man who is quickest to make out the shadows as they pass and best able to remember their customary precedences, sequences and co-existences, and so most successful in guessing at what was to come, do you think he would be very keen about such rewards, and that he would envy and emulate those who were honoured by these prisoners and lorded it among them, or that he would feel with Homer and greatly prefer while living on earth to be serf of another, a landless man, and endure anything rather than opine with them and live that life?" "Yes," he said, "I think that he would choose to endure anything rather than such a life." "And consider this also," said I, "if such a one should go down again and take his old place would he not get his eyes full of darkness, thus suddenly coming out of the sunlight?" "He would indeed." "Now if he should be required to contend with these perpetual prisoners in 'evaluating' these shadows while his vision was still dim and before his eyes were accustomed to the dark—and this time required for habituation would not be very short—would he not provoke laughter, and would it not be said of him that he had returned from his journey aloft with his eyes ruined and that it was not worth while even to attempt the ascent? And if it were possible to lay hands on and to kill the man who tried to release them and lead them up, would they not kill him?" "They certainly would," he said.

III. "This image then, dear Glaucon, we must apply as a whole to all that has been said, likening the region revealed through sight to the habitation of the prison, and the light of the fire in it to the power of the sun. And if you assume that the ascent and the contemplation of the things above is the soul's ascension to the intelligible region, you will not miss my surmise, since that is what you desire to hear. But God knows whether it is true. But, at any rate, my dream as it appears to me is that in the region of the known the last thing to be seen and hardly seen is the idea of good, and that when seen it must needs point us to the conclusion that this is indeed the cause for all things of all that is right and beautiful, giving birth in the visible world to light, and the author of light and itself in the intelligible world being the authentic source of truth and reason, and that anyone who is to act wisely in private or public must have caught sight of this." "I concur," he said, "so far as I am able." "Come then," I said, "and join me in this further thought, and do not be surprised that those who have attained to this height are not willing to occupy themselves with the affairs of men, but their souls ever feel the upward urge and the yearning for that sojourn above. For this, I take it, is likely if in this point too the likeness of our image holds." "Yes, it is likely." "And again, do you think it at all strange," said I, "if a man returning from divine contemplations to the petty miseries of men cuts a sorry figure and appears most ridiculous, if, while still blinking through the gloom and before he has become sufficiently accustomed to the environing darkness, he is compelled in courtrooms or elsewhere to contend about the shadows of justice or the images that cast the shadows and to wrangle in debate about the notions of these things in the minds of those who have never seen justice itself?" "It would be by no means strange," he said. "But a sensible man," I said, "would remember that there are two distinct disturbances of the eyes arising from two causes, according as the shift is from light to darkness or from darkness to light, and, believing that the same thing happens to the soul too, whenever he saw a soul perturbed and unable to discern something, he would not laugh unthinkingly, but would observe whether coming from a brighter life its vision was obscured by the unfamiliar darkness, or whether the passage from the deeper dark of ignorance into a more luminous world and the greater brightness had dazzled its vision. And so he would deem the one happy in its experience and way of life and pity the other, and if it pleased him to laugh at it, his laughter would be less laughable than that at the expense of the soul that had come down from the light above." "That is a very fair statement," he said.

IV. "Then, if this is true, our view of these matters must be this, that education is not in reality what some people proclaim it to be in their professions. What they aver is that they can put true knowledge into a soul that does not possess it, as if they were inserting vision into blind eyes." "They do indeed," he said. "But our present argument indicates," said I, "that the true analogy for this indwelling power in the soul and the instrument whereby each of us apprehends is that of an eye that could not be converted to the light from the darkness except by turning the whole body. Even so this organ of knowledge must be turned around from the world of becoming together with the entire soul, like the scene-shifting periact in the theatre, until the soul is able to endure the contemplation of essence and the brightest region of being. And this, we say, is the good, do we not?" "Yes." "Of this very thing, then," I said, "there might be an art, an art of the speediest and most effective shifting or conversion of the soul, not an art of producing vision in it, but on the assumption that it possesses vision but does not rightly direct it and does not look where it should, an art of bringing this about." "Yes, that seems likely," he said. "Then the other so-called virtues of the soul do seem akin to those of the body. For it is true that where they do not pre-exist, they are afterwards created by habit and practice. But the excellence of thought, it seems, is certainly of a more divine quality, a thing that never loses its potency, but, according to the direction of its conversion, becomes useful and beneficent, or, again, useless and harmful. Have you never observed in those who are popularly spoken of as bad, but smart men, how keen is the vision of the little soul, how quick it is to discern the things that interest it, a proof that it is not a poor vision which it has, but one forcibly enlisted in the service of evil, so that the sharper its sight the more mischief it accomplishes?" "I certainly have," he said. "Observe then," said I, "that this part of such a soul, if it had been hammered from childhood, and had thus been struck free of the leaden weights, so to speak, of our birth and becoming, which attaching themselves to it by food and similar pleasures and gluttonies turn downwards the vision of the soul—if, I say, freed from these, it had suffered a conversion towards the things that are real and true, that same faculty of the same men would have been most keen in its vision of the higher things, just as it is for the things toward which it is now turned." "It is likely," he said. "Well, then," said I, "is not this also likely and a necessary consequence of what has been said, that neither could men who are uneducated and inexperienced in truth ever adequately preside over a state, nor could those who had been permitted to linger on to the end in the pursuit of culture—the one because they have no single aim and purpose in life to which all their actions, public and private, must be directed, and the others, because they will not voluntarily engage in action, believing that while still living they have been transported to the Islands of the Blest." "True," he said. "It is the duty of us, the founders, then," said I, "to compel the best natures to attain the knowledge which we pronounced the greatest, and to win to the vision of the good, to scale that ascent, and when they have reached the heights and taken an adequate view, we must not allow what is now permitted." "What is that?" "That they should linger there," I said, "and refuse to go down again among those bondsmen and share their labours and honours, whether they are of less or of greater worth." "Do you mean to say that we must do them this wrong, and compel them to live an inferior life when the better is in their power?"

V. "You have again forgotten, my friend," said I, "that the law is not concerned with the special happiness of any class in the state, but is trying to produce this condition in the city as a whole, harmonizing and adapting the citizens to one another by persuasion and compulsion, and requiring them to impart to one another any benefit which they are severally able to bestow upon the community, and that it itself creates such men in the state, not that it may allow each to take what course pleases him, but with a view to using them for the binding together of the commonwealth." "True," he said, "I did forget it." "Observe, then, Glaucon," said I, "that we shall not be wronging, either, the philosophers who arise among us, but that we can justify our action when we constrain them to take charge of the other citizens and be their guardians. For we will say to them that it is natural that men of similar quality who spring up in other cities should not share in the labours there. For they grow up spontaneously from no volition of the government in the several states, and it is justice that the self-grown, indebted to none for its breeding, should not be zealous either to pay to anyone the price of its nurture. But you we have engendered for yourselves and the rest of the city to be, as it were, king-bees and leaders in the hive. You have received a better and more complete education than the others, and you are more capable of sharing both ways of life. Down you must go then, each in his turn, to the habitation of the others and accustom yourselves to the observation of the obscure things there. For once habituated you will discern them infinitely better than the dwellers there, and you will know what each of the 'idols' is and whereof it is a semblance, because you have seen the reality of the beautiful, the just and the good. So our city will be governed by us and you with waking minds, and not, as most cities now which are inhabited and ruled darkly as in a dream by men who fight one another for shadows and wrangle for office as if that were a great good, when the truth is that the city in which those who are to rule are least eager to hold office must needs be best administered and most free from dissension, and the state that gets the contrary type of ruler will be the opposite of this."

Phaedrus

The following selection is a long discourse on love presented as a myth. In the Meno, Phaedo, *and* Republic *Plato introduced the forms or essences as the ultimate constituents of reality and knowledge and as the ultimate principles of ethical judgment. Here, the forms are presented as the ultimate constituents of love and beauty. The theory of the soul presented in this context should be compared with the theories presented in the* Phaedo *and* Republic.

In considering its form let us proceed in the following manner. To explain what the soul is, would be a long and most assuredly a godlike labour; to say what it resembles, is a shorter and a human task. Let us attempt then the latter; let us say that the soul resembles the combined efficacy of a pair of winged steeds and a charioteer. Now the horses and drivers of the gods are all both good themselves and of good extraction, but the character and breed of all others is mixed. In the first place, with us men the supreme ruler has a pair of horses to manage, and then of these horses he finds one generous and of generous breed, the other of opposite descent and opposite character. And thus it necessarily follows that driving in our case is no easy or agreeable work. We must at this point endeavour to express what we mean respectively by a mortal and an immortal animal. All that is soul presides over all that is without soul, and patrols all heaven, now appearing in one form and now in another. When it is perfect and

SOURCE: *The Phaedrus, Lysis, and Protagoras of Plato*, translated by J. Wright (London: Macmillan and Co., 1909), pp. 47–67.

fully feathered, it roams in upper air, and regulates the entire universe; but the soul that has lost its feathers is carried down till it finds some solid resting-place; and when it has settled there, when it has taken to itself, that is, an earthly body, which seems capable of self-motion, owing to the power of its new inmate, the name of animal is given to the whole; to this compound, I mean, of soul and body, with the addition of the epithet mortal. The immortal, on the other hand, has received its name from the conclusion of no human reasoning; but without having either seen or formed any adequate conception of a god, we picture him to ourselves as an immortal animal, possessed of soul and possessed of body, and of both in intimate conjunction from all eternity. But this matter I leave to be and to be told as Heaven pleases—my task is to discover what is the cause that makes the feathers fall off the soul. It is something, I conceive, of the following kind.

The natural efficacy of a wing is to lift up heavy substances, and bear them aloft to those upper regions which are inhabited by the race of the gods. And of all the parts connected with the body it has perhaps shared most largely (with the soul) in the divine nature. Now of this nature are beauty, wisdom, virtue, and all similar qualities. By these then the plumage of the soul is chiefly fostered and increased; by ugliness, vice, and all such contraries, it is wasted and destroyed. Zeus, the great chieftain in heaven, driving a winged car, travels first, arranging and presiding over all things; and after him comes a host of gods and inferior deities, marshalled in eleven divisions, for Hestia stays at home alone in the mansion of the gods; but all the other ruling powers, that have their place in the number of the twelve, march at the head of a troop in the order to which they have been severally appointed. Now there are, it is true, many ravishing views and opening paths within the bounds of heaven, whereon the family of the blessed gods go to and fro, each in performance of his own proper work; and they are followed by all who from time to time possess both will and power; for envy has no place in the celestial choir. But whenever they go to feast and revel, they forthwith journey by an uphill path to the summit of the heavenly vault. Now the chariots of the gods being of equal poise, and obedient to the rein, move easily, but all others with difficulty; for they are burdened by the horse of vicious temper, which sways and sinks them towards the earth, if haply he has received no good training from his charioteer. Whereupon there awaits the soul a crowning pain and agony. For those which we called immortal go outside when they are come to the topmost height, and stand on the outer surface of heaven, and as they stand they are borne round by its revolution, and gaze on the external scene. Now of that region beyond the sky no earthly bard has ever yet sung or ever will sing in worthy strains. But this is the fashion of it; for sure I must venture to speak the truth, especially as truth is my theme. Real existence, colourless, formless, and intangible, visible only to the intelligence which sits at the helm of the soul, and with which the family of true science is concerned, has its abode in this region. The mind then of deity, as it is fed by intelligence and pure science, and the mind of every soul that is destined to receive its due inheritance, is delighted at seeing the essence to which it has been so long a stranger, and by the light of truth is fostered and made to thrive, until, by the revolution of the heaven, it is brought round again to the same point. And during the circuit it sees distinctly absolute justice, and absolute temperance, and absolute science; not such as they appear in creation, nor under the variety of forms to which we nowadays give the name of realities, but the justice, the temperance, the science, which exist in that which is real and essential being. And when in like manner it has seen all the rest of the world of essence, and feasted on the sight, it sinks down again into the interior of heaven, and returns to its own home. And on its arrival, the charioteer takes his horses to the manger, and sets before them ambrosia, and gives them nectar to drink with it. Such is the life of the gods; but of the other souls, that which follows a god most closely and resembles him most nearly, succeeds in raising the head of its charioteer into the outer region, and is carried round with the immortals in their revolution, though sore encumbered by its horses, and barely able to contemplate the real existences; while another rises and sinks by turns, his horses plunging so violently that he can discern no more than a part of these existences. But the common herd follow at a distance, all of them indeed burning with desire for the upper world, but, failing to reach it, they make the revolution in the moisture of the lower element, trampling on one another, and striking against one another, in their efforts to rush one before the other. Hence ensues the extremest turmoil and struggling and sweating; and herein, by the awkwardness of the drivers, many souls are maimed, and many lose many feathers in the crush; and all after painful labour go away without being blessed by admission to the spectacle of truth, and thenceforth live on the food of mere opinion.

And now will I tell you the motives of this great anxiety to behold the fields of truth. The suitable pasturage for the noblest portion of the soul is grown on the meadows there, and it is the nature of the wing, which bears aloft the soul, to be fostered thereby; and moreover, there is an irrevocable decree, that if any soul has followed a god in close companionship and discerned any of the true essences, it shall continue free from harm till the next revolution, and if it be ever thus successful, it shall be ever thus unharmed: but whenever, from inability to follow, it has missed that glorious sight, and, through some mishap it may have encountered, has become charged with forgetfulness and vice, and been thereby so burdened as to shed its feathers and fall to the earth, in that case there is a law that the soul thus fallen be not planted in any bestial nature during the first generation, but that if it has seen more than others of essential verity, it pass into the germ of a man who is to become a lover of wisdom, or a lover of beauty, or some votary of the Muses and Love; if it be of second rank, it is to enter the form of a constitutional ruler, a warrior, or a man fitted for command; the third will belong to a politician, or economist, or merchant; the fourth, to a laborious professor of gymnastics, or some disciple of the healing art; the fifth will be possessed by a soothsayer, or some person connected with mysteries; the sixth will be best suited by the life of a poet or some other imitative artist; the seventh, by the labour of an artisan or a farmer; the eighth, by the trade of a sophist or a demagogue; and the ninth, by the lot of an absolute monarch. And in all these various conditions those who have lived justly receive afterwards a better lot; those who have lived unjustly, a worse. For to that same place from which each soul set out, it does not return for ten thousand years; so long is it before it recovers its plumage, unless it has belonged to a guileless lover of philosophy, or a philosophic lover of boys. But these souls, during their third millennium, if only they have chosen thrice in succession this form of existence, do in this case regain their feathers, and at its conclusion wing their departure. But all the rest are, on the termination of their first life, brought to trial; and, according to their sentence, some go to the prison-houses beneath the earth, to suffer for their sins; while others, by virtue of their trial, are borne lightly upwards to some celestial spot, where they pass their days in a manner worthy of the life they have lived in their mortal form. But in the thousandth year both divisions come back again to share and choose their second life, and they select that which they severally please. And then it is that a human soul passes into the life of a beast, and from a beast who was once a man the soul comes back into a man again. For the soul which has never seen the truth at all can never enter into the human form; it being a necessary condition of a man that he should apprehend according to that which is called a generic form, which, proceeding from a variety of perceptions, is by reflection combined into unity. And this is nothing more nor less than a recollection of those things which in time past our soul beheld when it travelled with a god, and, looking high over what we now call real, lifted up its head into the region of eternal essence. And thus you see it is with justice that the mind of the philosopher alone recovers its plumage, for to the best of its power it is ever fixed in memory on that glorious spectacle, by the contemplation of which the godhead is divine. And it is only by the right use of such memorials as these, and by ever perfecting himself in perfect mysteries, that a man becomes really perfect. But because such an one stands aloof from human interests, and is rapt in contemplation of the divine, he is taken to task by the multitude as a man demented, because the multitude do not see that he is by God inspired.

It will now appear what conclusion the whole course of our argument has reached with regard to the fourth kind of madness, with which a man is inspired whenever, by the sight of beauty in this lower world, the true beauty of the world above is so brought to his remembrance that he begins to recover his plumage, and feeling new wings longs to soar aloft; but the power failing him gazes upward like a bird, and becomes heedless of all lower matters, thereby exposing himself to the imputation of being crazed. And the conclusion is this, that of all kinds of enthusiasm this is the best, as well in character as in origin, for those who possess it, whether fully or in part; and further, that he who loves beautiful objects must partake of this madness before he can deserve the name of lover. For though, as I said before, every man's soul has by the law of his birth been a spectator of eternal truth, or it would never have passed into this our mortal frame, yet still it is no easy matter for all to be reminded of their past by their present existence. It is not easy either for those who, during that struggle I told you of, caught but a brief glimpse of upper glories, nor for those who, after their fall to this world, were so unfortunate as to be turned aside by evil associations into the paths of wickedness, and so made to forget that holy spectacle. Few, few only are there left, with whom the world of memory is duly present. And these few, whenever they see here any resemblance of what they witnessed there, are struck with wonder, and can no longer contain themselves, though what it is that thus affects them they know not, for want of sufficient discernment. Now in the likenesses existing here of justice, and temperance, and all else which souls hold precious, there is no brightness; but through the medium of dull dim instruments it is but seldom and with difficulty that people are enabled on meeting with the copies to recognise the character of the original. But beauty not only shone brightly on our view at the time when in the heavenly choir we, for our part, followed in the band of Zeus, as others in the bands of other gods, and saw that blissful sight and spectacle, and were initiated into that mystery which I fear not to pronounce the most blessed of all mysteries; for we who celebrated it were perfect and untainted by the evil that awaited us in time to come, and perfect too, and simple, and calm, and blissful were the visions which we were solemnly admitted to gaze upon in the purest light, ourselves being no less pure, nor as yet entombed in that which we now drag about with us and call the body, being fettered to it as an oyster to his shell. Excuse my so far indulging memory, which has carried me to a greater length than I intended, in my yearning for a happiness that is past. I return to beauty. Not only, as I said before, did she shine brightly arteries, and prick each at the outlet which is shut against it; so that the soul, being stung all over, is frantic with pain. But then again it calls to mind the beautiful one, and rejoices. And both these feelings being combined, it is sore perplexed by the strangeness of its condition, and not knowing what to do with itself, becomes frenzied, and in its frenzy can neither sleep by night, nor by day remain at rest, but runs to and fro with wistful look wherever it may expect to see the possessor of the beauty. And after it has seen him, and drunk in fresh streams of desire, it succeeds in opening the stoppages which absence had made, and taking breath it enjoys a respite from sting and throe, and now again delights itself for the time being in that most delicious pleasure. And therefore, if it can help, it never quits the side of its beloved, nor holds any one of more account than him, but forgets mother, and brothers, and friends, and though its substance be wasting by neglect, it regards that as nothing, and of all observances and decorums, on which it prided itself once, it now thinks scorn, and is ready to be a slave and lie down as closely as may be allowed to the object of its yearnings; for, besides its reverence for the possessor of beauty, it has found in him the sole physician for its bitterest pains. Now this affection, my beautiful boy—you I mean to whom my speech is addressed—is called by mortals Eros (Love); on hearing its name among the gods, your young wit will naturally laugh. There are put forth, if I mistake not, by certain Homerids, out of their secret poems, two verses on Eros, of which the second is quite outrageous, and not at all particularly metrical. Thus they sing:

> Him mortals indeed call winged Eros,
> But immortals Pteros (Flyer), for his flighty nature.

Now these verses you may believe or not believe, as you think proper; but whatever is thought of them the cause of love, and the condition of lovers, is all the same, just such as has been here stated.

Now, if it be one of the former followers of Zeus who is seized by love, he is able to bear in greater weight than others the burden of the wing-named god. But all who were in the service of Ares, and patrolled the heavens in his company, when they are taken captive by Love, and fancy themselves in aught injured by the object of their love, are thirsty of blood, and ready to immolate both themselves and their favourites. And so it is with the followers of the other gods. Every man spends his life in honouring and imitating to the best of his power that particular god of whose choir he was a member, so long as he is exempt from decay, and living his first generation here; and in keeping with the bent thus acquired, he conducts his intercourse and behaviour towards the beloved object, as well as all the world. Accordingly, each man chooses himself his love out of the ranks of beauty to suit his peculiar turn; and then, as though his choice were his god, he builds him up for himself, and attires him like a holy image, for the purpose of doing him reverence, and worshipping him with ecstatic festival. They then that belong to Zeus seek to have for their beloved one who resembles Zeus in his soul. And so they look for a youth who is by nature a lover of wisdom, and fitted for command; and when they have found one, and become enamoured of him, they strive all they can to make him truly such. And if they have never previously entered upon this task, they now apply themselves to it, both seeking instruction from every possible quarter, and searching in their own souls. And this endeavour to discover the nature of their patron god, by following the track in themselves, is attended with success, by reason of their being ever constrained to gaze upon their god unflinchingly; and when they grasp him with their memory, they are inspired with his inspiration, and take from him their character and habits, so far as it is possible for man to partake of god. And attributing these blessings to their beloved, they love him still more dearly than ever; and whatever streams they may have drawn from Zeus, like the inspired draughts of the Bacchanals, they pour into their darling's soul, thereby making him resemble, as far as possible, the god whom they resemble themselves. Those again who followed in the train of Hera, search out a youth of kingly mould, and when he is found, act towards him in exactly the same manner as the former. And so it is with the adherents of Apollo, and all other gods. Walking themselves in the steps of their own proper god, they look for the youth whom they are to love to be of kindred nature; and when they have gained such an one, both by imitation on their own part, and by urging and attuning the soul of their beloved, they guide him into the particular pursuit and character of that god, so far as they are severally able, not treating him with jealous or illiberal harshness, but using every endeavour to bring him into all possible conformity with themselves and the god whom they adore. So beautiful is the desire of those who truly love; and if they accomplish their desire, so beautiful is the initiation, as I call it, into their holy mystery, and so fraught with blessing at the hand of the friend, whom love has maddened, to the object of the friendship, if he be but won. Now he who is won, is won in the following manner.

As at the commencement of this account I divided every soul into three parts, two of them resembling horses, and the third a charioteer, so let us here still keep to that division. Now of the horses one, if you remember, we said, was good, and the other bad; but wherein consists the goodness of the one, and the badness of the other, is a point which, not distinguished then, must be stated now. That horse of the two which occupies the nobler rank, is in form erect and firmly knit, high-necked, hook-nosed, white-coloured, black-eyed; he loves honour with temperance and modesty, and, a votary of genuine glory, he is driven without stroke of the whip by voice and reason alone. The bad horse, on the other hand, is crooked, bulky, clumsily put together, with thick neck, short throat, flat face, black coat, gray and bloodshot eyes, a friend to all riot and insolence, shaggy about the ears, dull of hearing, scarce yielding to lash and goad united. Whenever therefore the driver sees the sight which inspires love, and his whole soul being thoroughly heated by sense, is surcharged with irritation and the stings of desire, the obedient horse, yielding then as ever to the check of shame, restrains himself from springing on the loved one; but the other pays heed no longer to his driver's goad or lash, but struggles on with unruly bounds, and doing all violence to his yoke-fellow and master, forces them to approach the beautiful youth, and bethink themselves of the joys of dalliance. And though at first they resist him with indignation at the lawless and fearful crime he is urging, yet at last, when there is no end to the evil, they move onward as he leads them, having yielded him submission and agreed to do his bidding. So they come up to the beautiful boy, and see his face all gleaming with beauty. But at the sight the driver's memory is carried back to the essence of beauty, and again he sees her by the side of Continence standing on a holy pedestal. And at the sight he shudders, and with a holy awe falls backward to the ground, and falling cannot help pulling back the reins so violently that he brings both the horses on their haunches, the one indeed willingly, because he is not resisting, but the rebel in spite of struggling. And when they are withdrawn to some distance, the former in his shame and ravishment drenches all the soul with sweat; but the other, when he is recovered from the pain which the bit and the fall inflicted, and has with difficulty regained his breath, breaks out into passionate revilings, vehemently railing at his master and his comrade for their treacherous cowardice in deserting their ranks and agreement. And again he urges them, again refusing, to approach, and barely yields a reluctant consent when they beg to defer the attempt to another time. But soon as the covenanted time is come, though they affect forgetfulness, he reminds them of their engagement, and plunging and neighing and dragging, he again obliges them to approach the beautiful youth to make the same proposals. And when they are near, he stoops his head and gets the bit between his teeth, and drags them on incontinently. But the driver experiences, though still more strongly, the same sensation as at first; backward he falls like racers at the barrier, and with a wrench still more violent than before pulls back the bit from between the teeth of the riotous horse, thereby drenching his jaws and railing tongue with blood: and bruising against the ground his legs and haunches, consigns him to anguish. But as soon as by this treatment oft repeated the evil horse is recovered from his vice, he follows with humbled steps the guidance of his driver, and at sight of the fair one is consumed with terror. So that then, and not till then, does it happen that the soul of the lover follows his beloved with reverence and awe. And the consequence is, that the youth being now worshipped with all the worship of a god by a lover who does not feign the passion, but feels it in his soul, and being himself by nature fondly inclined to his worshipper, even though haply in time past he may have been set against lovers by the remarks of his schoolfellows or others on the scandal of allowing their approaches, and is therefore disposed to reject his present wooer, yet now that the latter is thus changed he is led in course of time, by the instinct of his years, and the law of destiny, to admit him to familiarity. For surely it was never destined for the bad to be friends of the bad, or the good aught but friendly to the good. But when the advances have been acccepted and speech and intercourse allowed, the affection of the lover being brought into near connection with the loved one, strikes him with wonder, as it compels him to feel that the friendship shown him by all the rest of his friends and relations put together is as nothing beside the love of his god-inspired friend. And if he continues long thus to indulge him, and allows him the closest contact both in gymnastic schools and other places of meeting, then it is that the stream of that effluence, to which Zeus when enamoured of Ganymedes gave the name of desire, pours upon the lover in a plenteous flood, and partly sinks within him, partly flows off him when he is full; and just as a wind or a noise rebounds from smooth and hard substances and is carried back again to the place from which it came; so the tide of beauty passes back into the beautiful boy through his eyes, the natural channel into his soul; and when it is come there and has fledged it anew, it waters the outlets of the feathers, and forcing them to shoot up afresh fills the soul of the loved one as well as that of his lover with love. He is in love therefore, but with whom he cannot say; nay, what it is that is come over him he knows not, neither can he tell, but like one who has caught a disease in the eye from the diseased gaze of another, he can assign no reason for the affection, but sees himself in his lover, as in a glass, without knowing who it is that he sees. And when they are together, he enjoys the same respite that his lover does from his anguish; but when they are parted, he yearns for him as he himself is yearned for, since he holds in his bosom love's reflected image, love returned. He calls it, however, and believes it to be not love but friendship, albeit, he feels the same desire as the other does, though in a feebler degree, for the sight, the touch, the kiss, the embrace. And consequently, as might be expected, his conduct henceforward is as follows. When they are lying side by side, the lover's unbridled horse has much to say to its driver, and claims as the recompense of many labours a short enjoyment; but the vicious horse of the other has nothing to say, but burning and restless clasps the lover and kisses him as he would kiss a dear friend, and when they are folded in each other's embrace, is just of such a temper as not for his part to refuse indulging the lover in any pleasure he might request to enjoy; but his yoke-fellow, on the other hand, joins the driver in struggling against him with chastity and reason. Should it appear then that the better part of their nature has succeeded in bringing both the lover and loved into a life of order and philosophy, and established its own ascendency, in bliss and harmony they live out their existence here, being masters of themselves and decorous before the world, having enslaved that portion of the soul wherein vice is contained, and liberated that where virtue dwells; and at last when they come to die, being winged and lightened, they have in one of their three truly Olympic combats achieved the prize, than which no greater good can either human prudence or godly madness bestow on man. But if they have given in to a coarser habit of life, and one unfriendly to wisdom, though not to honour, it may well happen that in a moment of drunkenness or like abandonment, those two unruly beasts will surprise the souls off their guard, and bringing them together into one place will choose and consummate that practice which the world deems happy, and once consummated will for the future indulge in it, though sparingly, as doing what is not approved by all their mind. Dear, therefore, to each other, though not so dear as the former two, do these continue both while their love is burning and when it is extinct; for they conceive themselves to have given and received the strongest pledges, which it were impious at any time to violate by becoming alienated. And in the end, without their wings it is true, but not without having started feathers, they go forth from the body, so that they carry off no paltry prize for their impassioned madness; for there is a law that the paths of darkness beneath the earth shall never again be trodden by those who have so much as set their foot on the heavenward road, but that walking hand in hand they shall live a bright and blessed life, and when they recover their wings, recover them together for their love's sake.

So great and so godly, my beautiful boy, are the blessings which the affection of a lover will bestow. But the commerce of one who does not love, being alloyed with mortal prudence, and dispensing only mortal and niggardly gifts, will breed in the soul of the loved one a sordidness which the vulgar laud as virtue, and doom it for nine thousand years to be tossed about the earth and under the earth without reason.

Philebus

In the Meno *Plato's method of dialectic was essentially Socrates' method of philosophical dialogue. By the time he wrote the* Republic, *Plato attached a more rigorous meaning to the term. In the following selection, Plato presents a new definition of dialectic.*

SOCRATES   The awe which I always feel, Protarchus, in mentioning the gods by name is not a mere human sentiment, but goes far beyond the greatest fear. So now I give to Aphrodite any name that may be pleasing to that goddess. But I am quite aware that pleasure is a Proteus that assumes many aspects; and, as I said, if we begin with her we are bound to consider well and see what kind of nature she has. For though Pleasure is, so far as mere name goes, abstractedly one, yet we all know that it takes forms many and varied, and in some sense, unlike to each other. For observe: we talk of the *pleasures* of the dissolute man; the *pleasure* that a sober man takes in the mere fact of his soberness; the *pleasures* of one who talks nonsense, and is brimful of nonsensical notions and hopes; the *pleasures* again that the Thinker takes in the act of thinking; and if we venture to say that these two classes of pleasures are like each other, surely we shall justly be thought to have very little sense ourselves.

PROTARCHUS   Very true, Socrates; but that is because these pleasures that you enumerate come from things that are opposite; yet it does not follow that the pleasures themselves are opposed to each other. For how can pleasure be anything else than as like as possible to pleasure,—the thing itself to itself?

SOC.   Well, my good friend, so is colour as like as possible to colour; so far as the mere fact is concerned, there will be no difference as to its being all *colour*. But we all know that black, besides being different from, is also most directly opposed to white. And so indeed is shape most like to shape, for the matter of that. It is all one *in kind;* but, parts compared with parts, some of them are most directly opposite to each other, and others, we know, have a very wide difference. Many other things too we shall find in the same position; so that you must not too far trust this kind of argument, which classes all the most opposite things under one head. I am afraid, indeed, that we shall find some pleasures to stand in direct opposition to others.

PROT.   Perhaps so; but what harm will that do to our argument?

SOC.   Because, we shall reply, you call them, as being unlike, by a wrong name. You assert that all that is pleasant is also good. Now, that things pleasant are pleasant, no reasoner denies; but, though some of them,—

SOURCE: *Philebus of Plato*, translated by F. A. Paley (Cambridge, England: Deighton, Bell & Co., 1873), pp. 3–18.

the greater part, I fear,—are bad, and some, as we admit, good, you call them all "good," though you are willing to allow that the pleasures themselves are unlike, if one should press you hard in the argument. What one condition or quality, then, is there in the bad and the good pleasures alike, that makes you say all pleasures are a good?

PROT. What, Socrates! Do you think any man would grant, when he has taken as his axiom that "Pleasure is the Chief Good,"—I say, do you suppose that any one will tolerate your assertion, that *some* pleasures only are good, and that there are some others which are bad?

SOC. Well, you will at least allow that pleasures are unlike each other, and some even contrary.

PROT. No, not in so far as they are *pleasures*.

SOC. We come back to the same assertion, my Protarchus. For if so, we must say that neither is pleasure different from pleasure, but all are alike; and the instances just cited do not affect us at all. Thus we shall have to bear a defeat from making random assertions, like the weakest and most inexperienced of reasoners.

PROT. What do you mean?

SOC. Why, if I, following your example, and determined to fight it out, venture to assert that nothing is so like its opposite as what is most unlike it, I shall be able to avail myself of your argument of "it's all the same." And thus we shall prove ourselves to be rather too young, and our reasoning will drift out of its course and be lost. So let us beat back, and perhaps if we start again from the point we began with, we may hope to come to an understanding with each other.

PROT. Tell me how you mean.

SOC. Conceive me again questioned by you, Protarchus.

PROT. On what point?

SOC. Whether intellect, exact knowledge, mind, and all those qualities which I at first assumed in my thesis as "good," when I was asked what "The Good" can be,—will not be open to the very same conclusions as your argument about pleasure.

PROT. How so?

SOC. All the kinds of knowledge, taken together, will seem so many, that some of them must be unlike to each other. And if some are even in some way opposed, surely I should not deserve the name of a sound reasoner on the present occasion, if through fear of this result of "contraries," I were to assert that no one kind of knowledge is unlike another, and so were to let this argument be lost, as if it were mere idle talk, and we ourselves were to get safe to the shore on the plank of a paradox.

PROT. Well, certainly *that* must not happen,—except indeed the getting off safe. However, I like the fairness of terms presented by your argument and mine. Granted that pleasures are many and unlike, and the kinds of knowledge many and diverse.

soc.   This diversity then, Protarchus, in the good which you and I respectively advocate, I propose that we should try not to disguise or conceal. Let us rather bring it forward to the notice of all, and not shrink from the conclusion, if our arguments on being examined should give evidence to show conclusively whether we ought to call Pleasure "The Good," or Intellect, or some other third thing. For now, of course, we are not contending with this object, that *my* view, or your view, shall be the winner; both of us, I suppose, are bound to aid that cause which is the truest.

prot.   Undoubtedly.

soc.   Then let us put this proposition on a still firmer footing by coming to an agreement upon it.

prot.   What proposition?

soc.   One which causes much trouble to all, whether they like or (as is sometimes the case with some people) dislike it.

prot.   Express yourself more clearly.

soc.   I mean, a proposition which has just now presented itself, by a kind of chance, to our notice, and the nature of which is very strange; for it *is* strange, when so stated, that "Many are One", and "One is Many"; and it is easy to argue against any one who takes either as his thesis.

prot.   Is this then your meaning,—when somebody says that I, Protarchus, who am by nature one, am also on the other hand several, thus assuming that there are ever so many *me's*, and some of them even contrary to each other,—the tall and the little, and the heavy and the light, in one and the same individual, and so on in numerous other relations?

soc.   What you have mentioned, Protarchus, is only the popular notion of the marvellous on the subject of the 'One and Many.' Such a notion now-a-days it is allowed, one might say, by all, that we ought not to take up; they regard it as puerile and obvious, and rather a hindrance than a help to argument. Indeed, they tell us that we should not entertain even such questions as this,—as when some one separately specifies the members or other parts of a particular thing, and then gets another to admit that all these members together form that original "One"; since he only laughs at him as he proves that he has been forced to make the portentous statements, that the One is many and infinite, and the Many but one!

prot.   And pray what other kinds of "One and Many" are there, which have *not* as yet been given up or become hackneyed on this same subject?

soc.   When, my son, we apply this doctrine of Unity not to things that are born and die, as in the case we just now took,—for in this instance, and in Unity of this sort, as I just now said, it is generally admitted that we should not take up such a subject for inquiry;—but when one essays to view Man as One, or Ox, or Beauty or Goodness, it is about these and suchlike unities that all the pains are taken, with careful subdivision, and all the real difficulty is felt.

PROT. In what respect?

SOC. In the first place, whether we must conceive that any such units have a *real* existence at all; in the next, in what sense, if each of these is One and ever the same, (that is, not admitting of either birth or destruction), we can conceive it still in the most unchangeable manner to remain this One and no other; then, whether we are to assume such a unit as separated into many parts and dispersed through the infinity of things created, or existing as a whole outside of itself,—which, of course, would seem the greatest impossibility of all, that what is One and the same should at the same time be in One and in Many. These, Protarchus, are the cases of "One and Many," viz. in abstracts, and not in those others, the concretes, which are the causes of all perplexity, if not carefully defined and understood, and on the other hand, if they are so, a source of great facility and convenience.

PROT. If so, Socrates, it is our duty first to work out this argument thoroughly in our present discussion.

SOC. I should myself certainly be inclined to say so.

PROT. Then take it for granted that all of us, the present company, are willing to accept your views on these subjects. As for Philebus, indeed, it is best perhaps not to rouse him by putting any question, since he is well out of the discussion.

SOC. Very well, then. Where shall one take up the fight that has raged so long and with such different results on the matters in dispute? . . . We say, if I mistake not, that this same "One and Many," called into being by discussions, goes the round of every subject of conversation, whether new or old. And as this did not begin in our time, so there is no chance of its ever ceasing; but something of this sort, as it seems to me, is an unfailing and eternal property of the subjects themselves that arises in our minds. And when any of our young men on any occasion has first tried it, he is as delighted with it as if he had discovered a treasury of wisdom, nay, he is transported with pleasure, and would fain allow no subject to rest, at one time giving it a turn in this direction, and lumping it together into one, at another, pulling it to pieces again and separating it into parts, thus perplexing himself first and principally, and next, whoever happens to be near him at the time, whether younger or older or of the same age with himself. And in doing this he spares neither father nor mother nor any other of his hearers,—I might almost say, of the animals in general, and not merely the human kind. For, of course, he would not be likely to spare any of the foreign people, if he could but get some one to make them understand him.

PROT. Do you not see, Socrates, how many we are, and that all of us are young? Have you no fear lest we should set upon you with Philebus, if you go on abusing us thus? However, we know what you mean; and if there is any way or any shift by which the confusion we are now in would goodnaturedly go and leave the argument to ourselves, or if we could find any better way than this for discovering the truth, do you take up the cause with zeal, and we will go with you to the best of our power. For the subject before us is no trifling one, Socrates.

SOC. Indeed it is not, my dear boys, as Philebus styles you in his address. There is, however, no better way, nor is there ever likely to be, than the one of which I have ever been an ardent admirer, though many a time 'ere now it has escaped from me and left me friendless and forlorn.

PROT. What way is this? Only let us hear it.

SOC. It is one which it is not very difficult to make intelligible to you, but which it is very hard indeed to adopt. It is one by which all the discoveries that were ever made in art have become known to us. Now mind what way I am speaking of.

PROT. Only tell us.

SOC. It was a gift of the gods to men, as it seems to me, that was flung down from some store-house in heaven by one Prometheus, together with very bright fire. And our forefathers,—better men than ourselves, and in closer converse with the gods,—have handed down to us this tradition, that all things which are said by us to *be*, are composed of both One and Many, and have in them the finite and the infinite as part of their nature. With this constitution then of things before us, it became our duty in all cases to propose to ourselves some one general view for investigation, since we are sure to find it at the bottom of every subject. When we have got hold of this, after *one* we should consider *two*, should there be two, or if not, then three, or some other number, and again each of these units in the same way, till we have clearly perceived the true nature of the original one, viz. not only that it is One and Many, and contains an indefinite number of parts, but also *how many* that can be counted up. But the note or character of infinity we must not apply to plurality, till one has fully seen all the number that plurality has between the original one and infinity. *Then* we may let each unit in them all pass into infinity, and concern ourselves no further with it. The gods then, as I said, so taught us to consider, to learn, and to inform each other. But the present degenerate race of philosophers arrive at the One and the Many too quickly and superficially; for after the One they immediately get to the Infinite, and take no account of intervening numbers. But it is in these very numbers that the difference consists between our conversing with each other like logicians, or on the other hand, like mere disputants.

PROT. Some of these views of yours I think, Socrates, that I begin to understand; but on other points I should like to hear more plainly what you mean.

SOC. Well, what I mean is clear enough, surely, in the letters of the alphabet. You may therefore get an idea of it from the very rudiments of your own education.

PROT.   How so?

SOC.   Articulate sound, you will grant, is one, as it proceeds from the mouth; and yet again it is infinite in the number of variations in each and from every individual.

PROT.   Certainly it is.

SOC.   And yet we are not fully informed by knowing either of these facts, viz. that there is Infinity or that there is Oneness in sound. No; it is the knowledge of the number and nature of sounds that makes each of us a grammarian.

PROT.   Most true.

SOC.   And surely what makes a man a musician is this very same knowledge.

PROT.   How so?

SOC.   Sound, we said, according to the former science, is One in itself.

PROT.   Assuredly.

SOC.   Now then let us assume two general kinds, the low-pitch and the high-pitch, and a third, the *homotone*, or note in unison. Is it not so?

PROT.   It is.

SOC.   Well, but you would not as yet be an accomplished musician if you knew only these facts. While, if you did not know them, you would be, one might almost say, good for nothing in musical science.

PROT.   Assuredly so.

SOC.   But when, my friends, you have mastered the number and the nature of the Intervals in sound, in respect of treble and bass, and the limits of these intervals, and the combinations that are made from them,—with a perfect knowledge of all which our predecessors taught us, their followers, to call them "harmonies"; when too, in the various movements of the body, you have discovered that other corresponding effects are produced, (which, numerically measured, they tell us we should call by other terms, "Time" and "Metre";) and when at the same time you begin to perceive that this is the view you ought to take about every "One and Many";—when, I repeat, you have fairly realised all these facts and in this way, then you become an adept; and when, by careful thought, you have apprehended any other truth, so too you are made intelligent in that. But this Infinity of number of and in each subject of thought makes you stray infinitely far from the right view, and does not allow you to become distinguished, or to make a figure in the world, as never having looked to any figures in anything.

PROT.   It seems to me, Philebus, that Socrates has admirably put what he has just now said.

PHIL.   So it seems to me also; as far as *this* subject goes. But why in the world is the argument addressed to *us*, and what is its purport?

SOC.   That indeed, Protarchus, Philebus has very properly asked.

PROT.   He has, in sooth; and therefore do you answer him.

SOC.   I will do so after a few more remarks on the subject itself. For as, when one has taken some one genus, he ought not, according to our view, to look at once to the nature of the Infinite, but to some number; so conversely, when one is obliged to take the Infinite first, he ought not to look to One immediately, but in this case too to a certain number containing in each term a certain plurality, and so try to take in that view, thus ending in *One* from *all*. But let us again illustrate our meaning by taking the case of letters.

SOC.   When *Voice* was found to be unlimited,—whether it was a god who perceived this first or some god-like man, as there is a tradition in Egypt which says that it was Theuth; for he seems to have been the first to notice the vowel-sounds in that infinite, not as a One, but as a plurality, and again, other sounds, not of the vowel-kind, yet partaking of the nature of voice, and to observe that these too had a certain number of their own; when moreover he had distinguished a third kind of letters which we now call *mutes*,—he next proceeded to class by themselves the consonants and the mutes, so far as to make each class One, and the vowels and the medials in the same way, until he had ascertained their precise number, and so gave the name of "letter" to each and all the primary sounds. Seeing however that none of us would ever comprehend any one genus of sound by itself, and without them all, he again considered this group or combination as One, and as making all these various sounds One, and so sounded the praise of one art by calling it Grammar.

PHIL.   I understand this more clearly than your former remarks, Protarchus, to compare the statements themselves with each other. But the same defect seems to present itself in the argument as I felt some time ago.

SOC.   Mean you, Philebus, again to ask, What has this to do with the subject?

PHIL.   Aye, that is what Protarchus and I have been asking ourselves for some time.

SOC.   And yet you have been all the time close to what you say you have long been trying to find.

PHIL.   How is that?

SOC.   Was it not Intellectuality and pleasure that we first undertook to discuss, in order to decide which of them we should prefer?

PHIL.   Certainly it was.

SOC.   But we affirm, I think, that each of these is a One in itself.

PHIL.   We do.

SOC.   Well then, this is the very point that our former argument requires us to determine; first, *how* each of them is at the same time One and Many; next, how it is that they do not pass at once into infinity, but what number of parts each of them has, before they become infinite in their forms or manifestations.

Statesman

In the Republic *Plato presents a political theory in which the ideal
state is directed by the wisdom of the philosopher-king. In the
following selection, Plato distinguishes between the ideal state and
the second best state: the former, ruled by reason, exists only as an
object for intellectual contemplation; the latter is governed by law
and can be established on earth.*

STRANGER   You have very rightly recalled that point. I think it follows that if
the art of government is to be found in this world at all in its pure form,
it will be found in the possession of one or two, or, at most, of a select few.

YOUNG SOCRATES   Yes.

STR.   On this principle it is the men who possess the art of ruling and these
only, whom we are to regard as rulers, whatever constitutional form
their rule may take. It makes no difference whether their subjects be
willing or unwilling; they may rule with or without a code of laws, they
may be poor or wealthy. It is the same with doctors. We do not assess
the medical qualification of a doctor by the degree of willingness on our
part to submit to his knife or cautery or other painful treatment.
Doctors are still doctors whether they work according to fixed prescriptions or without them and whether they be poor or wealthy. So
long as they control our health on a scientific basis, they may purge
and reduce us or they may build us up, but they still remain doctors.
The one essential condition is that they act for the good of our bodies
to make them better instead of worse, and treat men's ailments in every
case as healers acting to preserve life. We must insist that in this dis-
interested scientific ability we see the distinguishing mark of true
authority in medicine—and of true authority everywhere else as well.

Y. S.   Quite so.

STR.   Then the constitution *par excellence*, the only constitution worthy of the
name, must be the one in which the rulers are not men making a show
of political cleverness but men really possessed of scientific understanding of the art of government. Then we must not take into consideration on any sound principle of judgment whether their rule be by
laws or without them over willing or unwilling subjects or whether they
themselves be rich men or poor men.

Y. S.   No.

STR.   They may purge the city for its better health by putting some of the
citizens to death or banishing others. They may lessen the citizen body
by sending off colonies like bees swarming off from a hive, or they may
bring people in from other cities and naturalize them so as to increase

SOURCE: *Plato's Statesman*, translated by J. B. Skemp (London: Routledge & Kegan
Paul Ltd., 1952), pp. 194–210. Reprinted with permission of Routledge & Kegan
Paul Ltd., and Yale University Press.

the number of citizens. So long as they work on a reasoned scientific principle following essential justice and act to preserve and improve the life of the state so far as may be, we must call them real statesmen according to our standards of judgment and say that the state they rule alone enjoys good government and has a real constitution. We must go on to say that all the other state-fabrics called constitutions are not genuine, but counterfeit: they imitate the true constitution. Those which we call law-abiding copy it fairly closely, but the rest are more or less shocking caricatures of it.

Y. S.   All the rest, Sir, I believe to have been spoken in due measure—but the saying about ruling without laws is a hard saying for us to hear.

STR.   You are a little too quick for me, Socrates! I was just going to cross-examine you to see if you really accepted all I have said or felt some objection. I realize, however, from what you say that the point we are anxious to discuss in detail is this question whether a good governor can govern without laws.

Y. S.   Yes, it is.

STR.   In one sense it is evident that the art of Kingship does include the art of law-making. But the political ideal is not full authority for laws but rather full authority for a man who understands the art of Kingship and has kingly ability. Do you understand why?

Y. S.   No, please tell me why.

STR.   Law can never issue an injunction binding on all which really embodies what is best for each: it cannot prescribe with perfect accuracy what is good and right for each member of the community at any one time. The differences of human personality, the variety of men's activities and the inevitable unsettlement attending all human experience make it impossible for any art whatsoever to issue unqualified rules holding good on all questions at all times. I suppose that so far we are agreed.

Y. S.   Most emphatically.

STR.   But we find practically always that the law tends to issue just this in-variable kind of rule. It is like a self-willed, ignorant man who lets no one do anything but what he has ordered and forbids all subsequent questioning of his orders even if the situation has shown some marked improvement on the one for which he originally legislated.

Y. S.   Yes, that is just how the law treats us all.

STR.   It is impossible then, for something invariable and unqualified to deal satisfactorily with what is never uniform and constant.

Y. S.   I am afraid it is impossible.

STR.   But why then must there be a system of laws, seeing that law is not the ideal form of control? We must find out why a legal system is necessary.

Y. S.   We must.

STR.   You have courses of training here in Athens, have you not, just as they have in other cities—courses in which pupils are trained in a group to fit themselves for athletic contests in running or in other sports?

Y. S.   Of course. We have quite a number of them.

STR.   Let us call to mind the commands which professional trainers give to the athletes under their regimen in these courses.

Y. S   In what particular?

STR.   The view such trainers take is that they cannot do their work in detail and issue special commands adapted to the condition of each member of the group. When they lay down rules for physical welfare they find it necessary to give bulk instructions having regard to the general benefit of the average pupil.

Y. S.   Quite so.

STR.   That is why we find them giving the same exercises to whole groups of pupils, starting or stopping all of them at the same time in their running, wrestling or whatever it may be.

Y. S.   Yes.

STR.   Similarly we must expect that the legislator who has to give orders to whole communities of human creatures in matters of right and of mutual contractual obligation, will never be able in the laws he prescribes for the whole group to give every individual his due with absolute accuracy.

Y. S.   Very probably not.

STR.   But we shall find him making the law for the generality of his subjects under average circumstances. Thus he will legislate for all individual citizens, but it will be by what may be called a "bulk" method rather than an individual treatment; and this method of "bulk" prescription will be followed by him whether he makes a written code of law or refrains from issuing such a code, preferring to legislate by using unwritten ancestral customs.

Y. S.   Yes, and quite rightly so.

STR.   Of course he is right, Socrates. How could any law-giver be capable of prescribing every act of a particular individual and sit at his side, so to speak, all through his life and telling him just what to do? And if among the few who have really attained this true statesmanship there arose one who was free to give this detailed guidance to an individual, he would hardly put obstacles in his own way by deliberately framing legal codes of the kind we are criticizing.

Y. S.   That certainly follows, Sir, from what has been said.

STR.   I would rather say, Socrates, that it follows from what is going to be said.

Y. S.   And what is that?

STR.   Let us put this case to ourselves. A doctor or trainer plans to travel abroad and expects to be away from his charges for quite a long time. The doctor might well think that his patients would forget any verbal instructions he gave and the trainer might think likewise. In these circumstances each might want to leave written reminders of his orders—do you not think so yourself, Socrates?

Y. S.   Exactly so, Sir.

STR.   Well now, suppose our doctor did not stay abroad as long as he had expected and so came back the sooner to his patients. Would he hesitate to substitute different prescriptions for the original ones if his patients' condition happened to be better than anticipated because of a climatic improvement or some other unusual and unexpected development of that kind? Would the doctor feel it his duty to maintain stubbornly that there must be no transgression of the strict letter of those original prescriptions of his? Would he refuse to issue new prescriptions or conditions, or condemn a patient who was venturing to act contrary to the prescriptions he had written out for him? Would the doctor declare all such action must be wrong because those former prescriptions were the true canons of medicine and of health and therefore that all contravention of them must lead to disease and be contrary to medical science? Surely any such claims, in circumstances where a science is involved and a real art is at work, would only make the man who made the claim and his precious prescriptions supremely ridiculous.

Y. S.   Yes, it would indeed.

STR.   Imagine then the case of a scientific legislator. Suppose that by a written code or by support given to unwritten customs he has laid down what is just and honourable and what is not, and what benefits society and what hurts it. Suppose him to do this service for the several communities of the human flock who live in their cities as their appointed pasture shepherded by the codes their legislators have provided. If this man, who drew up his code by the art of statesmanship, wishes to amend it, or if another scientific legislator of this kind appears on the scene, will these be forbidden to enact new laws differing from the earlier ones? Surely such a prohibition would appear as ridiculous in the case of the legislator as it was in the case of the doctor, would it not?

Y. S.   Of course.

STR.   But are you familiar with the argument one usually hears advanced when an issue like this is raised?

Y. S.   No, I cannot remember it at the moment, at any rate.

STR.   It is quite a plausible argument: I grant that. They contend that if a man discovers better laws than those already enacted he is entitled to get them brought into effect, but only if in every instance he has first persuaded his own city to accept them.

Y. S.   But what of this? Surely this is a sound contention?

STR.   It may be: but answer this question. Suppose a man fails to persuade his city and forces his better laws upon it, what name are we to apply to force so used? But no, do not answer me that question yet, for there are others to be answered first.

Y. S.   What can they be?

STR. Consider once more the case of the patient under the doctor's treatment. Suppose that the doctor fails to persuade the patient but has a mastery of medical knowledge; and suppose that he forces a particular course of treatment which goes against written prescription but is actually more salutary on a child patient, may be, or on a man or a woman. What are we to call force of this kind? Whatever we decide to call it, we shall not call it "the sin against true medicine" or "a breach of the laws of health". Surely the very last thing a patient who is so constrained is entitled to say is that the doctor's act in applying the constraint was contrary to good medicine and an aggravation of his disease.

Y. S. You are quite right.

STR. .By what name then, do we call the sin against the art of statesmanship? Would it not be called Dishonour, Vice, Injustice?

Y. S. Assuredly.

STR. What then, shall we say of citizens of a state who have been forced to do things which are contrary to written laws and ancestral customs but are nevertheless juster, more effective and more noble than the directions of these traditional authorities? How shall we regard censure by these citizens of the force which has applied in these circumstances? Unless they wish to appear ridiculous in the extreme there is one thing they must refrain from saying. They must not assert in any such instance that in being subjected to compulsion they have suffered disgrace, injustice or evil at the hands of those who compelled them.

Y. S. That is quite true.

STR. Can it be the case that acts imposed under compulsion are right if the compeller is rich but wrong if he is poor? Surely what matters is that with or without persuasion, rich or poor, according to a code or against it, the ruler does what is really beneficial. These are the real issues and all is well if he passes this test, the only genuine test of good government in a community and the only principle by which the understanding and upright ruler will administer the affairs of those whom he rules. The ship's captain fixes his attention on the real welfare at any given time of his ship and his crew. He lays down no written enactments but supplies a law in action by practical application of his knowledge of seamanship to the needs of the voyage. It is in this way that he preserves the lives of all in his ship. Would not a true constitution be just like this and work in the same way if the rulers really understood what government is and employed their art as a stronger power for good than any written laws? By rulers with this sound attitude of mind no wrong can possibly be done so long as they keep firmly to the one great principle, that they must always administer impartial justice to their subjects under the guidance of intelligence and the art of government. Then they will not only preserve the lives of their subjects but reform their characters too, so far as human nature permits of this.

Y. S.   There can be no objection to your last remarks at any rate.

STR.   No, nor can there be to my earlier ones either.

Y. S.   To which are you referring?

STR.   You remember that we said that in no community whatsoever could it happen that a large number of people received this gift of political wisdom and the power to govern by pure intelligence which would accompany it. Only in the hands of the select few or of the enlightened individual can we look for that right exercise of political power which is itself the one true constitution. For we must call all other constitutions mere imitations of this. Some are more perfect copies of it, others are grosser and less adequate imitations.

Y. S.   What do you really mean by this? For I must admit that I did not really understand what you said before about these "imitations".

STR.   But I must make you understand. It would be a serious failing to start a discussion of this issue and then simply drop it without exposing the error which is rampant to-day in all that is said about it.

Y. S.   And what is this error?

STR.   That is what we must now seek out, though it involves a search over unfamiliar ground and the error is hard to discover. We may say, then, that there is only one constitution in the true sense—the one we have described. For the rest of them owe their very preservation to their following a code of laws enacted for this true state and to a strict adherence to a rule which we admit to be desirable though it falls short of the ideal.

Y. S.   What rule is this?

STR.   The rule that none of the citizens may venture to do any act contrary to the laws, and that if any of them ventures to do such act, the penalty is to be death or the utmost rigour of punishment. This is the justest and most desirable course as a second-best when the ideal we have just described has been set aside. We must now go on to say how this state of affairs we have just called second-best is achieved in practice, must we not?

Y. S.   Yes, we must.

STR.   Let us go back once again to the parallel cases with which we have constantly to compare the ruler who really is a statesman.

Y. S.   Who are they?

STR.   Our good friend the ship's captain and the doctor "worth a dozen other men". Let us picture to ourselves a situation in which they might find themselves and see how it all works out in their case.

Y. S.   What situation?

STR.   Suppose we all suddenly decided that we are the victims of the worst possible outrages at their hands. Every doctor, you see, can preserve the life of any he will among us, and can hurt any he will by knife or cautery or by demanding fees which are nothing but imposed taxes—for only the tiniest proportion of them is spent on medicaments for the patient and all the rest goes to keep the doctor and his household. Their final enormity is to accept bribes from the patient's relations or from his enemies and put him to death. Ships' captains are guilty of a different set of crimes, but they are just as heinous. They will enter into a conspiracy to put out to sea with you and then leave you stranded, or else they will scuttle the ship and throw the passengers overboard—and these are not all their misdeeds. Suppose we formed this view of doctors and captains and then held a Council at which the following decree was passed:

I. Neither medicine nor seamanship may be trusted in future with absolute control in its particular sphere, either over slaves or over free citizens.

II. We therefore resolve to gather together an Assembly of *all* (or *of the wealthy among*) the people.

III. It shall be lawful for men of no calling or men of any other calling to advise this Assembly on seamanship and medicine; that is to say:

(*a*) on the drugs and surgical instruments appropriate to the treatment of the sick;

(*b*) on ships and their tackle, on the handling of vessels and on perils of the sea, including

(*i*) risks arising from wind and tide;

(*ii*) risks arising from encountering pirates,

(*iii*) risks arising from manoeuvre of warships against enemy warships in the event of a naval engagement.

So much for the decree on these matters. The executive is to embody this decree of the Assembly of the People (based, you remember, on the advice of a few doctors and sailors maybe, but certainly on the advice of many unqualified people too) in laws which they are to inscribe on tablets of wood and of stone, and in the case of some of the rules so resolved upon, they must see that they find their place among the unwritten ancestral customs. Thereafter for ever medicine and navigation may only be practised according to these laws and customs.

Y.S.   A pretty state of affairs this!

STR.   But we have not done yet. Suppose that they resolve further to appoint magistrates chosen by lot annually from the citizen body (whether from the wealthy only or from all citizens). Some of these magistrates, once they are appointed, are to take command of ships and navigate them; others are to cure the sick according to the written code.

Y. S.   This is getting worse!

STR.   But we have not done—see what follows. When the year of office of each of these magistrates expires, a court must be established and a jury chosen by lot, perhaps from among wealthier citizens whose names are on a list of previously selected jurors, perhaps from the people as a whole. The magistrates are to be summoned before this court and it is to subject them to audit. It is open to anyone to lay an accusation against them that during their year of office they failed to sail the ships according to the written laws or the ancient custom of our forebears. Similar charges may be brought concerning the healers of the sick. If the verdict goes against any of them, the court must assess the penalty or the fine the convicted parties must pay.

Y. S.   Well then, the man who took office voluntarily in such a society would deserve any punishment and any fine that might be imposed.

STR.   Then there can be further misdemeanours, and we must enact a law to provide against them. It will be a law against independent research. If a man be found guilty of enquiry into seamanship or medicine in contravention of this law—of enquiry into nautical practice, for instance, or into climatic influences and bodily temperatures, and especially if he be guilty of airing theories of his own on such things, action must be taken to suppress him. First we must deny him the title of "Doctor" or "Captain." Instead we must call him a man with his head in the clouds, one of these chattering Sophists. Furthermore it will be lawful for any citizen so desiring to indict him before a court of justice (or what passes for such a court) on the charge of corrupting the younger men and influencing them to go in for seamanship and medicine in an illegal manner by setting up as doctors or captains on their own authority. If he is found guilty of influencing young or old against the laws and written enactments, he shall suffer the utmost penalties. For there can be no claim to possess wisdom greater than the wisdom of the laws. No one need be ignorant of seamanship or medicine, of sailing regulations or health regulations. The laws are there written out for our conning, the ancient customs are firmly established in our midst. Any who really desire to learn may learn.

Suppose, Socrates, that all the arts are treated like this. How do you imagine that generalship and hunting in all its forms would be effected? What would happen to painting and other representational arts, or to building and manufacture of all types of implements under such conditions; and how could farming or any cultivation whatever be carried on? Imagine the rearing of horses and other animals tied down to legal prescription, or divination and similar ministerial functions so controlled. What would legally-governed draughts be like or legal mathematics, whether simple arithmetic, plane geometry, stereometry or kinematics? What would the world be like if everything worked on this principle, organized throughout according to written laws instead of according to the relevant arts?

Y. S.   It is quite clear that the arts as we know them would be annihilated and that they could never be resurrected because of this law which puts an embargo on all research. The result would be that life which is hard enough as it is, would be quite impossible then and not to be endured.

STR. Yes, but there is a further possible degradation to consider. Suppose we compel each of these arts to function according to a legal code and place a magistrate in charge of this code either by election or by the fall of the lot, and make him rule according to it. Suppose then that he has no regard for the code and acts only from motives of ambition and favouritism. He embarks on a course of action contrary to law but does not act on any basis of scientific knowledge. Evil as the former state was, will not this latter one be still worse?

Y. S. It will indeed.

STR. The laws which have been laid down represent the fruit of experience— one must admit that. Each of them has been put forward by some advocate who has been fortunate enough to hit on the right method of commending it and who has thus persuaded the public assembly to enact it. Any man who dares by his action to infringe these laws is guilty of a wrong many times greater than the wrong done by strict laws, for such transgression, if tolerated, would do even more than a rigid code to pervert all ordered activity.

Y. S. Yes, of course it would.

STR. Then so long as men enact laws and written codes governing any depart- ment of life, our second-best method of government is to forbid any individual or any group to perform any act in contravention of these laws.

Y. S. True.

STR. Then laws would seem to be written copies of scientific truth in the various departments of life they cover, copies based as far as possible on the instructions received from those who really possess the scientific truth on these matters.

Y. S. Yes, of course.

STR. And yet we must never lose sight of the truth we stated before. The man with the real knowledge, the true Statesman, will in many instances allow his activities to be dictated by his art and pay no regard to written prescriptions. He will do this whenever he is convinced that there are measures which are better than the instructions he previously wrote and sent to people at a time when he could not be there to control them personally.

Y. S. Yes, that was what we said.

STR. So an individual or a group who possess a code of laws but try to intro- duce some change in them because they consider it an improvement are doing the same thing according to their lights as the true Statesman.

Y. S. Yes.

STR. But if they acted like this with minds unenlightened by knowledge, they

would indeed try to copy the true original, but would copy it very
badly. If on the other hand they possessed scientific knowledge, it
would no longer be a case of copying at all: it would be the real and
original statesmanship we are talking about.

Y. S.   Yes—or so I should say.

STR.   Now it has been argued already and we have agreed that no large group
of men is capable of acquiring any art, be it what you will.

Y. S.   That stands as our agreed conclusion.

.   .   .   .

STR.   Granted then, that an art of kingly rule exists, the wealthy group or the
whole citizen body would never be able to acquire this scientific art
of statesmanship.

Y. S.   How could they?

STR.   It seems to follow that there is an invariable rule which these imitative
constitutions must obey if they mean to reproduce as far as they can
that one real constitution, which is government by a real statesman
using real statecraft. They must all keep strictly to the laws once they
have been laid down and never transgress written enactments or
established national customs.

Timaeus

*Throughout his life Plato emphasized the value and importance of the
world of ideas to the exclusion of the vulgar, intransient world of
matter. In the* Timaeus, *however, he considers the nature of
physical reality; but remaining consistent with his belief that it was
impossible to have knowledge about nature, he wrote the entire work
in the form of a myth. In the following three excerpts, there are
two accounts of the creation of the world: the first is an account of
creation according to the principles of reason; the second takes into
account the principle of individuality of matter. Placed between
these two is the Platonic theory of time.*

TIMAEUS   Let me tell you then why the creator made this world of generation.
He was good, and the good can never have any jealousy of anything.
And being free from jealousy, he desired that all things should be as
like himself as they could be. This is in the truest sense the origin of
creation and of the world, as we shall do well in believing on the
testimony of wise men: God desired that all things should be good and
nothing bad, so far as this was attainable. Wherefore also finding the
whole visible sphere not at rest, but moving in an irregular and dis-
orderly fashion, out of disorder he brought order, considering that this
was in every way better than the other. Now the deeds of the best
could never be or have been other than the fairest; and the creator,

SOURCE: *The Dialogues of Plato*, translated by B. Jowett (3rd ed.; Oxford: Clarendon
Press, 1892), 5, pp. 450–451, 456, 462–469.

reflecting on the things which are by nature visible, found that no un-
intelligent creature taken as a whole was fairer than the intelligent
taken as a whole; and that intelligence could not be present in anything
which was devoid of soul. For which reason, when he was framing the
universe, he put intelligence in soul, and soul in body, that he might
be the creator of a work which was by nature fairest and best. Wherefore, using the language of probability, we may say that the world
became a living creature truly endowed with soul and intelligence by
the providence of God.

This being supposed, let us proceed to the next stage: In the likeness
of what animal did the Creator make the world? It would be an
unworthy thing to liken it to any nature which exists as a part only;
for nothing can be beautiful which is like any imperfect thing; but let
us suppose the world to be the very image of that whole of which all
other animals both individually and in their tribes are portions. For
the original of the universe contains in itself all intelligible beings, just
as this world comprehends us and all other visible creatures. For the
Deity, intending to make this world like the fairest and most perfect of
intelligible beings, framed one visible animal comprehending within
itself all other animals of a kindred nature. Are we right in saying
that there is one world, or that they are many and infinite? There
must be one only, if the created copy is to accord with the original.
For that which includes all other intelligible creatures cannot have a
second or companion; in that case there would be need of another living
being which would include both, and of which they would be parts,
and the likeness would be more truly said to resemble not them, but
that other which included them. In order then that the world might
be solitary, like the perfect animal, the creator made not two worlds
or an infinite number of them; but there is and ever will be one only-
begotten and created heaven.

.   .   .   .

When the father and creator saw the creature which he had made
moving and living, the created image of the eternal gods, he rejoiced,
and in his joy determined to make the copy still more like the original;
and as this was eternal, he sought to make the universe eternal, so far
as might be. Now the nature of the ideal being was everlasting, but to
bestow this attribute in its fulness upon a creature was impossible.
Wherefore he resolved to have a moving image of eternity, and when
he set in order the heaven, he made this image eternal but moving
according to number, while eternity itself rests in unity; and this image
we call time. For there were no days and nights and months and years
before the heaven was created, but when he constructed the heaven
he created them also. They are all parts of time, and the past and future
are created species of time, which we unconsciously but wrongly transfer

to the eternal essence; for we say that he "was," he "is," he "will be," but the truth is that "is" alone is properly attributed to him, and that "was" and "will be" are only to be spoken of becoming in time, for they are motions, but that which is immovably the same cannot become older or younger by time, nor ever did or has become, or hereafter will be, older or younger, nor is subject at all to any of those states which affect moving and sensible things and of which generation is the cause. These are the forms of time, which imitates eternity and revolves according to a law of number. Moreover, when we say that what has become *is* become and what becomes *is* becoming, and that what will become *is* about to become and that the non-existent *is* non-existent,—all these are inaccurate modes of expression. But perhaps this whole subject will be more suitable discussed on some other occasion.

. . . .

Thus far in what we have been saying, with small exceptions, the works of intelligence have been set forth; and now we must place by the side of them in our discourse the things which come into being through necessity—for the creation is mixed, being made up of necessity and mind. Mind, the ruling power, persuaded necessity to bring the greater part of created things to perfection, and thus and after this manner in the beginning, when the influence of reason got the better of necessity, the universe was created. But if a person will truly tell of the way in which the work was accomplished, he must include the other influence of the variable cause as well. Wherefore, we must return again and find another suitable beginning, as about the former matters, so also about these. To which end we must consider the nature of fire, and water, and air, and earth, such as they were prior to the creation of the heaven, and what was happening to them in this previous state; for no one has as yet explained the manner of their generation, but we speak of fire and the rest of them, whatever they mean, as though men knew their natures, and we maintain them to be the first principles and letters or elements of the whole, when they cannot reasonably be compared by a man of any sense even to syllables or first compounds. And let me say thus much: I will not now speak of the first principle or principles of all things, or by whatever name they are to be called, for this reason,—because it is difficult to set forth my opinion according to the method of discussion which we are at present employing. Do not imagine, any more than I can bring myself to imagine, that I should be right in undertaking so great and difficult a task. Remembering what I said at first about probability, I will do my best to give as probable an explanation as any other,—or rather, more probable; and I will first go back to the beginning and try to speak of each thing and of all. Once more, then, at the commencement of my discourse, I call upon God, and beg him to be our saviour out of a strange and unwonted enquiry, and to bring us to the haven of probability. So now let us begin again.

This new beginning of our discussion of the universe requires a fuller division than the former; for then we made two classes, now a third must be revealed. The two sufficed for the former discussion: one, which we assumed, was a pattern intelligible and always the same; and the second was only the imitation of the pattern, generated and visible. There is also a third kind which we did not distinguish at the time, conceiving that the two would be enough. But now the argument seems to require that we should set forth in words another kind, which is difficult of explanation and dimly seen. What nature are we to attribute to this new kind of being? We reply, that it is the receptacle, and in a manner the nurse, of all generation. I have spoken the truth; but I must express myself in clearer language, and this will be an arduous task for many reasons, and in particular because I must first raise questions concerning fire and the other elements, and determine what each of them is; for to say, with any probability or certitude, which of them should be called water rather than fire, and which should be called any of them rather than all or some one of them, is a difficult matter. How, then, shall we settle this point, and what questions about the elements may be fairly raised?

A STUDY GUIDE TO PLATO'S THOUGHT

1. In the *Meno*, what is the dramatic significance of the opening interchange between Socrates and Meno? Does it serve any philosophical significance?

2. What is the point of the slave-boy demonstration? Students object that Plato gives the boy the correct answers; is this a valid criticism?

3. What does the theory of knowledge called "recollection" entail? What is the connection between the immortality of the soul and recollection? Why does Plato use myth when discussing the immortality of the soul?

4. Plato often couples virtue and knowledge. In your own experience, have you found that when you know something is wrong you will not do it and that when you know that something is right you will do it? Is Plato's coupling accurate?

5. What is Socrates' view of death in the *Apology* and *Phaedo*? Why is he willing to die? What does the phrase, "those who rightly engage in philosophy study only dying and death," mean?

6. What is the theory of forms and how does it relate to the immortality of the soul?

7. In the *Republic*, what is Plato's definition of justice in the individual? In the state? How does justice differ from the other virtues?

8. What is the structure of reality depicted in the "parable of the caves?"

9. What is the role of philosopher in the state? Reason in the soul?

10. Compare Plato's treatment of the soul in the *Phaedo*, the *Republic*, and the *Phaedrus*; is there any essential difference? Why are different theories presented?

11. What is the Platonic theory of love and how does it relate to the theory of forms?

12. In the *Philebus*, what does Plato mean by dialectic? How does dialectic differ from dialogue?

13. In the *Statesman*, what is the distinction between the rule of reason and the rule of law? What do you imagine the second best Platonic state to be like?

14. Why does Plato describe two sequences of creation in the *Timaeus*? What is matter according to Plato? What is time? What are some of the principles Plato assumes but does not delineate in his creation myth?

4

SELECTIONS FROM ARISTOTLE'S WORK

The Principles of Form, Substance, and Action

The Logical Definition of Substance

*The five excerpts of this section attempt to present the complexity and
the characteristic style of Aristotle's thought by focusing attention
on three fundamental concepts—"form," "substance," and
"action"—and tracing their development through the theoretical
sciences. The first selection considers these concepts from the point of
view of language and gives the logical definition of substance. The
second and third both approach the problem from the perspective
of accounting for change: The second considers only those changes
which might be called modifications; and the third considers
absolute change, generation, and destruction. The fourth is a
metaphysical treatise and approaches the problem directly, asking,
What is substance? and What is form? And the last views the
problem from the point of view of accounting for the essential
properties of life.*

Things are said to be named "equivocally" when, though they have a
common name, the definition corresponding with the name differs for
each. Thus, a real man and a figure in a picture can both lay claim to
the name "animal"; yet these are equivocally so named, for, though
they have a common name, the definition corresponding with the name
differs for each. For should any one define in what sense each is an
animal, his definition in the one case will be appropriate to that case
only.

On the other hand, things are said to be named "univocally" which
have both the name and the definition answering to the name in common. A man and an ox are both "animal", and these are univocally
so named, inasmuch as not only the name, but also the definition, is
the same in both cases: for if a man should state in what sense each is

---

Source: "Categories," translated by E. M. Edghill, in *The Oxford Translation of
Aristotle*, edited by W. D. Ross (Oxford, England: The Clarendon Press, 1928),
1, pp. 1a–4b. Reprinted with permission of the publishers.

an animal, the statement in the one case would be identical with that in the other.

Things are said to be named "derivatively", which derive their name from some other name, but differ from it in termination. Thus the grammarian derives his name from the word "grammar", and the courageous man from the word "courage".

Forms of speech are either simple or composite. Examples of the latter are such expressions as "the man runs", "the man wins"; of the former "man", "ox", "runs", "wins".

Of things themselves some are predicable of a subject, and are never present in a subject. Thus "man" is predicable of the individual man, and is never present in a subject.

By being "present in a subject" I do not mean present as parts are present in a whole, but being incapable of existence apart from the said subject.

Some things, again, are present in a subject, but are never predicable of a subject. For instance, a certain point of grammatical knowledge is present in the mind, but is not predicable of any subject; or again, a certain whiteness may be present in the body (for colour requires a material basis), yet it is never predicable of anything.

Other things, again, are both predicable of a subject and present in a subject. Thus while knowledge is present in the human mind, it is predicable of grammar.

There is, lastly, a class of things which are neither present in a subject nor predicable of a subject, such as the individual man or the individual horse. But, to speak more generally, that which is individual and has the character of a unit is never predicable of a subject. Yet in some cases there is nothing to prevent such being present in a subject. Thus a certain point of grammatical knowledge is present in a subject.

When one thing is predicated of another, all that which is predicable of the predicate will be predicable also of the subject. Thus, "man" is predicated of the individual man; but "animal" is predicated of "man"; it will, therefore, be predicable of the individual man also: for the individual man is both "man" and "animal".

If genera are different and co-ordinate, their differentiae are themselves different in kind. Take as an instance the genus "animal" and the genus "knowledge". "With feet", "two-footed", "winged", "aquatic", are differentiae of "animal"; the species of knowledge are not distinguished by the same differentiae. One species of knowledge does not differ from another in being "two-footed".

But where one genus is subordinate to another, there is nothing to prevent their having the same differentiae: for the greater class is predicated of the lesser, so that all the differentiae of the predicate will be differentiae also of the subject.

Expressions which are in no way composite signify substance, quantity, quality, relation, place, time, position, state, action, or affection. To sketch my meaning roughly, examples of substance are "man" or "the horse", of quantity, such terms as "two cubits long" or "three cubits long", of quality, such attributes as "white", "grammatical". "Double", "half", "greater", fall under the category of relation; "in the market place", "in the Lyceum", under that of place; "yesterday", "last year", under that of time. "Lying", "sitting", are terms indicating position; "shod", "armed", state; "to lance", "to cauterize", action; "to be lanced", "to be cauterized", affection.

No one of these terms, in and by itself, involves an affirmation; it is by the combination of such terms that positive or negative statements arise. For every assertion must, as is admitted, be either true or false, whereas expressions which are not in any way composite, such as "man", "white", "runs", "wins", cannot be either true or false.

Substance, in the truest and primary and most definite sense of the word, is that which is neither predicable of a subject nor present in a subject; for instance, the individual man or horse. But in a secondary sense those things are called substances within which, as species, the primary substances are included; also those which, as genera, include the species. For instance, the individual man is included in the species "man", and the genus to which the species belongs is "animal"; these, therefore—that is to say, the species "man" and the genus "animal"— are termed secondary substances.

It is plain from what has been said that both the name and the definition of the predicate must be predicable of the subject. For instance, "man" is predicated of the individual man. Now in this case the name of the species "man" is applied to the individual, for we use the term "man" in describing the individual; and the definition of "man" will also be predicated of the individual man, for the individual man is both man and animal. Thus, both the name and the definition of the species are predicable of the individual.

With regard, on the other hand, to those things which are present in a subject, it is generally the case that neither their name not their definition is predicable of that in which they are present. Though, however, the definition is never predicable, there is nothing in certain cases to prevent the name being used. For instance, "white" being present in a body is predicated of that in which it is present, for a body is called white: the definition, however, of the color "white" is never predicable of the body.

Everything except primary substances is either predicable of a primary substance or present in a primary substance. This becomes evident by reference to particular instances which occur. "Animal" is predicated of the species "man", therefore of the individual man, for if there were no individual man of whom it could be predicated, it could not be predicated of the species "man" at all. Again, colour is present in body, therefore in individual bodies, for if there were no individual body in which it was present, it could not be present in body at all. Thus everything except primary substances is either predicated of primary substances, or is present in them, and if these last did not exist, it would be impossible for anything else to exist.

Of secondary substances, the species is more truly substance than the genus, being more nearly related to primary substance. For if any one should render an account of what a primary substance is, he would render a more instructive account, and one more proper to the subject, by stating the species than by stating the genus. Thus, he would give a more instructive account of an individual man by stating that he was man than by stating that he was animal, for the former description is peculiar to the individual in a greater degree, while the latter is too general. Again, the man who gives an account of the nature of an individual tree will give a more instructive account by mentioning the species "tree" than by mentioning the genus "plant".

Moreover, primary substances are most properly called substances in virtue of the fact that they are the entities which underlie everything else, and that everything else is either predicated of them or present in them. Now the same relation which subsists between primary substance and everything else subsists also between the species and the genus: for the species is to the genus as subject is to predicate, since the genus is predicated of the species, whereas the species cannot be predicated of the genus. Thus we have a second ground for asserting that the species is more truly substance than the genus.

Of the species themselves, except in the case of such as are genera, no one is more truly substance than another. We should not give a more appropriate account of the individual man by stating the species to which he belonged, than we should of an individual horse by adopting the same method of definition. In the same way, of primary substances, no one is more truly substance than another; an individual man is not more truly substance than an individual ox.

It is, then, with good reason that of all that remains, when we exclude primary substances, we concede to species and genera alone the name "secondary substance", for these alone of all the predicates convey a knowledge of primary substance. For it is by stating the species or the genus that we appropriately define any individual man; and we shall make our definition more exact by stating the former than by stating the latter. All other things that we state, such as that he is white, that he runs, and so on, are irrelevant to the definition. Thus it is just that these alone, apart from primary substances, should be called substances.

Further, primary substances are most properly so called, because they underlie and are the subjects of everything else. Now the same relation that subsists between primary substance and everything else subsists also between the species and the genus to which the primary substance belongs, on the one hand, and every attribute which is not included within these, on the other. For these are the subjects of all such. If we call an individual man "skilled in grammar", the predicate is applicable also to the species and to the genus to which he belongs. This law holds good in all cases.

It is a common characteristic of all substance that it is never present in a subject. For primary substance is neither present in a subject nor predicated of a subject; while, with regard to secondary substances, it is clear from the following arguments (apart from others) that they are not present in a subject. For "man" is predicated of the individual man, but is not present in any subject: for manhood is not present in the individual man. In the same way, "animal" is also predicated of the individual man, but is not present in him. Again, when a thing is present in a subject, though the name may quite well be applied to that in which it is present, the definition cannot be applied. Yet of secondary substances, not only the name, but also the definition, applies to the subject: we should use both the definition of the species and that of the genus with reference to the individual man. Thus substance cannot be present in a subject.

Yet this is not peculiar to substance, for it is also the case that differentiae cannot be present in subjects. The characteristics "terrestrial" and "two-footed" are predicated of the species "man", but not present in it. For they are not *in* man. Moreover, the definition of the differentia may be predicated of that of which the differentia itself is predicated. For instance, if the characteristic "terrestrial" is predicated of the species "man", the definition also of that characteristic may be used to form the predicate of the species "man": for "man" is terrestrial.

The fact that the parts of substances appear to be present in the whole, as in a subject, should not make us apprehensive lest we should have to admit that such parts are not substances: for in explaining the phrase "being present in a subject", we stated that we meant "otherwise than as parts in a whole".

It is the mark of substances and of differentiae that, in all propositions of which they form the predicate, they are predicated univocally. For all such propositions have for their subject either the individual or the species. It is true that, inasmuch as primary substance is not predicable of anything, it can never form the predicate of any proposition. But of secondary substances, the species is predicated of the individual, the genus both of the species and of the individual. Similarly the differentiae are predicated of the species and of the individuals. Moreover, the definition of the species and that of the genus are applicable to the primary substance, and that of the genus to the species. For all that is predicated of the predicate will be predicated also of the subject. Similarly, the definition of the differentiae will be applicable to the species and to the individuals. But it was stated above that the word "univocal" was applied to those things which had both name and definition in common. It is, therefore, established that in every proposition, of which either substance or a differentia forms the predicate, these are predicated univocally.

All substance appears to signify that which is individual. In the case of primary substance this is indisputably true, for the thing is a unit. In the case of secondary substances, when we speak, for instance, of "man" or "animal", our form of speech gives the impression that we are here also indicating that which is individual, but the impression is not strictly true; for a secondary substance is not an individual, but a class with a certain qualification; for it is not one and single as a primary substance is; the words "man", "animal", are predicable of more than one subject.

Yet species and genus do not merely indicate quality, like the term "white"; "white" indicates quality and nothing further, but species and genus determine the quality with reference to a substance: they signify substance qualitatively differentiated. The determinate qualification covers a larger field in the case of the genus than in that of the species: he who uses the word "animal" is herein using a word of wider extension than he who uses the word "man".

Another mark of substance is that it has no contrary. What could be the contrary of any primary substance, such as the individual man or animal? It has none. Nor can the species or the genus have a contrary. Yet this characteristic is not peculiar to substance, but is true of many other things, such as quantity. There is nothing that forms the contrary of "two cubits long" or of "three cubits long", or of "ten", or of any such term. A man may contend that "much" is the contrary of "little", or "great" of "small", but of definite quantitative terms no contrary exists.

Substance, again, does not appear to admit of variation of degree. I do not mean by this that one substance cannot be more or less truly substance than another, for it has already been stated that this is the case; but that no single substance admits of varying degrees within itself. For instance, one particular substance, "man", cannot be more or less man either than himself at some other time or than some other man. One man cannot be more man than another, as that which is white may be more or less white than some other white object, or as that which is beautiful may be more or less beautiful than some other beautiful object. The same quality, moreover, is said to subsist in a thing in varying degrees at different times. A body, being white, is said to be whiter at one time than it was before, or, being warm, is said to be warmer or less warm than at some other time. But substance is not said to be more or less that which it is: a man is not more truly a man at one time than he was before, nor is anything, if it is substance, more or less what it is. Substance, then, does not admit of variation of degree.

The most distinctive mark of substance appears to be that, while remaining numerically one and the same, it is capable of admitting contrary qualities. From among things other than substance, we should find ourselves unable to bring forward any which possessed this mark. Thus, one and the same colour cannot be white and black. Nor can the same one action be good and bad: this law holds good with everything that is not substance. But one and the self-same substance, while retaining its identity, is yet capable of admitting contrary qualities. The same individual person is at one time white, at another black, at one time warm, at another cold, at one time good, at another bad. This capacity is found nowhere else, though it might be maintained that a statement or opinion was an exception to the rule. The same statement, it is agreed, can be both true and false. For if the statement "he is sitting" is true, yet, when the person in question has risen, the same statement will be false. The same applies to opinions. For if any one thinks truly that a person is sitting, yet, when that person has risen, this same opinion, if still held, will be false. Yet although this exception may be allowed, there is, nevertheless, a difference in the manner in which the thing takes place. It is by themselves changing that substances admit contrary qualities. It is thus that that which was hot becomes cold, for it has entered into a different state. Similarly that which was white becomes black, and that which was bad good, by a process of change; and in the same way in all other cases it is by changing that substances are capable of admitting contrary qualities. But statements and opinions themselves remain unaltered in all respects: it is by the alteration in the facts of the case that the contrary quality comes to be theirs. The statement "he is sitting" remains unaltered, but it is at one time true, at another false, according to circumstances. What has been said of statements applies also to opinions. Thus, in respect of the manner in which the thing takes place, it is the peculiar mark of substance that it should be capable of admitting contrary qualities; for it is by itself changing that it does so.

If, then, a man should make this exception and contend that statements and opinions are capable of admitting contrary qualities, his contention is unsound. For statements and opinions are said to have this capacity, not because they themselves undergo modification, but because this modification occurs in the case of something else. The truth or falsity of a statement depends on facts, and not on any power on the part of the statement itself of admitting contrary qualities. In short, there is nothing which can alter the nature of statements and opinions. As, then, no change takes place in themselves, these cannot be said to be capable of admitting contrary qualities.

But it is by reason of the modification which takes place within the substance itself that a substance is said to be capable of admitting contrary qualities; for a substance admits within itself either disease or health, whiteness or blackness. It is in this sense that it is said to be capable of admitting contrary qualities.

To sum up, it is a distinctive mark of substance, that, while remaining numerically one and the same, it is capable of admitting contrary qualities, the modification taking place through a change in the substance itself.

Let these remarks suffice on the subject of substance.

The Individual as a Composite of Form and Matter: A Theory of Change

In all sciences that are concerned with principles or causes or elements, it is acquaintance with these that constitutes knowledge or understanding. For we conceive ourselves to know about a thing when we are acquainted with its ultimate causes and first principles, and have got down to its elements. Obviously, then, in the study of Nature too, our first object must be to establish principles.

Now the path of investigation must lie from what is more immediately cognizable and clear to us, to what is clearer and more intimately cognizable in its own nature; for it is not the same thing to be directly accessible to our cognition and to be intrinsically intelligible. Hence, in advancing to that which is intrinsically more luminous and by its nature accessible to deeper knowledge, we must needs start from what is more immediately within our cognition, though in its own nature less fully accessible to understanding.

Now the things most obvious and immediately cognizable by us are concrete and particular, rather than abstract and general; whereas elements and principles are only accessible to us afterwards, as derived from the concrete data when we have analysed them. So we must advance from the concrete whole to the several constituents which it embraces; for it is the concrete whole that is the more readily cognizable by the senses. And by calling the concrete a "whole" I mean that it embraces in a single complex a diversity of constituent elements, factors, or properties.

SOURCE: Aristotle, *The Physics*, translated by Philip Wicksteed and F. M. Cornford (Cambridge, Mass.: Harvard University Press, 1957), *1*, pp. 9–39, and *2*, pp. 7–43. Reprinted with permission of the publishers.

The relation of names to definitions will throw some light on this point; for the name gives an unanalysed indication of the thing ("circle," for instance), but the definition analyses out some characteristic property or properties. A variant of the same thing may be noted in children, who begin by calling every man "father" and every woman "mother," till they learn to sever out the special relation to which the terms properly apply.

Well, then, there must be either one principle of Nature or more than one. And if only one, it must be either rigid, as Parmenides and Melissus say, or modifiable, as the Physicists say, some declaring air to be the first principle, and others water. If, on the other hand, there are more principles than one, they must be either limited or unlimited in number. And if limited, though more than one, they must be two or three or four, or some other definite number. And if they are unlimited, they must either be, as Democritus held, all of the same kind generically, though differing in shape and sub-characteristics, or of contrasted nature as well.

The thinkers who inquire into the number of "absolute entities," again, follow the same line. For their first question is whether the constituents of which things are composed are one or more than one; and, if more than one, are they limited or unlimited? So they, too, are inquiring whether there is one principle or ultimate constituent, or many.

Now, as to the contention that all existence is one and is rigidly unchanging, we might say that it does not really concern the student of Nature, and he need not investigate it; any more than it concerns the geometer to argue with one who denies the geometrical axioms. Such questions must be dealt with either by some other special science or by a fundamental discipline that underlies all the sciences. And so it is in this matter of the unity of the natural principle, for if it is only one, and one in the sense of rigidity, it is not a principle at all; for a principle must be the principle of some thing or things other than its naked self. To consider, therefore, whether the natural principle is one in this sense, is like discussing any other paradox that is set up just for the sake of arguing, like the paradox of Heracleitus, or the contention (should anyone advance it) that the totality of existence is one single man. If their fundamental paradox is admitted, there is nothing strange in all their other paradoxes following from it. Let us then start from the datum that things of Nature, or (to put it at the lowest) some of them, do move and change, as is patent to observation; and let us make a note that we are not bound to answer every kind of objection we may meet, but only such as are erroneously deduced from the accepted principles of the science in question. Thus, it is the geometer's business to refute the squaring of the circle that proceeds by way of equating the segments, but he need not consider Antipho's solution. And yet, after all, though their (the Eleatics') contention does not concern the study of Nature, it does incidentally raise points that are of interest to the physicist; so perhaps it will be as well to examine it briefly,—especially as it has a certain philosophical interest of its own.

Now since the term "existent" is itself ambiguous, it lies at the very heart of the matter to inquire whether (1) they who assert all existing things to be "one" are thinking of all existing things substantively or quantitively or qualitively. Or (2) are all existing things "one substance," like "one man" or "one horse" or "one soul"? Or is it that they are all one in quality, (say) all the same "white," or "hot," or so forth, so that the same qualitive predication can be made of them all? For though all such assertions are impossible, yet they are far from being all identical.

(1) Thus (a) if all things are to be one both substantively, quantitively, and qualitively, then (whether we consider these forms of "being" as objectively separable from each other or not) in any case existences are many and not only one. Whereas (b) if it be meant that all things are one *magnitude*, or one *quality*, then, whether there be any substantive existence at all or no, the assertion is absurd—if we may so call the impossible. For none of the categories except "substance" can exist independently, since all the rest must necessarily be predicated of some substance as their *subjectum*. But Melissus says that the Universe is unlimited, which would make it a magnitude or *quantum*, since "limited" and "unlimited" pertain to *quanta* only, so that no substantive being and no quality or affection can, as such, be called unlimited (though it may incidentally be a *quantum* also); for the conception of a *quantum* enters into the definition of "unlimited," whereas the conception of substantive existence, or quality, does not. If then (a) the "existent" is both a substance and a magnitude, it is two and not one; whereas (b) if it is a substance only, it cannot be unlimited, nor indeed can it have any dimension at all, for otherwise it would be quantitive as well as substantive.

(2) Again, since "one" is itself quite as ambiguous a term as "existent," we must ask in what sense the "All" is said to be *one*. (a) Continuity establishes one kind of unity; (b) indivisibility another; (c) identity of definition and of constituent characteristics yet a third; as for instance (the Greek) *methy* and *oinos* (both of which mean "wine") are "one and the same" thing.

So then, (a) if a single *continuum* is what is meant by "one," it follows that "the One" is many, for every *continuum* is divisible without limit. (And this suggests the question—not to our present purpose, perhaps, but interesting on its own account: whether the part and the whole of a *continuum* are to be regarded as a unity or as existing severally, and in either case in what sense they are a unity or plurality, and if they are regarded as a plurality in what sense a plurality. And the question arises again with respect to a discontinuous whole, consisting of unlike parts: In what sense do such parts exist, as several from the whole? Or if each is indivisibly one with the whole, are they so with each other?)

Whereas (*b*) if "one" signifies an "indivisible," then it excludes quantity (as well as quality); and therefore, the One Being, not being a *quantum*, cannot be "unlimited" as Melissus declares it to be; nor indeed "limited" as Parmenides has it, for it is the limit only, not the *continuum* which it limits, that complies with the condition of indivisibility.

Lastly (*c*) if the contention is that all things are identically "one and the same" by definition (as "clothes" and "garments" are) we are back again at the Heracleitean paradox; for, in that case, being good and being bad will be the same and being not good the same as being good—with the consequence that the same thing will be both good and not good, or both a man and a horse, and we shall no longer be maintaining that all existences are one, so much as that none of them is anything—and being of a certain quality will be the same thing as being of a certain magnitude.

Indeed some of the later ancients were themselves disturbed by the danger of finding themselves admitting that the same thing is both one and many; and therefore some of them, like Lycophron, banned the word "is" altogether; while others did such violence to language as to substitute for "the man is pale-complexioned" the phrase "the man has complexion-paled," or to admit "the man walks" but not "the man is walking," for fear of making the one existent appear many by affixing the word "is"; which nervousness resulted from their equating "is" with "exists" and ignoring the different senses of "one" or of "being." But the fact is that one thing obviously *can* be many, either in the sense of being several conceptually distinct things at once (for though it is one thing to be pale-complexioned and another to be cultivated, yet one and the same man can be both, so that "one" is "many"); or in the sense in which a whole can be regarded as being the sum of the parts into which it can be divided. This latter case brought our philosophers to a stand; and they had to admit multiplicity in unity, unwillingly, as though it were a paradox. And so, of course, it would be, if "one" and "many" were used in the sense in which they contradict each other, but not if, for instance, we are regarding the "one" both in its actual unity and its potential multiplicity. . . .

The false reasoning of Melissus is palpable; for, assuming that "all that comes into existence has a beginning," he deduces from it "all that does not come into existence has no beginning." And, moreover, the assumption itself "whatever comes into existence has a beginning" is untenable, in so far as "began some-when" is taken (as Melissus takes it) to be equivalent to "begin some-where" (so that if the Universe "had no beginning" it "can have no limit," and is "unbounded"): and again in so far as no distinction is made between the thing itself having to begin-to-be at "some particular point of time," and a modification of the thing having to start from "some particular point within the thing itself,"—as if there could not be a simultaneous modification over the whole field affected.

And again why should unity involve rigidity? For if a definite body of water, regarded as a unit without internal distinctions of quality, may have currents of motion within itself, why not the Universe? And, in any case, why not modifications other than those of local movement? But of course the Universe cannot really be homogeneous, like a mass of water (except in the sense of its ultimate constituent being uniform; in which sense, though not in the other, some of the Physicists also have maintained its unity); for a man is patently different in kind from a horse, and opposites are different in kind from each other.

The same kind of argument will apply to Parmenides, as well as such other arguments as particularly apply to his treatment; for here too the refutation turns on the falsity of his assumption and the unsoundness of his deductions. His assumption is false inasmuch as he treats "being" as having only one meaning, whereas in reality it has several. And his inferences are false, because, even if we accepted such a proposition as "nothing that is not white exists," and if "white" had only one meaning, still the white things would be many and not one. Obviously not one in the sense of a homogeneous *continuum*. Nor in the sense of a conceptual identity, for there remains a conceptual distinction between the subject in which the whiteness is seated, and the qualification of "being white," and that distinction does not involve the separate existence of anything alongside of "that which is white"; because the plurality is established not by there being something separate, but by there being a conceptual distinction between white and the subject in which it inheres. But Parmenides had not yet arrived at this principle.

Parmenides, then, must assume not only that the word "is," whatever it may be predicated of, has only one meaning, but also that it means "is identical-with-Being," and that "is one" means "is identical-with-Unity." ("Being" will then no longer be regarded as an attribute); for an attribute is ascribed to some subject (other than itself); consequently, the subject to which "being" (supposing it to be an attribute) is ascribed will have no being at all; for it will be other than "being" (the attribute ascribed to it) and so will be something which (simply) is not. Accordingly "identical-with-Being" (the sole meaning we have given to the word "is") cannot be an attribute of some subject other than itself. For in that case its subject cannot be a thing which is, unless "being" denotes a plurality of things in the sense that each is some thing that is. But it has been assumed that "being" denotes only one thing. If, then, what is identical-with-Being is not an attribute of anything else, but (a subject, so that other things are attributes) of it, is there any reason to say that "identical-with-Being" denotes that which *is* (a real entity) any more than that which *is not* (a nonentity)? (I can show that there is no reason.) For suppose the thing which is identical-with-Being also has the attribute "white," and that "being white" is not identical-with-Being—(the only sense in which it can "be" at all), for it cannot even have "being" as an attribute, because (*ex hypothesi*) nothing except what is identical-with-Being has any being at all—then it follows that white *is not*, and that not merely in the sense that it *is not this or that*, but in the sense of an absolute nonentity. Accordingly, that which is identical-with-Being (our subject) will be a nonentity; for (we assumed that) it is true to say of it that it is white, and this means that it is a nonentity. So that even if (to escape this difficulty) we say that the term "white" denotes what is identical-with-Being, then "being" has more than one meaning.

[Nor can "the existent" have any magnitude, if it is to exclude plurality; for one part of it will have an existence distinguishable from that of another.]

But the analysing of a substantive entity into other substantive entities (so far from being anything startling) is clearly illustrated by definitions. For instance, if "man" signifies a substantive existence, so must "animal" and "biped" also. Otherwise they would be accidental attributes, whether of "man" or of some other subject. But that is impossible, for an accidental attribute must either be separable, so as sometimes to apply and sometimes not (*e.g.* that the man is "sitting down"), or else must include its subject in its own definition (as "snub" includes in its definition the definition of "nose," of which we say that snubness is an attribute). Now, the terms of the definition (which are the constituent principles of the thing defined) do not themselves severally contain, in *their* definitions, any mention of the whole thing which they combine to define. For instance, "man" does not enter into the definition of "biped," nor does that of "white man" enter into the definition of "white." Therefore, if "biped" were an attribute of man at all, it would have to be a separable one, so that the man might, on occasion, not be a biped; the only alternative (as we have said) being that "man" should be included in the definition of "biped"; and this is not so, for it is the other way about, "biped" being included in the definition of "man". And if both "biped" and "animal" were attributes of some other subject than man and were not themselves, severally, subjects at all, then man himself would belong to the class of "things attributed to a subject." We must, then, absolutely lay it down, that the substantively existent is not an attribute of something else; and also that what is true in this respect of the elements of a definition, severally and collectively, is also true of the thing which they define. The universe then is composed of a plurality of distinct individual entities.

Note that some thinkers have given in to both the Eleatic arguments —to the argument that, if "being" has only one meaning, all things are one, by conceding that "what is not" exists; and also to the argument from dichotomy by supposing the existence of indivisible magnitudes. Now it is obvious that, from the premises "being has only one meaning" and "contradictories cannot co-exist," it is not a true inference that there is nothing which "is not"; for "what is not" may very well (not "exist" absolutely, but) be "what is *not this or that*." But to assert that, if there is to be nothing over and above "just what is," it will follow that all things are one, is absurd. For who would take this expression "just what is" to mean anything but "something that substantively exists"? But if it means that, there is nothing against the things that exist being a plurality, as we have seen.

It is clear, then, that the existent cannot be all "one" in this sense.

. . . .

In advancing now to the formulation of a positive theory, let us begin with the general conception of "change" (that is to say, of things "coming into existence" altogether, or "becoming this or that" in particular which they were not before). For the natural order of exposition, as we have seen, is to start from the general principle and proceed to the special applications.

Note, then, that in speaking of one thing becoming another, or one thing coming out of, or in the place of, another, we may use either (1) simple or (2) complex terms. I mean that we can say either (1) that a "man" becomes cultured, or that the "uncultured" in him is replaced by culture, or (2) that the "uncultured man" becomes a "cultivated man." In this case (1) the "man" (who acquires culture), and his state of "unculture" (which is replaced by culture) and the "culture" itself (which was not, but has "come to be") are all what I call "simple" terms; whereas (2) both the "uncultivated man," who became something he was not, and the "cultivated man" that he became, are what I call "composite" terms.

And note that in some of these cases we can say, not only that a thing "becomes so-and-so," but also that it does so "*from being* so-and-so"; *e.g.* a man becomes cultivated from being uncultivated. But we cannot use this expression in all cases; for he does not become cultivated "*from being* a man"; on the contrary, he becomes a cultivated *man*.

And of the two simple terms, "man" and "uncultivated" (both of which we said "became" something), one (the "man") persists when he has become a cultivated man; but the other (the "uncultivated" or "non-cultivated" in him) does not persist either in the simple "cultivated" which we say it has "become" or in the composite "cultivated man."

Observing these distinctions, we may reach a principle of universal application (if we "observingly distil it out," as they say), namely that in all cases of becoming there must always be a subject—the thing which becomes or changes, and this subject, though constituting a unit, may be analysed into two concepts and expressed in two terms, with different definitions; for the definition of "man" is distinct from the definition of "uncultivated." And the one persists while the other disappears—the one that persists being the one that is *not* embraced in an antithesis; for it is the "man" that persists, and neither the simple "cultured" or uncultivated" nor the composite "uncultivated man."

When we speak of something "becoming *from* or *out of*" whatever it may be (rather than of its "becoming so-and-so"), we generally mean by the thing *from* or *out of* which the becoming takes place, the non-persistent term or aspect: thus, we speak of becoming cultivated from being uncultivated, not from being a man. Still the expression "out of" is used sometimes of the factor which persists: we say a statue is made *out of* bronze, not that the bronze *becomes* a statue (in the sense of ceasing to be bronze). When, however, the thing *from* or *out of* which the becoming occurs is the contrasted, nonpersistent term, both expressions are used: we can say of a thing, *e.g.* "the uncultivated" (man), either that he "becomes this" (cultivated) or that he "becomes this (cultivated) *from being* that (uncultivated)." Hence it is the same with the composite terms: we say that the "uncultivated man" becomes cultivated and also that he becomes so "*from being* an uncultivated man."

But there is (in Greek) a further ambiguity; for the same word (*gignesthai*) is employed either of a thing "coming to be" in the absolute sense of "coming into existence," or in the sense of "coming to be this or that" which it was not before; and it is only of a concrete thing, as such, that we can speak of its "coming to be" in the full sense of coming into existence. Now in all other cases of change, whether of quantity or quality or relation or time or place, it is obvious that there must be some underlying subject which undergoes the change, since it is only a concrete something that can have that "substantive existence," the characteristic of which is that it can itself be predicated of no other subject, but is itself the subject of which all the other categories are predicated; but on further consideration it will be equally obvious that a substance also, or anything, whether natural or artificial, that exists independently, proceeds from something that may be regarded as the subject of that change which results in its coming into being; for in every case there is something already there, out of which the resultant thing comes; for instance the sperm of a plant or animal. The processes by which things "come into existence" in this absolute sense may be divided into (1) change of shape, as with the statue made of bronze, or (2) additions, as in things that grow, or (3) subtractions, as when a block of marble is chipped into a Hermes, or (4) combination, as in building a house, or (5) such modifications as affect the properties of the material itself. Clearly, then, all the processes that result in anything "coming to exist" in this absolute sense start with some subject that is already there to undergo the process.

From all this it is clear that anything that "becomes" is always complex: there is (1) something that begins to exist (the new element of form), and (2) something that "comes to be this" (comes to have this form); and this second thing may be regarded under two aspects— as the subject which persists, or as the contrasted qualification (which the new form will replace). For instance, in the uncultivated man who becomes cultivated, "uncultivated" is the contrasted qualification, "man," the subject; or, when the statue is made, the contrasted qualification is the unshapeliness, formlessness, want of purposeful arrangement; the subject is the bronze or marble or gold. If, then, we grant that the things of Nature have ultimate determinants and principles which constitute them, and also that we can speak of them "coming to be" not in an incidental but in an essential sense—so as to come to be the things they are and which their names imply, not having been so before—then it is obvious that they are composed, in every case, of the underlying subject and the "form" which their defining properties give to it; for the cultivated man is in a way "compact" of the subject "man" and the qualification "cultivated," for the definition of such a *compositum* may always be resolved into the definitions of these two components. Clearly then these are the elements, or factors, out of which things that "come to be" arise.

Now the subject is numerically one thing, but has two conceptually distinct aspects, for the man, or the gold, or the material factor in general is a thing that can be counted, since it may almost be regarded as a concrete individual thing and is not an incidental factor in the generation of what comes into being; whereas the negation of the emergent qualification or the presence of its opposite is incidental. On the other hand, the form—*e.g.* the "order" or the "culture" or any other such predicable qualification—is also one thing. So there is a sense in which the ultimate principles of the sum of changing things are two, but a sense in which they are three; for the actual change itself takes place between the terms of an antithesis, such as cultivated and uncultivated, hot and cold, articulated and unarticulated, and so forth; but from another point of view these two principles are inadequate, for they cannot possibly act or be acted upon directly by each other. This difficulty, however, disappears if we admit, as a third principle, a non-antithetical "subject." So in a sense there are no principles except the terms of opposition, and it may be said that they are two in number and no more; but there is a sense also in which we cannot quite admit this and must go on to three, because of the conceptual distinction that exists in them; for instance in the uncultivated man, between his being a man and his being uncultivated, or in the unshaped bronze, between its being unshaped and its being bronze.

It is now clear, then, how many are the principles of things in the changing world of Nature, and in what sense; namely that there is something that underlies all opposites, and that opposition involves two terms.

But, if we take it another way, we may escape the duality of the opposition by considering one of its terms taken singly as competent, by its absence or presence, to accomplish the whole change. Then there will only be the "ultimately underlying" factor in Nature in addition to this formal principle to reckon with. And of this "underlying" factor we can form a conception by analogy; for it will bear the same relation to concrete things in general, or to any specific concrete thing, which the bronze bears to the statue before it has been founded, or the wood to the couch, or the crude material of any object that has determined form and quality to that object itself. This ultimate material will count as one principle (not, of course, one in the sense of a concrete "individual"); and the collectivity of determining qualities implied by the thing's definition is also one principle; and further there is the opposite of this, namely the "being without" or "shortage" of it.

How the principles, then, can be taken as two, and how that enumeration appears to need supplementing, has now been shown. First it appeared as though the "terms of an antithesis" constituted all the principles necessary; but then we saw that something must underlie them, constituting a third. And now we see that the two terms of the opposition itself stand on a different footing from each other; and we see how all the principles are related to each other, and what we are to understand by the "underlying subject." It remains to consider whether the modifying "form" or the modified "matter" is to be regarded as the more "essential" factor of a thing; but that there are three principles altogether, and in what sense they are three, has already been demonstrated.

Let this, then, suffice as to the number of the principles and as to what they are.

It remains to show that the conclusion we have reached not only solves the problem of genesis, but furnishes the only escape from the blind alley into which the first speculations on the subject led their authors. For when first they began to reason on the truth of things and the nature of all that exists, pioneers as they were, they fell upon a false track for want of a clue, and maintained that nothing at all could either come into existence or pass out of it; for they argued that, if a thing comes into existence, it must proceed either out of the existent or out of the non-existent, both of which were impossible; for how could anything "come out of" the existent, since it is already there? and obviously it could not come out of the non-existent, for what it comes out of must be there for it to come out of, and the non-existent is not there at all. And so, developing the logical consequences of this, they went on to say that the actually and veritably "existent" is not many, but only one.

Such then is their dogma; but, as for us, we maintain that when we speak of anything "coming to be," whether out of existence or non-existence, or of the non-existent or the existent acting or being acted on in any way, or of anything at all "becoming this or that," one explanation is as follows: It is much the same as saying that a "physician" does or experiences something, or that he has "become" (and now is) something that he has "turned into," instead of remaining a physician. For all these expressions are ambiguous, and this ambiguity is clearly analogous to the ambiguity concealed under our language when we speak of what "the existent has turned into," or of the existent "doing" this or "experiencing" that. For if the physician builds a house, it is not *qua* physician but *qua* builder that he does so; or if he becomes light in complexion, it is *qua* dark in complexion not *qua* physician that he changes; whereas if he exercises the healing art, or drops or loses that art, so as to become a non-physician, it is *qua* physician that he does so. And so, just as strange conceptions might be formed as to what a physician could or could not do or suffer or become, if we were always thinking of him in his primary and direct capacity as a physician, but applied our conclusions to him in *all* his actual or possible capacities, so, obviously, if we always argue from the non-existent *qua* non-existent, but apply our conclusions to the incidentally non-existent as well, we shall fall into analogous errors. And it was just because the earlier thinkers failed to grasp this analytical distinction, that they piled misconception upon misconception to the pitch of actually concluding that there was no such thing as genesis and that nothing at all ever came to be, or was, except the one and only "existent."

Now we, too (who recognize both "form" and "lack of form," or "shortage," as factors in becoming), assert that nothing can "come to be," in the absolute sense, out of the non-existent, but we declare nevertheless that all things which come to be owe their existence to the incidental non-existence of something; for they owe it to the "shortage" from which they started "being no longer there." And if it seems an amazing paradox to maintain that anything derives in this way from the non-existent, yet it is really quite true. Moreover, it is equally true that it is only in this same incidental sense that anything can derive from the existent either, or "what is" can come into being. In this sense, however, this does occur in the same way as (for instance) if "an animal" should turn into "an animal," or a particular animal—say, a horse—should turn into another particular animal—say, a dog. The dog would come into being, not only "out of" a particular animal, but out of "an animal" (and it would become "an animal"), but only incidentally, not *qua* animal, since it was already an animal and could not "turn into" what it already was. If anything, then, is to "turn into" an animal, otherwise than incidentally, it must be non-animal at the start and must come to be animal in the process. Similarly, if a thing is to become or turn into an existent otherwise than incidentally, it cannot start from what exists;—though neither can it start from the non-existent, for we have explained that this means "from the non-existent as such." At the same time we do not do away with the principle that everything must either be or not be.

This then is one way of formulating the solution of the problem. But there is also an alternative formula based on the distinction between existing as a potentiality and existing as an actuality. But this is developed more fully elsewhere.

. . . .

What I mean by matter is precisely the ultimate underlying subject, common to all the things of Nature, presupposed as their substantive, not incidental, constituent. And again, the destruction of a thing means the disappearance of everything that constitutes it except just that very underlying subject which its existence presupposes, and if this perished, then the thing that presupposes it would have perished with it by anticipation before it came into existence.

. . . .

When we say that anything moves or changes, (1) it may be that the change mentioned is incidental to some other change or dependent on it; as we might say "here comes Culture," when it is really the apostle of culture who "comes," and incidentally brings culture with him. Or (2) it may be that we ascribe to a whole a change that has taken place in some one of its parts; for "the body is healed" when the diseased eye or chest is cured. But (3) there must always be something that moves or changes, neither incidentally nor in the sense that some part of it moves, but in that it is in motion itself and directly. This last is what is *essentially* capable of movement or change. It is different for each kind of change; for instance, there is that which is capable of qualitive change, and within the field of qualitive change, there is a distinction between "what can be healed" and "what can be warmed."

Again, the distinctions now drawn apply to that which causes motion, as well as to that which moves; for the healer is primarily a physician and incidentally a man; and the contusion raised by the fist is said to be raised by the man whose fist it is.

Now, if there is always a thing that causes movement directly and a subject that is moved, and there is also a time *in which* the movement takes place, and further a *whence* and a *whither* (for every movement is "from that to this," and the thing that *passes* from "that" to "this" is distinct from both of them; the kindling log, for instance, is not itself either the "heat" into which, nor the "coldness" out of which, it passes) —all this being so, the movement, or passing, clearly pertains to the log itself and not to the condition of heat or coldness; for no quality or place or magnitude either causes movement or experiences it. We have, then, a mover and a moved and the "whither" of the movement. (I say the "whither" rather than the "whence," because it is from its "whither" that a process of change takes its name. Thus we call a change into non-existence "perishing," though the "whence" of the change is existence no less truly than its "whither" is non-existence, and we call it "genesis" if its "whither" is existence, in spite of non-existence being its "whence.") Thus, to our previous account of movement, we may now add that the "forms" and "conditions" and "place," which are all goals of movement, are themselves without movement, as for instance "knowledge" and "heat." (Yet the question might occur whether anything that affects a subject should not be regarded as a movement, and whether "whiteness" does not so affect its subject—in which case there would be a movement, the goal or "whither" of which would itself be a movement. But, I take it, it is not really the affection "whiteness" that is a movement, but the process of "whitening.")

Note, further, that in these unmoving goals of movement also the distinctions hold between incidental and primary and between "in virtue of a part other than the whole" and "in its own entirety." Thus, a thing that is turning white may incidentally pass into being an object of thought (for the "being an object of thought" is incidental to its colour); and it progresses into "colour" in virtue of the whiteness it passes into being a "part" (species) of the genus "colour" (just as one might say that so and so had "gone to Europe" if he had gone to Athens); whereas the primary fact is that the subject has progressed into "white colour."

So now all is clear as to a movement of a subject as such "on its own account," as contrasted with movement that is "incidental" or "in virtue of a part"; as to what is meant by a thing moving or being moved "itself directly"; and as to the applicability of these distinctions alike to the cause of movement and the subject of movement; and further it is clear that movement takes place not in the form (which is its "whence" or "whither") but in the subject itself which, being potentially movable, is at the time actually in motion.

Here, then, we may dismiss the "incidental" change; because it is always at work in subjects of all sorts and in respect of any of their properties. But change which is not incidental is not found in subjects of all sorts but moves on the line between terms which are either (a) contraries (or their intermediates), or (b) contradictories; as is evident by a survey of instances. A change may start from an intermediate between two contraries because for the purposes of change the intermediate can be treated as opposed to either extreme, so that it may be regarded as a kind of contrary to them, and they to it. Thus, baritone may be contrasted with either bass or alto, and grey is light compared to black and dark compared to white.

Well then, since every transition is from something to something else (for the very word "trans-ition" implies a "going across" from where you were before to where you are afterwards), there seem to be four ways of transit, as follows. Using "positive" to mean something denoted by an affirmative term, a transition may be (1) from positive (A) to positive (B), or (2) from positive (A) to negative (not-A), or (3) from negative (not-A) to positive (A), or (4) from negative (not-A) to negative (not-B). But since a transition from not-A to not-B would not be a change at all, because there is no opposition (there are no contraries and no contradiction), it drops out with our exclusion of the "incidental." This leaves only three transitions or changes to consider.

Of these (3) the transition from not-A to its contradictory A is genesis —either an unqualified "coming into being" out of the mere negation or a qualified "coming to be this or that" from being not this or that. Thus the transition of x from "not-white" to "white" is a coming-to-be *of white*; whereas the transition of x from simple non-existence to existence is an unqualified coming into being: we mean that x has simply come into existence, not that it has "come-to-be (become) this or that." In like manner (2) the transition from A to not-A is "perishing"— either unqualified if it be from existence to simple non-existence or qualified if it be to the negation of some specified thing asserted of the subject, just as in the case of genesis.

And though "is" and "isn't" have other significations in addition to "exists" and "does not exist," yet in no case can that which "is not" partake of motion. In assertion or negation it is a relation and not a subject of any kind, of which we say that it "is" or "isn't," and a relation cannot "move." Nor again is the potentially existent, that "does not exist" actually, capable of motion—except indeed incidentally, in the sense that, if the man moves, his non-paleness or non-excellence incidentally moves with him. Lastly, that which is absolutely "not anything" can in no sense move. From all this it follows that genesis cannot be a movement, for, if it were, the non-existent in its transit to existence would have to move. So (however much incidental genesis there may be) the case of absolute genesis would imply that the non-existent was already there and moving. But it cannot be in motion, nor, for that matter, at rest either. Besides these obstacles to any movement of "that which is not," it may be urged, further, that anything that moves must have position, which the non-existent cannot have, since it is not anywhere. Neither can perishing be a movement; for the opposite of a movement is either movement or rest, whereas the opposite of perishing is genesis.

Since, then, every movement is a transition, and two of the three forms of transition, viz. genesis and perishing (which are transits to and from contradictory opposites) are not movements, it remains that the only transition that is a movement is that from positive to positive. And these positive terms may be either contrary or intermediate; for we must count shortage (which can often be expressed by a positive term, such as "naked," "toothless," or "black") as a contrary.

If, then, the categories are enumerated as substantive existence, quality, whereness, whenness, relation, quantity, action, and being-acted-on, it follows that there are three kinds of movement—qualitive, quantitive, and local.

The field on which movement takes place is not that of substantive existence; for movement is between contraries, and there is nothing contrary to substance.

Nor is it relation; for, when one of two related subjects changes, the relative term may cease to be true of the other, though that other has not changed at all. All changed relation, then, must be incidental to something else.

Nor is it action and passion, whether in the wide sense of the terms or as they are applied to the agent and patient of movement; for there can be neither movement of movement, nor generation of generation, nor, in general, change of change.

For (1) in the first place, there can only be two conceivable senses in which movement of movement could be understood. (*a*) It might mean that a movement was itself the subject or mobile, corresponding to the man who changes from fair to dark, so that in the same way movement is warmed or chilled, or removes to another place, or expands or contracts. But this is impossible, for movement is not a subject at all. Or (*b*) it might mean that some subject, other than the movement itself, might pass out of one process of change into another, as a man may pass from disease to health. But neither is this possible except incidentally; for this movement itself must be along a definite line from one "form" to another. (The same principle applies to genesis and perishing as well as to movement, only that the terms in the former case are direct contradictories and in the latter case not so, though contrasted.) We are to suppose, then, that the subject changes from health to sickness and at the same time changes out of this change into some other. Now it is obvious enough that when he has actually become sick, he may start upon any other change or cease to change at all; but this is one change *succeeding* (or not) another, it is not one change *changing into* another. And each successive change must always be along a definite line, though it might be along any one of all the possible lines, including the direct opposite of the one it succeeds—in this case the change from sickness to health. But naturally the *subject* of change may incidentally carry with him his change of one kind into a change of another kind that he enters into while the first change is going on; for instance, he may shift from the process of recollecting something and so arriving at knowledge to the process of forgetting it and so arriving at ignorance.

(2) Again, if genesis is to have a genesis, and there is to be change of change, then we must go back *ad infinitum*. The consequent necessarily presupposes the antecedent, so that if the ultimate genesis was once in the course of being generated, the ultimate generand was at best only in process of being generated and was not in itself there, even though the subject that was in course of becoming the generand was. And again, taking the ultimate genesis as itself a generand, *its* genesis was once in process of generation, so that it was not itself yet generated, and so forth. And since there is no first link of our infinitely receding chain, neither is there the next or any following link; so it would be impossible that anything should ever come into existence, or move, or change.

(3) Again, the subject of any specific movement is identically the subject of the contrary movement (and of its cessation in rest) and what is capable of being generated is also capable of being destroyed. If, then, genesis is capable of being generated, it is capable of being destroyed. But when? As it begins? As it ends? No; for to be destroyed a thing must be there to destroy. Genesis, then, would have to be being destroyed while it was being generated; which is impossible.

(4) Again, in a case of genesis, as in all cases of change, there must be a subject which passes from the starting-point to the goal. Thus, in all modifications there must be a body that undergoes the modification, if it be physical, or a mind, if it be mental; but what is the corresponding thing that becomes a movement or a genesis? Besides, what goal can we assign to the genesis of a genesis or the movement of a movement? The goal can only be the movement or genesis of something from something to something else. And how could the motion be at the same time the station in which it ceases? If the generating process were coming to

know, the goal would be knowledge, not coming to it. So with all else, and so with genesis: the goal cannot be genesis, but the something generated.

(5) Again, if there are only three kinds of "movement" in the wide sense, both the movement which is supposed to undergo the change and the movement into which it changes can only be a movement of one of these three kinds; thus a local movement must undergo a process of qualitive modification or be itself locally moved.

In conclusion, then, since any subject of movement moves in one of three ways—either incidentally, or in virtue of a part, or primarily, it is only in the incidental sense that a change can be changing, as, for instance, when a man who is recovering his health carries his "recovering" with him as he changes his place in a race or passes from ignorance to knowledge of something. And we have already agreed to dismiss the "incidental" sense of change from our consideration.

Since, then, movement can pertain neither to substantive being nor to relation not to acting and being acted on, it remains that it pertain exclusively to quality, quantity, and locality, each of which embraces contrasts. Movement in quality is what we call "modification," which is a common term applicable to change in either direction between the contraries concerned. By quality I do not mean any quality that is of the essence of the thing that undergoes the change (though its differentia is of course a quality in the general sense of the word), but that passive quality with regard to which it is said to be "affected" or to be incapable of being affected. As to quantity, there is no general term that applies equally to changes in either direction between greater and less; but "increase" is used for the movement towards the full size, "decrease" for movement in the contrary direction. As to motion from place to place, we have neither common nor particular terms, but let "locomotion" pass as the common term, though the Greek word in its strict sense applies only to things which, in changing their place, have not the power to stop, and to things that do not move *themselves* from place to place.

The change towards a greater or a less degree of the same quality is a "modification"; for the movement from contrary to contrary may be either complete or partial. If a thing moves towards the lesser degree of one contrary it is said to be changing towards the other, and if towards the greater degree, to be changing from the other. Nor is there any difference between complete and partial change save in the partial persistence of both contraries in the latter; and the difference of degree means the presence or absence in it of more or less of the other contrary.

The conclusion is now established that the three movements examined are the only ones that there are.

We say a thing is "moveless" either because by its nature it is insusceptible of motion (as a sound is invisible); or because its movement is so slow as to be hardly perceptible, or because it is "slow to begin," which is equivalent to "inapt to move," or lastly because, though it could move under given conditions of time, place, and manner, it is not actually moving. And it is only to this last class of "moveless" things that I apply the term "rest." For rest is the contrary of motion and must therefore be the shortage of that which might by nature be present to the subject in question.

We have now elucidated the questions, what motion is, and what station or rest, and how many kinds of change there are, and how many of motion.

Let us proceed to consider the meaning of the terms "together," "apart," "touching," "between," "next in succession (but not touching)," "contiguous," and "continuous," and the question to what each of the qualifications so described naturally belongs.

Things are said to be "*together*" in place when the immediate and proper place of each is identical with that of the other, and "*apart*" (or "severed") when this is not so.

They "*touch*" each other when their extremes are in this sense "together."

Since all change is between opposites, and opposites are either contraries or contradictories, and there is nothing between contradictories, it is clear that the intermediate or "between" can only exist when there are two contraries. B is "*between*" A and C if anything passing (locally or otherwise) by a continuous change in accordance with its nature must necessarily come to B before it reaches the extreme C on its way thereto from A. "Between" implies at least three terms: the "whence" of the passing, the opposite of the whence, namely the "whither," and something on the line of passage, nearer to the whence than the whither is; and the passage is "continuous" if there is no break or leap in the course—or, if any, only the minimum. I am speaking of a break not in time, but in that with respect to which the changing thing is changing; for in time the bottom note of the diapason may be followed by the top note (which constitutes the maximum possible break or leap in the scale) just as immediately as any two notes severed by the smallest conceivable interval. All which applies not only to changes of place but the other kinds of change as well. In the local application of the word, one thing is the "contrary" of another, if it is farther from it, in a straight line, than any other individual thing of the same order in the field under consideration. The straight line is chosen because, as the shortest, it is the only definite one between any two positions, and a measure or standard must be definite.

One thing is "*next in succession*" to another if it comes after the point you start from in an order determined by position, or "form," or whatsoever it may be, and if there is nothing of its own kind between it and that to which it is said to be next in succession. (By "nothing of its own kind" I mean, for instance, that there must be no other line or lines between one line and the line to which it is next in succession; or no monad or monads, or no house or houses, between the one next in succession and the one it is next in succession to. But there is nothing against a thing being said to be next in succession to another because things of a different kind to themselves intervene between them.) For what is next in succession must succeed *something* and be a thing that comes later; for no one would say that "one" comes next in succession to "two," or the first of the month to the second, but the other way round.

"Contiguous" means next in succession and touching.

Lastly, the *"continuous"* is a subdivision of the contiguous; for I mean by one thing being continuous with another that those limiting extremes of the two things in virtue of which they touch each other become one and the same thing, and (as the very name indicates) are "held together," which can only be if the two limits do not remain two but become one and the same. From this definition it is evident that continuity is possible in the case of such things as can, in virtue of their natural constitution, become one by touching; and the whole will have the same sort of union as that which holds it together, *e.g.* by rivet or glue or contact or organic union.

It is further evident that of these terms—"next-in-succession," "contiguous," "continuous"—"next-in-succession" is the first in logical order. For things that touch each other must be nexts-in-succession, but nexts-in-succession need not be touching; and accordingly "next-in-succession" is a property of things of a higher order of abstraction, such as numbers, where there is no question of contact. And again, if things make a continuous whole, there must be touching; but if they touch, it does not follow that they become continuous; for it does not follow that their extremities become identical if they come together, but they must have come together if they have become identical. Thus, genetically, natural coalescence comes last of all; for if the extremities are to coalesce, they must come into contact; but not all extremities that come into mutual contact therefore become identified, while obviously things incapable of touching each other are also incapable of natural coalescence.

It follows that if, as they say, there were such things as sejunct points and monads, then the point and the monad could not be identical; for two points could touch each other, but two monads can only be next-in-succession to each other. And between any two points there can be found intermediate points, for between every two points there is a line, and in every line there are points; but there can be nothing between two successive numbers, the monad and the dyad for instance.

So now the meaning of "together" and "apart," "touching," "between" and "next-in-succession," "contiguous" and "continuous" has been set forth, and also of what things these several terms can be predicated.

Distinction Between Qualified and Unqualified Change, Implying Notion of Form as "This"

Our next task is to study coming-to-be and passing-away. We are to distinguish the causes, and to state the definitions, of these processes considered in general—as changes predicable uniformly of all the things that come-to-be and pass-away by nature. Further, we are to study growth and "alteration". We must inquire what each of them is; and whether "alteration" is to be identified with coming-to-be, or whether to these different names there correspond two separate processes with distinct natures.

On this question, indeed, the early philosophers are divided. Some of them assert that the so-called "unqualified coming-to-be" is "alteration", while others maintain that "alteration" and coming-to-be are distinct. For those who say that the universe is one something (i. e. those who generate all things out of one thing) are bound to assert that coming-to-be is "alteration", and that whatever "comes-to-be" in the proper sense of the term is "being altered": but those who make the matter of things more than one must distinguish coming-to-be from "alteration". To this latter class belong Empedocles, Anaxagoras, and Leucippus. And yet Anaxagoras himself failed to understand his own utterance. He *says*, at all events, that coming-to-be and passing-away are the same as "being altered": yet, in common with other thinkers, he affirms that the elements are many. Thus Empedocles holds that the corporeal elements are four, while all the elements—including those which initiate movement—are six in number; whereas Anaxagoras agrees with Leucippus and Democritus that the elements are infinite.

(Anaxagoras posits as elements the "homoeomeries", viz. bone, flesh, marrow, and everything else which is such that part and whole are the same in name and nature; while Democritus and Leucippus say that there are indivisible bodies, infinite both in number and in the varieties of their shapes, of which everything else is composed—the compounds differing one from another according to the shapes, "positions", and "groupings" of their constituents.)

For the views of the school of Anaxagoras seem diametrically opposed to those of the followers of Empedocles. Empedocles says that

SOURCE: "On Generation and Corruption," translated by H. H. Joachim, in *The Oxford Translation of Aristotle*, edited by W. D. Ross (Oxford, England: The Clarendon Press, 1928), 2, pp. 314a–315a, 315b–319b. Reprinted with permission of the publishers.

Fire, Water, Air, and Earth are four elements, and are thus "simple" rather than flesh, bone, and bodies which, like these, are "homoe-omeries". But the followers of Anaxagoras regard the "homoeomeries" as "simple" and elements, whilst they affirm that Earth, Fire, Water, and Air are composite; for each of these is (according to them) a "common seminary" of all the "homoeomeries".

Those, then, who construct all things out of a single element, must maintain that coming-to-be and passing-away are "alteration." For they must affirm that the underlying something always remains identical and one; and change of such a *substratum* is what we call "altering". Those, on the other hand, who make the ultimate kinds of things more than one, must maintain that "alteration" is distinct from coming-to-be: for coming-to-be and passing-away result from the consilience and the dissolution of the many kinds. That is why Empedocles too uses language to this effect, when he says "There is no coming-to-be of anything, but only a mingling and a divorce of what has been mingled". Thus it is clear (i) that to describe coming-to-be and passing-away in these terms is in accordance with their fundamental assumption, and (ii) that they do in fact so describe them: nevertheless, they too must recognize "alteration" as a fact distinct from coming-to-be, though it is impossible for them to do so consistently with what they say.

That we are right in this criticism is easy to perceive. For "alteration" is a fact of observation. While the substance of the thing remains unchanged, we *see* it "altering" just as we *see* in it the changes of magnitude called "growth" and "diminution". Nevertheless, the statements of those who posit more "original reals" than one make "alteration" impossible. For "alteration", as we assert, takes place in respect to certain qualities: and these qualities (I mean, e. g., hot-cold, white-black, dry-moist, soft-hard, and so forth) are, all of them, differences characterizing the "elements". The actual words of Empedocles may be quoted in illustration—

> The sun everywhere bright to see, and hot;
> The rain everywhere dark and cold;

and he distinctively characterizes his remaining elements in a similar manner. Since, therefore, it is not possible for Fire to become Water, or Water to become Earth, neither will it be possible for anything white to become black, or anything soft to become hard, and the same argument applies to all the other qualities. Yet this is what "alteration" essentially is.

It follows, as an obvious corollary, that a single matter must always be assumed as underlying the contrary "poles" of any change—whether change of place, or growth and diminution, or "alteration"; further, that the being of this matter and the being of "alteration" stand and fall together. For if the change is "alteration", then the *substratum* is a single element; i.e. all things which admit of change into one another have a single matter. And, conversely, if the *substratum* of the changing things is one, there is "alteration".

. . . .

We have therefore to discuss the whole subject of "unqualified" coming-to-be and passing-away; we have to inquire whether these changes do or do not occur and, if they occur, to explain the precise conditions of their occurrence. We must also discuss the remaining forms of change, viz. growth and "alteration". For though, no doubt, Plato investigated the conditions under which things come-to-be and pass-away, he confined his inquiry to these changes; and he discussed not *all* coming-to-be, but only that of the elements. He asked no questions as to how flesh or bones, or any of the other similar compound things, come-to-be; nor again did he examine the conditions under which "alteration" or growth are attributable to things.

A similar criticism applies to all our predecessors with the single exception of Democritus. Not one of them penetrated below the surface or made a thorough examination of a single one of the problems. Democritus, however, does seem not only to have thought carefully about all the problems, but also to be distinguished from the outset by his method. For, as we are saying, none of the other philosophers made any definite statement about growth, except such as any amateur might have made. They said that things grow "by the accession of like to like", but they did not proceed to explain the manner of this accession. Nor did they give any account of "combination": and they neglected almost every single one of the remaining problems, offering no explanation, e.g., of "action" or "passion"—how in physical actions one thing acts and the other undergoes action. Democritus and Leucippus, however, postulate the "figures", and make "alteration" and coming-to-be result from them. They explain coming-to-be and passing-away by their "dissociation" and "association", but "alteration" by their "grouping" and "position". And since they thought that the truth lay in the appearance, and the appearances are conflicting and infinitely many, they made the "figures" infinite in number. Hence—owing to the changes of the compound—*the same* thing seems different and conflicting to different people: it is "transposed" by a small additional ingredient, and appears utterly other by the "transposition" of a single constituent. For Tragedy and Comedy are both composed of *the same* letters.

Since almost all our predecessors think (i) that coming-to-be is distinct from "alteration", and (ii) that whereas things "alter" by change of their qualities, it is by "association" and "dissociation" that they come-to-be and pass-away, we must concentrate our attention on these theses. For they lead to many perplexing and well-grounded dilemmas. If, on the one hand, coming-to-be *is* "association", many impossible consequences result: and yet there are other arguments, not easy to unravel, which force the conclusion upon us that coming-to-be cannot possibly be anything else. If, on the other hand, coming-to-be *is not* "association", either there is no such thing as coming-to-be at all or it is "alteration": or else we must endeavour to unravel this dilemma too— and a stubborn one we shall find it.

The fundamental question, in dealing with all these difficulties, is this: "Do things come-to-be and alter and grow, and undergo the contrary changes, because the primary reals are indivisible magnitudes? Or is no magnitude indivisible?" For the answer we give to this question makes the greatest difference. And again, if the primary "reals" are indivisible magnitudes, are these *bodies*, as Democritus and Leucippus maintain? Or are they *planes*, as is asserted in the *Timaeus*?

To resolve bodies into planes and no further—this, as we have also remarked elsewhere, is in itself a paradox. Hence there is more to be said for the view that there are indivisible bodies. Yet even these involve much of paradox. Still, as we have said, it is possible to construct "alteration" and coming-to-be with them, if one "transposes" *the same* by "turning" and "intercontact", and by "the varieties of the figures", as Democritus does. (His denial of the reality of colour is a corollary from this position: for, according to him, things get coloured by "turning" of the "figures".) But the possibility of such a construction no longer exists for those who divide bodies into planes. For nothing except solids results from putting planes together: they do not even attempt to generate any quality from them.

Lack of experience diminishes our power of taking a comprehensive view of the admitted facts. Hence those who dwell in intimate association with nature and its phenomena grow more and more able to formulate, as the foundations of their theories, principles such as to admit of a wide and coherent development: while those whom devotion to abstract discussions has rendered unobservant of the facts are too ready to dogmatize on the basis of a few observations. The rival treatments of the subject now before us will serve to illustrate how great is the difference between a "scientific" and a "dialectical" method of inquiry. For, whereas the Platonists argue that there must be atomic magnitudes "because otherwise The Triangle will be more than one", Democritus would appear to have been convinced by arguments appropriate to the subject, i. e. drawn from the science of nature. Our meaning will become clear as we proceed.

For to suppose that a body (i. e. a magnitude) is divisible through and through, and that this division is possible, involves a difficulty. What will there be in the body which escapes the division?

If it is divisible through and through, and if this division is possible, then it might *be*, at one and the same moment, *divided* through and through, even though the dividings had not been effected simultaneously: and the actual occurrence of this result would involve no impossibility. Hence the same principle will apply whenever a body is by nature divisible through and through, whether by bisection, or generally by any method whatever: nothing impossible will have resulted if it has actually been divided—not even if it has been divided into innumerable parts, themselves divided innumerable times. Nothing impossible will have resulted, though perhaps nobody in fact could so divide it.

Since, therefore, the body is divisible through and through, let it have been divided. What, then, will remain? A magnitude? No: that is impossible, since then there will be something not divided, whereas *ex hypothesi* the body was divisible *through and through*. But if it be admitted that neither a body nor a magnitude will remain, and yet division is to take place, the constituents of the body will *either* be points (i. e. without magnitude) *or* absolutely nothing. If its constituents are nothings, then it might both come-to-be out of nothings and exist as a composite of nothings: and thus presumably the whole body will be nothing but an appearance. But if it consists of points, a similar absurdity will result: it will not possess any magnitude. For when the points were in contact and coincided to form a single magnitude, they did not make the whole any bigger (since, when the body was divided into two or more parts, the whole was not a bit smaller or bigger than it was before the division): hence, even if all the points be put together, they will not make any magnitude.

But suppose that, as the body is being divided, a minute section—a piece of sawdust, as it were—is extracted, and that in this sense a body "comes away" from the magnitude, evading the division. Even then the same argument applies. For in what sense is that section divisible? But if what "came away" was not a body but a separable form or quality, and if the magnitude *is* "points or contacts thus qualified": it is paradoxical that a magnitude should consist of elements which are not magnitudes. Moreover, *where* will the points be? And are they motionless or moving? And every contact is always a contact of two somethings, i. e. there is always something besides the contact or the division or the point.

These, then, are the difficulties resulting from the supposition that any and every body, whatever its size, is divisible through and through. There is, besides, this further consideration. If, having divided a piece of wood or anything else, I put it together, it is again equal to what it was, and is one. Clearly this is so, whatever the point at which I cut the wood. The wood, therefore, has been divided *potentially* through and through. What, then, is there in the wood besides the division? For even if we suppose there is some quality, yet how is the wood dissolved into such constituents and how does it come-to-be out of them? Or how are such constituents separated so as to exist apart from one another?

Since, therefore, it is impossible for magnitudes to consist of contacts or points, there must be indivisible bodies and magnitudes. Yet, if we *do* postulate the latter, we are confronted with equally impossible consequences, which we have examined in other works. But we must try to disentangle these perplexities, and must therefore formulate the whole problem over again.

On the one hand, then, it is in no way paradoxical that every perceptible body should be indivisible as well as divisible at any and every point. For the second predicate will attach to it *potentially*, but the first *actually*. On the other hand, it would seem to be impossible for a body to be, even potentially, divisible at all points simultaneously. For if it were possible, then it might actually occur, with the result, not that the body would simultaneously be actually *both* (indivisible and divided), but that it would be simultaneously divided at any and every point. Consequently, nothing will remain and the body will have passed-away into what is incorporeal: and so it might come-to-be again either out of points or absolutely out of nothing. And how is that possible?

But now it is obvious that a body is in fact divided into separable magnitudes which are smaller at each division—into magnitudes which fall apart from one another and are actually separated. Hence (it is urged) the process of dividing a body part by part is not a "breaking up" which could continue *ad infinitum*; nor can a body be simultaneously divided at every point, for that is not possible; but there is a limit, beyond which the "breaking up" cannot proceed. The necessary consequence—especially if coming-to-be and passing-away are to take place by "association" and "dissociation" respectively—is that a body must contain atomic magnitudes which are invisible.

Such is the argument which is believed to establish the necessity of atomic magnitudes: we must now show that it conceals a faulty inference, and exactly where it conceals it.

For, since point is not "immediately-next" to point, magnitudes are "divisible through and through" in one sense, and yet not in another. When, however, it is admitted that a magnitude is "divisible through and through", it is thought there is a point not only anywhere, but also everywhere, in it: hence it is supposed to follow, from the admission, that the magnitude must be divided away into nothing. For—it is supposed—there is a point everywhere within it, so that it consists either of contacts or of points. But it is only *in one sense* that the magnitude is "divisible through and through", viz. in so far as there is one point *anywhere* within it and all its points are *everywhere* within it if you take them singly one by one. But there are not more points than one *anywhere* within it, for the points are not "consecutive": hence it is not simultaneously "divisible through and through". For if it were, then, if it be divisible at its centre, it will be divisible also at a point "immediately-next" to its centre. But it is not so divisible: for position is not "immediately-next" to position, nor point to point—in other words, division is not "immediately-next" to division, nor composition to composition.

Hence there are both "association" and "dissociation", though neither (*a*) into, and out of, atomic magnitudes (for that involves many impossibilities), nor (*b*) so that division takes place through and through—for this would have resulted only if point had been "immediately-next" to point: but "dissociation" takes place into small (i.e. relatively small) parts, and "association" takes place out of relatively small parts.

It is wrong, however, to suppose, as some assert, that coming-to-be and passing-away in the unqualified and complete sense are distinctively defined by "association" and "dissociation", while the change that takes place in what is continuous is "alteration". On the contrary, this is where the whole error lies. For unqualified coming-to-be and passing-away are not effected by "association" and "dissociation". They take place when a thing changes, from *this* to *that*, as a whole. But the philosophers we are criticizing suppose that all such change is "alteration": whereas in fact there is a difference. For in that which underlies the change there is a factor corresponding to the definition and there is a material factor. When, then, the change is in these constitutive factors, there will be coming-to-be or passing-away: but when it is in the thing's qualities, i. e. a change of the thing *per accidens*, there will be "alteration".

"Dissociation" and "association" affect the thing's susceptibility to passing-away. For if water has first been "dissociated" into smallish drops, air comes-to-be out of it more quickly: while, if drops of water have first been "associated", air comes-to-be more slowly. Our doctrine will become clearer in the sequel. Meantime, so much may be taken as established—viz. that coming-to-be cannot be "association", at least not the kind of "association" some philosophers assert it to be.

Now that we have established the preceding distinctions, we must first consider whether there is anything which comes-to-be and passes-away in the unqualified sense: or whether nothing comes-to-be in this strict sense, but everything always comes-to-be *something* and *out of something*—I mean, e. g., comes-to-be-healthy out of being-ill and ill out of being-healthy, comes-to-be-small out of being-big and big out of being-small, and so on in every other instance. For if there is to be coming-to-be without qualification, "something" must—without qualification—"come-to-be out of not-being", so that it would be true to say that "not-being is an attribute of some things". For *qualified* coming-to-be is a process out of *qualified* not-being (e. g. out of not-white or not-beautiful), but *unqualified* coming-to-be is a process out of *unqualified* not-being.

Now "unqualified" means either (i) the primary predication within each Category, or (ii) the universal, i. e. the all-comprehensive, predication. Hence, if "unqualified not-being" means the negation of "being" in the sense of the primary term of the Category in question, we shall have, in "unqualified coming-to-be", a coming-to-be of a substance out of not-substance. But that which is not a substance or a "this" clearly cannot possess predicates drawn from any of the other Categories either—e. g. we cannot attribute to it any quality, quantity, or position. Otherwise, properties would admit of existence in separation from substances. If, on the other hand, "unqualified not-being" means "what is not in any sense at all", it will be a universal negation of all forms of being, so that what comes-to-be will have to come-to-be out of nothing.

Although we have dealt with these problems at greater length in another work, where we have set forth the difficulties and established the distinguishing definitions, the following concise restatement of our results must here be offered:—

In one sense things come-to-be out of that which has no "being" without qualification: yet in another sense they come-to-be always out of "what is". For coming-to-be necessarily implies the pre-existence of something which *potentially* "is", but *actually* "is not"; and this something is spoken of both as "being" and as "not-being".

These distinctions may be taken as established: but even then it is extraordinarily difficult to see how there can be "unqualified coming-to-be" (whether we suppose it to occur out of what potentially "is", or in some other way), and we must recall this problem for further examination. For the question might be raised whether substance (i. e. the "this") comes-to-be at all. Is it not rather the "such", the "so-great", or the "somewhere", which comes-to-be? And the same question might be raised about "passing-away" also. For if a substantial thing comes-to-be, it is clear that there will "be" (not actually, but potentially) a substance, out of which its coming-to-be will proceed and into which the thing that is passing-away will necessarily change. Then will any predicate belonging to the remaining Categories attach *actually* to this presupposed substance? In other words, will that which is only potentially a "this" (which only potentially *is*), while without the qualification "potentially" it is not a "this" (i. e. *is not*), possess,

e. g., any determinate size or quality or position? For (i) if it possesses none of these determinations actually, but all of them only potentially, the result is *first* that a being, which is not a determinate being, is capable of separate existence; and *in addition* that coming-to-be proceeds out of nothing pre-existing—a thesis which, more than any other, preoccupied and alarmed the earliest philosophers. On the other hand (ii) if, although it is not a "this somewhat" or a substance, it is to possess some of the remaining determinations quoted above, then (as we said) properties will be separable from substances.

We must therefore concentrate all our powers on the discussion of these difficulties and on the solution of a further question—viz. What is the cause of the perpetuity of coming-to-be? Why is there always unqualified, as well as *partial*, coming-to-be?

"Cause" in this connexion has two senses. It means (i) the source from which, as we say, the process "originates", and (ii) the matter. It is the material cause that we have here to state. For, as to the other cause, we have already explained (in our treatise on Motion) that it involves (*a*) something immovable through all time and (*b*) something always being moved. And the accurate treatment of the first of these— of the immovable "originative source"—belongs to the province of the other, or "prior", philosophy: while as regards "that which sets everything else in motion by being itself continuously moved", we shall have to explain later which amongst the so-called "specific" causes exhibits this character. But at present we are to state the material cause—the cause classed under the head of matter—to which it is due that passing-away and coming-to-be never fail to occur in Nature. For perhaps, if we succeed in clearing up this question, it will simultaneously become clear what account we ought to give of that which perplexed us just now, i. e. of *unqualified* passing-away and coming-to-be.

Our new question too—viz. "what is the cause of the unbroken continuity of coming-to-be?"—is sufficiently perplexing, if in fact what passes-away vanishes into "what is not" and "what is not" is nothing (since "what is not" is neither a thing, nor possessed of a quality or quantity, nor in any place). If, then, some one of the things "which are" is constantly disappearing, why has not the whole of "what is" been used up long ago and vanished away—assuming of course that the material of all the several comings-to-be was finite? For, presumably, the unfailing continuity of coming-to-be cannot be attributed to the infinity of the material. That is impossible, for nothing is actually infinite. A thing is infinite only potentially, i. e. the dividing of it can continue indefinitely: so that we should have to suppose there is only one kind of coming-to-be in the world—viz. one which never fails, because it is such that what comes-to-be is on each successive occasion smaller than before. But in fact this is not what we see occurring.

Why, then, is this form of change necessarily ceaseless? Is it because the passing-away of *this* is a coming-to-be of *something else*, and the coming-to-be of *this* a passing-away of *something else?*

The cause implied in this solution must no doubt be considered adequate to account for coming-to-be and passing-away in their general character as they occur in all existing things alike. Yet, if the same process is a coming-to-be of *this* but a passing-away of *that*, and a passing-away of *this* but a coming-to-be of *that*, why are some things said to come-to-be and pass-away without qualification, but others only with a qualification?

This distinction must be investigated once more, for it demands some explanation. <It is applied in a twofold manner.> For (i) we say "it is now passing-away" without qualification, and not merely "*this* is passing-away": and we call *this* change "coming-to-be", and *that* "passing-away", without qualification. And (ii) so-and-so "comes-to-be-something", but does not "come-to-be" without qualification; for we say that the student "comes-to-be-learned", not "comes-to-be" without qualification.

(i) Now we often divide terms into those which signify a "this somewhat" and those which do not. And <the first form of> the distinction, which we are investigating, results from a similar division of terms: for it makes a difference *into what* the changing thing changes. Perhaps, e. g., the passage into Fire is "coming-to-be" *unqualified*, but "passing-away-of-something" (e. g. of Earth): whilst the coming-to-be of Earth is *qualified* (not *unqualified*) "coming-to-be", though *unqualified* "passing-away" (e. g. of Fire). This would be the case on the theory set forth in Parmenides: for he says that the things into which change takes place are two, and he asserts that these two, viz. *what is* and *what is not*, are Fire and Earth. Whether we postulate these, or other things of a similar kind, makes no difference. For we are trying to discover not what undergoes these changes, but what is their characteristic manner. The passage, then, into what "is not" except with a qualification is unqualified passing-away, while the passage into what "is" without qualification is unqualified coming-to-be. Hence whatever the contrasted "poles" of the changes may be—whether Fire and Earth, or some other couple—the one of them will be a "being" and the other "a not-being".

We have thus stated one characteristic manner in which *unqualified* will be distinguished from *qualified* coming-to-be and passing-away; but they are also distinguished according to the special nature of the material of the changing thing. For a material, whose constitutive differences signify more a "this somewhat", is itself more "substantial" or "real": while a material, whose constitutive differences signify privation, is "not real". (Suppose, e. g., that "the hot" is a positive predication, i. e. a "form", whereas "cold" is a privation, and that Earth and Fire differ from one another by these constitutive differences.)

The opinion, however, which most people are inclined to prefer, is that the distinction depends upon the difference between "the perceptible" and "the imperceptible". Thus, when there is a change into perceptible material, people say there is "coming-to-be"; but when there is a change into invisible material, they call it "passing-away". For they distinguish "what is" and "what is not" by their perceiving and not-perceiving, just as what is knowable "is" and what is unknowable "is not"—perception on their view having the force of knowledge. Hence, just as they deem themselves to live and to "be" in virtue of their perceiving or their capacity to perceive, so too they deem the things to "be" *qua* perceived or perceptible—and in this they are in a sense on the track of the truth, though what they actually say is not true.

Thus unqualified coming-to-be and passing-away turn out to be different according to common opinion from what they are in truth. For Wind and Air are in truth more real—more a "this somewhat" or a "form"—than Earth. But they are less real to perception—which explains why things are commonly said to "pass-away" without qualification when they change into Wind and Air, and to "come-to-be" when they change into what is tangible, i. e. into Earth.

We have now explained why there is "unqualified coming-to-be" (though it is a passing-away-of-something) and "unqualified passing-away" (though it is a coming-to-be-of-something). For this distinction of appellation depends upon a difference in the material out of which, and into which, the changes are effected. It depends *either* upon whether the material is or is not "substantial", *or* upon whether it is more or less "substantial", *or* upon whether it is more or less perceptible.

(ii) But why are some things said to "come-to-be" without qualification, and others only to "come-to-be-so-and-so", in cases different from the one we have been considering where two things come-to-be reciprocally out of one another? For at present we have explained no more than this:—why, when two things change reciprocally into one another, we do not attribute coming-to-be and passing-away *uniformly* to them both, although every coming-to-be is a passing-away of something else and every passing-away some other thing's coming-to-be. But the question subsequently formulated involves a different problem—viz. why, although the learning thing is said to "come-to-be-learned" but not to "come-to-be" without qualification, yet the growing thing *is* said to "come-to-be".

The distinction here turns upon the difference of the Categories. For some things signify a *this somewhat*, others a *such*, and others a *so-much*. Those things, then, which do not signify substance, are not said to "come-to-be" without qualification, but only to "come-to-be-so-and-so". Nevertheless, in all changing things alike, we speak of "coming-to-be" when the thing comes-to-be something in *one* of the two Columns—e. g. in Substance, if it comes-to-be Fire but not if it comes-to-be Earth; and in Quality, if it comes-to-be learned but not when it comes-to-be ignorant.

We have explained why some things come-to-be without qualification, but not others—both in general, and also when the changing things are substances and nothing else; and we have stated that the *substratum* is the material cause of the continuous occurrence of coming-to-be, because it is such as to change from contrary to contrary and because, in substances, the coming-to-be of one thing is always a passing-away of another, and the passing-away of one thing is always another's coming-to-be. But there is no need even to discuss the other question we raised—viz. why coming-to-be continues though things are constantly being destroyed. For just as people speak of "a passing-away" without qualification when a thing has passed into what is imperceptible and what in that sense "is not", so also they speak of "a coming-to-be out of a not-being" when a thing emerges from an imperceptible. Whether, therefore, the *substratum* is or is not something, what comes-to-be emerges out of a "not-being": so that a thing "comes-to-be out of a not-being" just as much as it "passes-away into what is not". Hence it is reasonable enough that coming-to-be should never fail. For coming-to-be is a passing-away of "what is not" and passing-away is a coming-to-be of "what is not".

But what about that which "is" not except with a qualification? Is it one of the two contrary poles of the change—e. g. is Earth (i. e. the heavy) a "not-being", but Fire (i. e. the light) a "being"? Or, on the contrary, does "what is" include Earth as well as Fire, whereas "what is not" is matter—the matter of Earth and Fire alike? And again, is the matter of each different? Or is it the same, since otherwise they would not come-to-be reciprocally out of one another, i. e. contraries out of contraries? For these things—Fire, Earth, Water, Air—are characterized by "the contraries."

Perhaps the solution is that their matter is in one sense the same, but in another sense different. For that which underlies them, whatever its nature may be *qua* underlying them, is the same: but its actual being is not the same.

Consideration of Substance and Form

1

We have said that it is of substances that we seek the causes and principles and elements. As to what objects are substances, some are agreed

SOURCE: *Aristotle's Metaphysics*, translated by H. G. Apostle, (Bloomington, Ind.: Indiana University Press, 1966), pp. 108–114, 134–145. Reprinted with permission of the publishers.

upon by all thinkers, but also certain others are advocated by some thinkers. Those agreed upon are physical substances, such as fire, earth, water, air, and the other simple bodies, and next, plants and their parts, and animals and parts of animals, and finally, the heavens and its parts, but some thinkers say that also the Forms and the Mathematical Objects are substances. From certain arguments it turns out that the essence and the underlying subject are also substances. Moreover, from other arguments the genus is to a higher degree a substance than the species, and the universal is to a higher degree a substance than the individual; and to the universal and the genus we may attach also the Ideas, for these are thought to be substances according to the same argument.

Since the essence is a substance, and the formula of this is a definition, for this reason we have given a description of a definition and of that which exists in virtue of itself. Since a definition is a formula, and a formula has parts, it was also necessary with respect to parts to examine what sort of objects are parts of *substances* and what are not, and also if to a part of a *substance* there is a corresponding part in the definition of the *substance*. Moreover, we have shown that neither a universal nor a genus is a substance; as for the Ideas and the Mathematical Objects, we must examine them later, for some thinkers say that these exist in addition to the sensible substances.

Let us now proceed to discuss those which are agreed upon as being substances. These are the sensible substances, and all sensible substances have matter. Now a substance is an underlying subject; and in one sense, this is matter (by "matter" I mean that which is not a *this* in *actuality* but is potentially a *this*); in another sense, it is the formula or the *form*, which is a *this* and separable in formula; in a third sense, it is the composite of the two, of which alone there is generation and destruction, and which is separate without qualification, for of substances according to formula some are separable but others are not.

It is clear that also matter is a substance, for in all opposite changes there is some subject which underlies the changes; for example, with respect to place there is something which is now here but after elsewhere; with respect to increase there is something which is now of a certain quantity but after less or greater; with respect to alteration there is something which is now healthy but later sick; and similarly with respect to substance, there is something which is now in generation but later in destruction, and something which is now a subject as a *this* but later a subject with respect to a privation. And the other changes follow this change [with respect to substance], but one or two of the other changes is not followed by this change; for if something has matter which can change with respect to place, it is not necessary for it to have matter which can change with respect to generation or

destruction. The difference between unqualified and qualified generation has been stated in the *Physics*.

2

Since the existence of a substance as an underlying subject and as
matter is agreed upon, and this is what exists potentially, it remains
for us to state what a substance as the *actuality* of a sensible thing is.
Democritus seems to think that there are three differentiae; that the
underlying body, which is matter, is one and the same, but that it
differs either in contour, which is shape, or in turning, which is position,
or in arrangement, which is order. But many differences appear to exist.
For example, some things are spoken of as being combinations of matter, as in the case of things formed by fusion, such as honey-water,
others as being bound together, such as a bundle, others as being glued
together, such as a book, others as being nailed together, such as a
casket, others in more than one of these ways; and some things differ
in position, such as a threshold and a lintel (for these differ by lying in
a certain way), others in time, such as dinner and breakfast, others in
place, such as winds; and some things differ in sensible attributes, such
as hardness or softness, density or rarity, dryness or wetness, and they
differ either in some or in all of these, and in general, some differ by
excess and others by deficiency. Hence it is clear that the "is" has as
many senses [as there are differences]; for a thing *is* a threshold in view
of the fact that it lies in a certain position, and "to be" for this thing
means to lie in that position, and "to be ice" means to be condensed
in a certain way. In some cases, the being of a thing will be defined
even by all of these attributes, since the thing may be partly blended,
partly fused, partly bound together, partly condensed, and partly
formed by the use of other differentiae, as in the case of a hand or
a foot. Accordingly, we should posit the genera of differentiae (for these
will be the principles of existence), that is, those in virtue of which
things differ by being more or less dense or rare, or the others of this
sort; for all these come under excess and deficiency. And if anything
differs in shape, or smoothness or roughness, then it differs in straight-
ness or curvature. And for other things, *to be* will be *to be blended*,
and *not to be* will be the opposite.

It is evident from these that if the *substance* is the cause of the being
of each thing, then it is in these differentiae that we must seek the
cause of the being of each of these things. Now none of these differentiae is a substance, not even if combined, but in each case it is
something analogous to *substance;* and just as in substances that which
is a predicate of matter is the *actuality* itself, so also in the other definitions, that which is a predicate is to the highest degree the *actuality*.
For example, if we are to define a threshold, we should say "wood or

stone in such-and-such a position", and we should define a house as "bricks and timber in such-and-such a position" (or, also the final cause is present in some cases), and ice as "water frozen or condensed in such-and-such a way"; and we should define a harmony as "such-and-such a combination of high and low", and the rest in the same manner.

It is evident from these that there is a distinct *actuality* for distinct matter, and a distinct formula; for in some cases it is the combination, in others the blend, and in others some one of the others which we have named. On account of this, in defining what a house is, those who say that it is stones and bricks and wood speak of what is potentially a house, for these are matter; those who say that it is a receptacle for sheltering animals or goods, or some other such thing, speak of the *actuality* of the house. But those who combine both, speak of the third kind of substance, the one composed of matter and form (for it seems that the formula by means of the differentiae is that of the form and of the *actuality*, but the formula of the constituents is rather that of the matter); and this is similar to the kind of definitions which Archytas used to accept, for they are of both matter and form. For example, what is windlessness? Stillness in a large expanse of air. Air is the matter, stillness is the *actuality* and the *substance*. What is a calm? Smoothness of the sea. The underlying subject as matter is the sea, the *actuality* or the *shape* is smoothness.

From what has been said it is evident what a sensible substance is and how it exists; in one sense it is matter, in another it is the *form* or *actuality*, and in a third it is the composite of these two.

3

We should not ignore the fact that sometimes we are unaware of whether a name signifies the composite substance, or the *actuality* or *shape*, for example, whether "a house" signifies the composite, that is, a covering made of bricks and stones laid in such-and-such a manner, or, the *actuality* or form, that is, a covering, whether "a line" signifies twoness in length or twoness, and whether "an animal" signifies a soul in a body or a soul; for it is the soul which is the *substance* or the *actuality* of a certain body. The name "an animal" may also be applied to both, not as having the same formula when asserted of both, but as being related to one thing. But, although these distinctions contribute something to another inquiry, they contribute nothing to the inquiry into sensible *substances;* for the essence belongs to the form or *actuality*. For a soul and the essence of a soul are the same, but the essence of a man is not the same as the man, unless also the soul is called "a man"; accordingly, in some cases a thing and its essence are the same, in others this is not so.

From our inquiry it appears that the constituents of a syllable are not its letters plus their combination, nor, in the case of a house, are they bricks and combination. And this is right; for a combination or blend does not consist of those objects of which it is the combination or the blend. And in the other cases, it is similar; for example, if a threshold exists by virtue of its position, the position does not consist of the threshold, but it is rather the threshold which is composed of the position. Nor is a man an animal plus two-footedness, but there must be something which exists besides these, if these are matter, and this something is neither an element, nor does it consist of elements, but is the *substance;* and it is this that some thinkers leave out and state only the matter. So if this is the cause of the existence and of the substance, then it is this that they should be calling "a substance".

Now this *substance* must either be eternal or be destructible without being in the process of being destroyed and generable without being in the process of being generated. It was shown and made clear elsewhere that no one makes or generates the form, but what is made is a *this*, and what is generated is something from these.

It is not yet clear if the *substances* of destructible things can exist apart, but it is clear that in some cases they cannot, for example, in cases where they cannot exist apart from the individuals, as in a house or utensil. Perhaps these things themselves are not substances, nor anything else except the things which are formed by nature; for one might posit only nature as a *substance* in destructible things.

The problem which the followers of Antisthenes and other such uneducated men used to raise has some value here, namely, that it is not possible to define the whatness of a thing, for a definition according to them is a long rigmarole, but that it is possible to state and even teach what kind of a thing something is; for example, in the case of silver, that it is not possible to define its whatness, but that one may say that it is like tin. If so, then there can be a definition and a formula of a substance, if it be composite, whether sensible or intelligible; but there can be no such of its primary constituents, if the defining formula signifies that something is attributed to something else, where one part is to be like matter and the other part like *shape*.

It is also evident, if *substances* are in a sense numbers, why they are numbers in this sense and not composed of units as some say. For (1) a definition is a number of a sort; for it is divisible and into indivisibles, since no formula is infinite, and a number is a thing of this sort. And (2) just as, if anything which is a part of a number is subtracted from or added to a number, even if that part is the smallest, the number formed is no longer the same but distinct, so the definition or the essence will not be the same but distinct if something is added to or subtracted from it. And (3) there must be something in a number by which the number is one, but these thinkers say nothing about what it is that makes a number one, if indeed it is one. For either it is not one but a heap as it were, or if it is indeed one, they should state what it is that makes a unity out of many. And a definition is one, but similarly they have nothing to say about its unity. And this is to be expected; for a *substance* is one in this way for the same reason, not one as a sort of unit or point, but as an actuality and a nature of some kind. And (4) just as a number does not admit the more or the less, so neither does a substance in the sense of form; and if a substance does so admit, it will be a substance which includes matter.

Concerning the generation and destruction of the so-called substances, how they are possible and how they are not, and also the reference of substances to numbers, let the discussion up to now suffice.

4

Concerning material substance, we must not forget that even if all generated things are generated from the same primary constituent or constituents and if the matter as a principle is the same for all, still there is matter which is *proper* to each thing; for example, for phlegm the proximate matter is the sweet or the fatty, for the bile it is the bitter or some others, and perhaps all these come from the same matter. And the same thing comes from many matters, if among these one comes from the other; for example, phlegm comes from the fatty and the sweet, if the fatty comes from the sweet; and it comes from the bile when this is decomposed into its ultimate matter. For one thing may come from a second in two ways, either when the second is earlier on the way to generation, or when it is analyzed into its principles.

If the matter is one, distinct things may be generated because of distinct moving causes; for example, from wood a chest and a bed may be made. In some cases, if the things are distinct their matter must be distinct; for example, a saw could not be made of wood, nor is this up to the moving cause; for no such cause could make a saw out of wool or wood. But if it is at all possible for the same thing to be made from distinct matters, it is clear that the art or the moving principle must be the same; for if both the matter and the moving principle are distinct, so will be the thing generated.

So when one seeks the cause of something, since "cause" has several senses, all the possible causes in each case should be stated. For example, what is the material cause of a man? Let us say, the menses. What is the moving cause? Let us say, the seed. What is the cause as form? It is his essence. What is the final cause? His end. Perhaps the latter two are the same. But we should state the proximate causes. What is the material cause? Not fire or earth, but what is proper to the thing. Accordingly, with regard to physical and generable substances we should proceed in this manner, if we are to proceed rightly, that is, if indeed the causes are these and so many and if we are to know the causes.

As for the physical but eternal substances, this requires another discussion. For perhaps some of them have no matter, or not matter of this kind but only matter which is movable with respect to place. Nor is there matter in those things which exist by nature but are not substances; however, their underlying subject is a substance. For example, what is the cause of an eclipse, and what is its matter? There is no matter, but it is the Moon which is affected by the eclipse. What is the moving cause which has destroyed the light? The Earth. Perhaps there is no final cause. The cause as form is the formula, but this is not made clear unless it includes the cause. For example, what is an eclipse? A privation of light. But if we add "caused by the Earth moving in between", what results is the formula which includes the cause. In the case of sleep it is not clear what is the primary part that is affected. Is it the animal? Yes, but in virtue of what part, or which is the primary part? The heart, or some other part. Next, by what moving cause? Next, what is the affection of the primary part, but not of the whole animal? Let us say, such-and-such immobility. Yes, but this occurs in virtue of what affection of the primary part?

5

Since some things now exist and now do not exist but are not in the process of being generated or of being destroyed, as for example points, if they exist indeed, and in general forms and *shapes* (for it is not whiteness that is generated but it is the wood that becomes white, if everything generated comes to be from something and comes to be something), not all contraries can be generated from each other, but the generation of a light man from a dark man is distinct from that of lightness from darkness. Nor have all things matter, but only those which are generated from or change to each other. Those things which exist and do not exist, without being in the process of changing, have no matter.

There is a *difficulty* as to how the matter of each thing is related to the contraries. For example, if the body is potentially healthy, and disease is contrary to health, is the body potentially both? And is water potentially both wine and vinegar? Or is it that, in the one case, it is matter with respect to a possession or a form, and in the other, with respect to privation or destruction, which are contrary to nature?

There is also the *difficulty* as to why wine is not the matter of vinegar nor potentially vinegar, although vinegar is generated from wine, and why a living animal is not potentially dead. Indeed they are not, but destructions are accidental, and it is the animal's matter itself which, in virtue of the destruction, is the potency and matter of a corpse, and it is water which is the matter of vinegar. For generation in these cases is like generation of night from day. And all things which change to each other in this manner must go back to their matter; for example, if a corpse is to become an animal, it must first go back to its matter and then in this way become an animal, and vinegar must first go back to water and then become wine.

6

Returning to the *difficulty* stated earlier concerning definitions and numbers, we may ask: What causes each of them to be one? For in anything which has many parts and whose totality is not just a heap but is some whole besides just the parts, there is some cause, inasmuch as in bodies, too, the cause of unity is in some cases contact, in others viscosity, or some other such affection. Now a definition is one formula not by the placing of things together, as in the *Iliad*, but by being a formula of one thing. What is it, then, that makes a man one, and why is he one and not many, such as an animal and also a biped, if indeed there exists, as some say, Animal Itself and Biped Itself. For why are these two not Man, so that men may exist by participating not in Man or one Idea but in two, Animal and Biped? And, in general, a man would then be not one but more than one, an animal and a biped. It is evident, then, if we proceed in this manner, as these thinkers are accustomed to define and speak, we cannot answer or solve the *difficulty*. But if, as we maintain, the one is matter and the other *form*, and the former exists potentially but the latter as *actuality*, what we seek no longer seems to be a *difficulty*. For this is the same *difficulty* as the one which would arise if the definition of a *cloak* were to be "a round bronze"; for the name would be a sign of this formula, so that we would be inquiring into the cause of the unity of roundness and bronze. The difficulty indeed no longer appears, in view of the fact that the one is matter and the other form. What causes that which exists potentially to be in *actuality*, then, aside from that which acts in the case of things which are generated? Doubtless, nothing else causes that which is potentially a sphere to be a sphere in actuality, but this is the essence in each.

Of matter, some is intelligible and some sensible, and in a formula it is always the case that one part is matter and one part is *actuality;* for example, in the case of a circle, "a plane figure." But of the things which have no matter, whether intelligible or sensible, each is immediately just a unity as well as just a being, such as a *this*, or a quality, or a quantity. And so in their definitions, too, neither "being" nor "one" is present, and the essence of each is immediately a unity as well as a being. Consequently, nothing else is the cause of oneness or of being in each of them; for each is immediately a being and a unity, not in the sense that "being" and "unity" are their genera, nor in the sense that they exist apart from individuals.

It is because of this *difficulty* that some thinkers speak of participation but are perplexed as to what causes participation and what it is to participate, and others speak of communion with the soul, as when Lycophron says that *knowledge* is the communion of *knowing* with the soul, and still others call life a composition or connection of soul with body. However, the same argument applies to all; for being healthy, too, will be a communion or a connection or a composition of soul and health, and the being of a triangular bronze will be a composition of bronze and a triangle, and being white will be a composition of surface and whiteness. They are speaking in this manner because they are seeking a unifying formula of, and a difference between, potentiality and actuality. But, as we have stated, the last matter and the *form* are one and the same; the one exists potentially, the other as *actuality*. Thus, it is like asking what the cause of unity is and what causes something to be one; for each thing is a kind of unity, and potentiality and actuality taken together exist somehow as one. So there is no other cause, unless it be the mover which causes the motion from potency to *actuality*. But all things which have no matter are without qualification just unities of one kind or another.

Form Identified with the Capacity for Action

So much for the theories of soul handed down by our predecessors. Let us, then, make a fresh start and try to determine what soul is and what will be its most comprehensive definition. Now there is one class of existent things which we call substance, including under the term, firstly, matter, which in itself is not this or that; secondly, shape or form, in virtue of which the term this or that is at once applied; thirdly, the whole made up of matter and form. Matter is identical with potentiality, form with actuality. And there are two meanings of actuality: knowledge illustrates the one, exercise of knowledge the other. Now bodies above all things are held to be substances, particularly such bodies as are the work of nature; for to these all the rest owe their origin. Of natural bodies some possess life and some do not: where by life we mean the power of self-nourishment and of independent growth and decay. Consequently every natural body possessed of life must be substance, and substance of the composite order. And since in fact we have here body with a certain attribute, namely, the possession of life, the body will not be the soul: for the body is not an attribute of a subject, it stands rather for a subject of attributes, that is, matter.

SOURCE: "On the Soul," translated by R. D. Hicks, in *Aristotle: De Anima* (Cambridge, England: Cambridge University Press, 1907), pp. 51–59.

It must follow, then, that soul is substance in the sense that it is the form of a natural body having in it the capacity of life. Such substance is actuality. The soul, therefore, is the actuality of the body above described. But the term "actuality" is used in two senses; in the one it answers to knowledge, in the other to the exercise of knowledge. Clearly in this case it is analogous to knowledge: for sleep, as well as waking, implies the presence of soul; and, whilst waking is analogous to the exercise of knowledge, sleep is analogous to the possession of knowledge without its exercise; and in the same individual the possession of knowledge comes in order of time before its exercise. Hence soul is the first actuality of a natural body having in it the capacity of life. And a body which is possessed of organs answers to this description. We may note that the parts of plants, as well as those of animals, are organs, though of a very simple sort: for instance, a leaf is the sheath of the pod and the pod of the fruit. 'The roots, again, are analogous to the mouths of animals, both serving to take in nourishment. If, then, we have to make a general statement touching soul in all its forms, the soul will be the first actuality of a natural body furnished with organs. Hence there is no need to enquire whether soul and body are one, any more than whether the wax and the imprint are one; or, in general, whether the matter of a thing is the same with that of which it is the matter. For, of all the various meanings borne by the terms unity and being, actuality is the meaning which belongs to them by the fullest right.

It has now been stated in general terms what soul is, namely, substance as notion or form. And this is the quiddity of such and such a body. Suppose, for example, that any instrument, say, an axe, were a natural body, its axeity would be its substance, would in fact be its soul. If this were taken away, it would cease, except in an equivocal sense to be an axe. But the axe is after all an axe. For it is not of a body of this kind that the soul is the quiddity, that is, the notion or form, but of a natural body of a particular sort, having in itself the origination of motion and rest.

Further, we must view our statement in the light of the parts of the body. For, if the eye were an animal, eyesight would be its soul, this being the substance as notion or form of the eye. The eye is the matter of eyesight, and in default of eyesight it is no longer an eye, except equivocally, like an eye in stone or in a picture. What has been said of the part must be understood to apply to the whole living body; for, as the sensation of a part of the body is to that part, so is sensation as a whole to the whole sentient body as such. By that which has in it the capacity of life is meant not the body which has lost its soul, but that which possesses it. Now the seed in animals, like the fruit in plants, is that which is potentially such and such a body. As, then, the cutting of the axe or the seeing of the eye is full actuality, so, too, is the waking state; while the soul is actuality in the same sense as eyesight and the capacity of the instrument. The body, on the other hand, is simply that which is potentially existent. But, just as in the one case the eye means the pupil in conjunction with the eyesight, so in the other soul and body together constitute the animal.

Now it needs no proof that the soul—or if it is divisible into parts, certain of its parts—cannot be separated from the body, for there are cases where the actuality belongs to the parts themselves. There is, however, no reason why some parts should not be separated, if they are not the actualities of any body whatever. Again, it is not clear whether the soul may not be the actuality of the body as the sailor is of the ship. This, then, may suffice for an outline or provisional sketch of soul.

But, as it is from the things which are naturally obscure, though more easily recognized by us, that we proceed to what is clear and, in the order of thought, more knowable, we must employ this method in trying to give a fresh account of soul. For it is not enough that the defining statement should set forth the fact, as most definitions do; it should also contain and present the cause: whereas in practice what is stated in the definition is usually no more than a conclusion. For example, what is quadrature? The construction of an equilateral rectangle equal in area to a given oblong. But such a definition expresses merely the conclusion. Whereas, if you say that quadrature is the discovery of a mean proportional, then you state the reason.

We take, then, as our starting-point for discussion that it is life which distinguishes the animate from the inanimate. But the term life is used in various senses; and, if life is present in but a single one of these senses, we speak of a thing as living. Thus there is intellect, sensation, motion from place to place and rest, the motion concerned with nutrition and, further, decay and growth. Hence it is that all plants are supposed to have life. For apparently they have within themselves a faculty and principle whereby they grow and decay in opposite directions. For plants do not grow upwards without growing downwards; they grow in both directions equally, in fact in all directions, as many as are constantly nourished and therefore continue to live, so long as they are capable of absorbing nutriment. This form of life can be separated from the others, though in mortal creatures the others cannot be separated from it. In the case of plants the fact is manifest: for they have no other faculty of soul at all.

It is, then, in virtue of this principle that all living things live, whether animals or plants. But it is sensation primarily which constitutes the animal. For, provided they have sensation, even those creatures which are devoid of movement and do not change their place are called animals and are not merely said to be alive. Now the primary sense in all animals is touch. But, as the nutritive faculty may exist without touch or any form of sensation, so also touch may exist apart from the other senses. By nutritive faculty we mean the part of the soul in which even plants share. Animals, however, are found universally to have the sense of touch: why this is so in each of the two cases will be stated hereafter.

For the present it may suffice to say that the soul is the origin of the functions above enumerated and is determined by them, namely, by capacities of nutrition, sensation, thought, and by motion. But whether each one of these is a soul or part of a soul and, if a part, whether it is only logically distinct or separable in space also is a question, the answer to which is in some cases not hard to see: other cases present difficulties. For, just as in the case of plants some of them are found to live when divided and separated from each other (which implies that the soul in each plant, though actually one, is potentially several souls), so, too, when insects or annelida are cut up, we see the same thing happen with other varieties of soul: I mean, each of the segments has sensation and moves from place to place, and, if it has sensation, it has also imagination and appetency. For, where there is sensation, there is also pleasure and pain: and, where these are, desire also must of necessity be present. But as regards intellect and the speculative faculty the case is not yet clear. It would seem, however, to be a distinct species of soul, and it alone is capable of separation from the body, as that which is eternal from that which is perishable. The remaining parts of the soul are, as the foregoing consideration shows, not separable in the way that some allege them to be: at the same time it is clear that they are logically distinct. For the faculties of sensation and of opinion taken in the abstract are distinct, since to have sensation and to opine are distinct. And so it is likewise with each of the other faculties above mentioned. Again, while some animals possess all these functions, others have only some of them, others only one. It is this which will differentiate animal from animal. The reason why this is so must be investigated hereafter. The case is similar with the several senses: some animals have all of them, others some of them, others again only one, the most indispensable, that is, touch.

Now "that by which we live and have sensation" is a phrase with two meanings, answering to the two meanings of "that by which we know" (the latter phrase means, firstly, knowledge and, secondly, soul, by either of which we say we know). Similarly that by which we have health means either health itself or a certain part, if not the whole, of the body. Now of these knowledge and health are the shape and in some sort form, the notion and virtual activity, of that which is capable of receiving in the one case knowledge, in the other health: that is to say, it is in that which is acted upon or conditioned that the activity of the causal agencies would seem to take effect. Now the soul is that whereby primarily we live, perceive, and have understanding: therefore it will be a species of notion or form, not matter or substratum. Of the three meanings of substance mentioned above, form, matter and the whole made up of these two, matter is potentiality and form is actuality. And, since the whole made up of the two is endowed with soul, the body is not the actuality of soul, but soul the actuality of a particular body. Hence those are right who regard the soul as not independent of body and yet at the same time as not itself a species of body. It is not body, but something belonging to body, and therefore resides in body and, what is more, in such and such a body. Our predecessors were wrong in endeavouring to fit the soul into a body without further determination of the nature and qualities of that body: although we do not even find that of any two things taken at random the one will admit the other. And this result is what we might expect. For the actuality of each thing comes naturally to be developed in the potentiality of each thing: in other words, in the appropriate matter. From these considerations, then, it is manifest that soul is a certain actuality, a notion or form, of that which has the capacity to be endowed with soul.

On Man

The Nature of Human Happiness

The following selection, from the last book of the Ethics, *not only provides Aristotle's ideal of human happiness, which is essentially the same as Plato's, but also explains the relationship between politics and ethics.*

After this discussion of the kinds of virtue and friendship and pleasure it remains to give a sketch of happiness, since we defined happiness as the end of human things. We shall shorten our account of it if we begin by recapitulating our previous remarks.

We said that happiness is not a moral state; for, if it were, it would be predicable of one who spends his whole life in sleep, living the life of a vegetable, or of one who is utterly miserable. If then we cannot accept this view if we must rather define happiness as an activity of some kind, as has been said before, and if activities are either necessary and

SOURCE: *Nicomachean Ethics of Aristotle*, translated by J. E. C. Welldon (London, England: Macmillan & Co. Ltd., 1908), pp. 332–350. Reprinted with permission of the publishers.

desirable as a means to something else or desirable in themselves, it is clear that we must define happiness as belonging to the class of activities which are desirable in themselves, and not desirable as means to something else; for happiness has no want, it is self-sufficient.

Again, activities are desirable in themselves, if nothing is expected from them beyond the activity. This seems to be the case with virtuous actions, as the practice of what is noble and virtuous is a thing desirable in itself. It seems to be the case also with such amusements as are pleasant, we do not desire them as means to other things; for they often do us harm rather than good by making us careless about our persons and our property. Such pastimes are generally the resources of those whom the world calls happy. Accordingly people who are clever at such pastimes are generally popular in the courts of despots, as they make themselves pleasant to the despot in the matters which are the objects of his desire, and what he wants is to pass the time pleasantly.

The reason why these things are regarded as elements of happiness is that people who occupy high positions devote their leisure to them. But such people are not, I think, a criterion. For a high position is no guarantee of virtue or intellect, which are the sources on which virtuous activities depend. And if these people, who have never tasted a pure and liberal pleasure, have recourse to the pleasures of the body, it must not be inferred that these pleasures are preferable; for even children suppose that such things as are valued or honoured among them are best. It is only reasonable then that, as men and children differ in their estimate of what is honourable, so should good and bad people.

As has been frequently said, therefore, it is the things which are honourable and pleasant to the virtuous man that are really honourable and pleasant. But everybody feels the activity which accords with his own moral state to be most desirable, and accordingly the virtuous man regards the activity in accordance with virtue as most desirable.

Happiness then does not consist in amusement. It would be paradoxical to hold that the end of human life is amusement, and that we should toil and suffer all our life for the sake of amusing ourselves. For we may be said to desire all things as means to something else except indeed happiness, as happiness is the end *or perfect state.*

It appears to be foolish and utterly childish to take serious trouble and pains for the sake of amusement. But to amuse oneself with a view to being serious seems to be right, as Anacharsis says; for amusement is a kind of relaxation, and it is because we cannot work for ever that we need relaxation.

Relaxation then is not an end. We enjoy it as a means to activity; but it seems that the happy life is a life of virtue, and such a life is serious, it is not one of mere amusement. We speak of serious things too (*for serious things are virtuous*) as better than things which are ridiculous and amusing, and of the activity of the better part of man's being or of the better man as always the more virtuous. But the activity of that which is better is necessarily higher and happier. Anybody can enjoy bodily pleasures, a slave can enjoy them as much as the best of men; but nobody would allow that a slave is capable of happiness unless he is capable of life; for happiness consists not in such pastimes as I have been speaking of, but in virtuous activities, as has been already said.

If happiness consists in virtuous activity, it is only reasonable to suppose that it is the activity of the highest virtue, or in other words, of the best part of our nature. Whether it is the reason or something else which seems to exercise rule and authority by a natural right, and to have a conception of things noble and divine, either as being itself divine or as relatively the most divine part of our being, it is the activity of this part in accordance with its proper virtue which will be the perfect happiness.

It has been already stated that it is a speculative activity, *i.e. an activity which takes the form of contemplation.* This is a conclusion which would seem to agree with our previous arguments and with the truth itself; for the speculative is the highest activity, as the intuitive reason is the highest of our faculties, and the objects with which the intuitive reason is concerned are the highest of things that can be known. It is also the most continuous; for our speculation can more easily be continuous than any kind of action. We consider too that pleasure is an essential element of happiness, and it is admitted that there is no virtuous activity so pleasant as the activity of wisdom or philosophic reflexion; at all events it appears that philosophy possesses pleasures of wonderful purity and certainty, and it is reasonable to suppose that people who possess knowledge pass their time more pleasantly than people who are seekers after truth.

Self-sufficiency too, as it is called, is preeminently a characteristic of the speculative activity; for the wise man, the just man, and all others, need the necessaries of life; but when they are adequately provided with these things, the just man needs people to whom and with whom he may do justice, so do the temperate man, the courageous man and everyone else; but the wise man is capable of speculation by himself, and the wiser he is, the more capable he is of such speculation. It is perhaps better for him in his speculation to have fellow-workers; but nevertheless he is in the highest degree self-sufficient.

It would seem too that the speculative is the only activity which is loved for its own sake as it has no result except speculation, whereas from all moral actions we gain something more or less besides the action itself.

Again, happiness, it seems, requires leisure; for the object of our business is leisure, as the object of war is the enjoyment of peace. Now the activity of the practical virtues is displayed in politics or war, and actions of this sort seem incompatible with leisure. This is absolutely true of military actions, as nobody desires war, or prepares to go to war, for its own sake. A person would be regarded as absolutely bloodthirsty if he were to make enemies of his friends for the mere sake of fighting and bloodshed. But the activity of the statesman too is incompatible with leisure. It aims at securing something beyond and apart from politics, viz. the power and honour or at least the happiness of the statesman himself and his fellow citizens, which is different from the political activity and is proved to be different by our search for it *as something distinct*.

If then political and military actions are preeminent among virtuous actions in beauty and grandeur, if they are incompatible with leisure and aim at some end, and are not desired for their own sakes, if the activity of the intuitive reason seems to be superior in seriousness as being speculative, and not to aim at any end beyond itself, and to have its proper pleasure, and if this pleasure enhances the activity, it follows that such self-sufficiency and power of leisure and absence of fatigue as are possible to a man and all the other attributes of felicity are found to be realized in this activity. This then will be the perfect happiness of Man, if a perfect length of life is given it, for there is no imperfection in happiness. But such a life will be too good for Man. He will enjoy such a life not in virtue of his humanity but in virtue of some divine element within him, and the superiority of this activity to the activity of any other virtue will be proportionate to the superiority of this devine element in man to his composite *or material* nature.

If then the reason is divine in comparison with *the rest of* Man's nature, the life which accords with reason will be divine in comparison with human life in general. Nor is it right to follow the advice of people who say that the thoughts of men should not be too high for humanity or the thoughts of mortals too high for mortality; for a man, as far as in him lies, should seek immortality and do all that is in his power to live in accordance with the highest part of his nature, as, although that part is insignificant in size, yet in power and honour it is far superior to all the rest.

It would seem too that this is the true self of everyone, if a man's true self is his supreme or better part. It would be absurd then that a man should desire not the life which is properly his own but the life which properly belongs to some other being. The remark already made will be appropriate here. It is what is proper to everyone that is in its nature best and pleasantest for him. It is the life which accords with reason then that will be best and pleasantest for Man, as a man's reason is in the highest sense himself. This will therefore be also the happiest life.

It is only in a secondary sense that the life which accords with other, *i.e. non-speculative*, virtue can be said to be happy; for the activities of such virtue are human, *they have no divine element.* Our just or courageous actions or our virtuous actions of any kind we perform in relation to one another, when we observe the law of propriety in contracts and mutual services and the various moral actions and in our emotions. But all these actions appear to be human affairs. It seems too that moral virtue is in some respects actually the result of physical organization and is in many respects closely associated with the emotions. Again, prudence is indissolubly linked to moral virtue, and moral virtue to prudence, since the principles of prudence are determined by the moral virtues, and moral rectitude is determined by prudence. But the moral virtues, as being inseparably united with the emotions, must have to do with the composite *or material* part *of our nature*, and the virtues of the composite part *of our nature* are human, *and not divine*, virtues. So too therefore is the life which accords with these virtues; so too is the happiness *which accords with them.*

But the happiness *which consists in the exercise* of the reason is separated *from these emotions.* It must be enough to say so much about it; for to discuss it in detail would take us beyond our present purpose. It would seem too to require external resources only to a small extent or to a less extent than moral virtue. It may be granted that both will require the necessaries of life and will require them equally, even if the politician devotes more trouble to his body and his bodily welfare than the philosopher; for the difference will not be important. But there will be a great difference in respect of their activities. The liberal man will want money for the practice of liberality, and the just man for the requital of services which have been done him; for our wishes, *unless they are manifested in actions*, must always be obscure, and even people who are not just pretend that it is their wish to act justly. The courageous man too will want physical strength if he is to perform any virtuous action, and the temperate man liberty, as otherwise it will be impossible for him or for anybody else to show his character.

But if the question be asked whether it is the purpose or the performance that is the surer determinant of virtue, as virtue implies both, it is clear that both are necessary to perfection. But action requires various conditions, and the greater and nobler the action, the more numerous will the conditions be.

In speculation on the other hand there is no need of such conditions, at least for its activity; it may rather be said that they are actual impediments to speculation. It is as a human being and as living in society that a person chooses to perform virtuous actions. Such conditions then will be requisite if he is to live as a man.

That perfect happiness is a species of speculative activity will appear from the following consideration among others. Our conception of the Gods is that they are preeminently happy and fortunate. But what kind of actions do we properly attribute to them? Are they just actions? But it would make the Gods ridiculous to suppose that they form contracts, restore deposits, and so on. Are they then courageous actions? Do the Gods endure dangers and alarms for the sake of honour? Or liberal actions? But to whom should they give money? It would be absurd to suppose that they have a currency or anything of the kind. Again, what will be the nature of their temperate actions? Surely to praise the gods for temperance is to degrade them; they are exempt from low desires. We may go through the whole category of virtues, and it will appear that whatever relates to moral action is petty and unworthy of the Gods.

Yet the Gods are universally conceived as living and therefore as displaying activity; they are certainly not conceived as sleeping like Endymion. If then action and still more production is denied to one who is alive, what is left but speculation? It follows that the activity of God being preeminently blissful will be speculative, and if so then the human activity which is most nearly related to it will be most capable of happiness.

It is an evidence of this truth that the other animals, as being perfectly destitute of such activity, do not participate in happiness; for while the whole life of the Gods is fortunate or blessed, the life of men is blessed in so far as it possesses a certain resemblance to their speculative activity. But no other animal is happy, as no other animal participates at all in speculation.

We conclude then that happiness is coextensive with speculation, and that the greater a person's power of speculation, the greater will be his happiness, not as an accidental fact but in virtue of the speculation, as speculation is honourable in itself. Hence happiness must be a kind of speculation.

Man, as being human, will require external prosperity. His nature is not of itself sufficient for speculation, it needs bodily health, food, and care of every kind. It must not however be supposed that, because it is impossible to be fortunate without external goods, a great variety of such goods will be necessary to happiness. For neither self-sufficiency nor moral action consists in excess; it is possible to do noble deeds without being lord of land and sea, as moderate means will enable a person to act in accordance with virtue. We may clearly see that it is so; for it seems that private persons practise virtue not less but actually more than persons in high place. It is enough that such a person should possess as much as is requisite for virtue; his life will be happy if he lives in the active exercise of virtue. Solon was right perhaps in his description of the happy man as one "who is moderately supplied with external goods, and yet has performed the noblest actions,"—such was his opinion—"and had lived a temperate life," for it is possible to do one's duty with only moderate means. It seems too that Anaxagoras did not conceive of the happy man as possessing wealth or power when he said that he should not be surprised if the happy man proved a puzzle in the eyes of the world; for the world judges by externals alone, it has no perception of anything that is not external.

The opinions of philosophers then seem to agree with our theories. Such opinions, it is true, possess a sort of authority; but it is the facts of life that are the tests of truth in practical matters, as they possess a supreme authority. It is right then to consider the doctrines which have been already advanced in reference to the facts of life, to accept them if they harmonize with those facts, and to regard them as mere theories if they disagree with them.

Again, he whose activity is directed by reason and who cultivates reason, and is in the best, *i.e. the most rational*, state of mind is also, as it seems, the most beloved of the Gods. For if the Gods care at all for human things, as is believed, it will be only reasonable to hold that they delight in what is best and most related to themselves, i.e. in reason, and that they requite with kindness those who love and honour it above all else, as caring for what is dear to themselves and performing right and noble actions.

It is easy to see that these conditions are found preeminently in the wise man. He will therefore be most beloved of the Gods. We may fairly suppose too that he is most happy; and if so, this is another reason for thinking that the wise man is preeminently happy.

Supposing then that our sketch of these subjects and of the virtues, and of friendship too, and pleasure, has been adequate, are we to regard our object as achieved? Or are we to say in the old phrase that in practical matters the end is not speculation and knowledge but action? It is not enough to know the nature of virtue; we must endeavour to possess it, and to exercise it, and to use whatever other means are necessary for becoming good.

Now, if theories were sufficient of themselves to make men good, they would deserve to receive any number of handsome rewards, as Theognis said, and it would have been our duty to provide them. But it appears in fact that, although they are strong enough to inspire the mass of men to chivalrous action; for it is not the nature of such men to obey honour but terror, nor to abstain from evil for fear of disgrace but for fear of punishment. For, as their life is one of emotion, they pursue their proper pleasures and the means of gaining these pleasures, and eschew the pains which are opposite to them. But of what is noble and truly pleasant they have not so much as a conception, because they have never tasted it. Where is the theory or argument which can reform such people as these? It is difficult to change by argument the settled features of character. We must be content perhaps if, when we possess all the means by which we are thought to become virtuous, we gain some share of virtue.

Some people think that men are made good by nature, others by habit, others again by teaching.

Now it is clear that the gift of Nature is not in our own power, but is bestowed through some divine providence upon those who are truly fortunate. It is probably true also that reason and teaching are not universally efficacious; the soul of the pupil must first have been cultivated by habit to a right spirit of pleasure and aversion, like the earth that is to nourish the seed. For he whose life is governed by emotion would not listen to the dissuasive voice of reason, or even comprehend it, and if this is his state, how is it possible to convert him? Emotion, it seems, never submits to reason but only to force. It is necessary then to presuppose a character which is in a sense akin to virtue, which loves what is noble and dislikes what is dishonourable. But it is difficult for one to receive from his early days a right inclination to virtue, unless he is brought up under virtuous laws; for a life of temperance and steadfastness is not pleasant to most people, least of all to the young. It follows that the nurture and pursuits *of the young* should be regulated by law, as they will not be painful, if he becomes used to them.

But it is not enough, I think, that we should receive a right nurture and control in youth; we must practise what is right and get the habit of doing it when we have come to man's estate. We shall need laws then to teach us what is right, and so to teach us all the duty of life; for most people are moved by necessity rather than by reason, and by the fear of punishment rather than by the love of nobleness.

Accordingly it is sometimes held that legislators should on the one hand invite and exhort men to pursue virtue because it is so noble, as they who have been already trained in virtue will pay heed to them, and on the other hand, if they are disobedient and degenerate, should inflict punishments and chastisements on them and utterly expel them, if they are incurable; for so the good man who lives by the rule of honour will obey reason, and the bad man whose aim is pleasure must be chastened by pain like a beast of burden. Hence too it is said that the pains ought to be such as are most opposed to a person's favourite pleasures.

If then, as has been said, he who is to be a good man should receive a noble nurture and training and then should live accordingly in virtuous pursuits and never voluntarily or involuntarily do evil, this result will only be attained if we live, so to say, in accordance with reason and right order resting upon force.

Now the authority of a father does not possess such force or compulsion, nor indeed does that of any individual, unless he is a king or some such person. But the law has a compulsory power, as being itself in a sense the outcome of prudence and reason; and whereas we hate people who oppose our inclinations, even if they are right in so doing, we do not feel the law to be grievous in its insistence upon virtue.

It is only in the state of Lacedaemon and a few other states that the legislator seems to have undertaken to control the nurture and pursuits of the citizens. In the great majority of states there is an absolute neglect of such matters, and everybody lives as he chooses, "being lawgiver of wife and children" like the Cyclops.

It is best then that the state should undertake the control of these matters and should exercise it rightly and should have the power of giving effect to its control. But if the state altogether neglects it, it would seem to be the duty of every citizen to further the cause of virtue in his own children and friends, or at least to set before himself the purpose of furthering it. It would seem too from what has been said that he will be best able to do this, if he has learnt the principles of legislation; for the control of the state is clearly exercised through the form of laws, and is good if the laws are virtuous. Whether they are written or unwritten laws, and whether they are suited to the education of an individual or of a number of people is apparently a matter of indifference, as it is in music or gymnastic or other studies. For as in a state it is law and custom which are supreme, so in a household it is the paternal precepts and customs, and all the more because of the father's relationship to the members of his family, and of the benefits which he has conferred upon them; for the members of a family are naturally affectionate and obedient to the father from the first.

Again, there is a superiority in the individual as against the general methods of education; it is much the same as in medicine where, although it is the general rule that a feverish patient needs to be kept quiet and to take no food, there may perhaps be some exceptions. Nor does a teacher of boxing teach all his pupils to box in the same style.

It would seem then that a study of individual character is the best way of perfecting the education of the individual, as then everyone has a better chance of receiving such treatment as is suitable. Still the individual case may best be treated, whether in medicine or in gymnastic or in any other subject, by one who knows the general rule applicable to all people or to people of a particular kind; for the sciences are said to deal, and do deal, with general laws. At the same time there is no reason why even without scientific knowledge a person should not be successful in treating a particular case if he has made an accurate, although empirical, observation of the results which follow from a particular course of treatment, as there are some doctors who seem to be excellent doctors in their own cases, although they would be unable to relieve anybody else.

Nevertheless if a person wishes to succeed in art or speculation, it is, I think, his duty to proceed to a universal principle and to make himself acquainted with it as far as possible; for sciences, as has been said, deal with universals. Also it is the duty of any one who wishes to elevate people, whether they be few or many, by his treatment, to try to learn the principles of legislation, if it is laws that are the natural means of making us good. So in education it is not everybody—it is at the most only the man of science—who can create a noble disposition in all who come to him as patients, as it is in medicine or in any other art which demands care and prudence.

Is it not then our next step to consider the sources and means of learning the principles of legislation? It may be thought that here as elsewhere we must look *to the persons who practise the principles, i.e.* to statesmen; for legislation, as we saw, is apparently a branch of politics. But there is this difference between politics and all other sciences and faculties. In these it is the same people who are found to teach the faculties and to make practical use of them, e.g. doctors and painters; whereas in politics it is the sophists who profess to teach, but it is never they who practise. The practical people are the active statesmen who would seem to be guided in practical life by a kind of faculty or experience rather than by intelligence; for we see that they never write or speak on these subjects, although it is perhaps a nobler task than the composition of forensic or parliamentary speeches, nor have they ever made their own sons or any other people whom they care for into statesmen. Yet it might be expected that they should do so, if it were in their power, for they could not have bequeathed any better legacy to their state, nor is there anything which they would have preferred for themselves or their dearest friends to such a faculty. Still it must be admitted that experience does much good; otherwise people could not be made statesmen by familiarity with politics. It follows that, if people desire to understand politics, they need experience as well as theory.

These sophists however who are lavish in their professions appear to be far from teaching *statesmanship;* in fact they are absolutely ignorant of the sphere or nature of statesmanship. If it were not so they would not have made statesmanship identical with, or inferior to, rhetoric; they would not have thought it easy work to form a legislative code by merely collecting such laws as are held in high repute; they would not have supposed that all they have to do is to make a selection of the best laws, as if the selection itself did not demand intelligence, and as if a right judgment were not a thing of the greatest difficulty in legislation no less than in music. For it is only such persons as possess experience of particular arts who can form a correct judgment of artistic works, and understand the means and manner of executing them, and the harmony of particular combinations. Inexperienced persons on the other hand are only too glad if they are alive to the fact that a work has been well or badly executed, as in painting. But laws are like the artistic works of political science. How then should *a mere collection of* laws make a person capable of legislating, or of deciding upon the best laws? It does not appear that *the study* of medical books makes people good doctors; yet medical books affect not only to state methods of treatment, but to state the way of curing people, and the proper method of treating particular cases by classifying the various states of health. But all this, although it seems useful to the experienced, is useless to those who are ignorant of medical science. It may be supposed then that collections of laws and politics would be useful to those who are capable of considering and deciding what is right or wrong, and what is suitable to particular cases; but if people who examine such questions have not *the proper* frame of mind, they will find it impossible to form a right judgment unless indeed by accident, although they may gain a more intelligent appreciation of them.

As previous writers have failed to investigate the subject of legislation, it will perhaps be better to examine it ourselves, and indeed to examine the whole subject of politics, in order that the philosophy of human life may be made as complete as possible.

Let us try then, first of all, to recount such particular opinions as have been rightly expressed by our predecessors, then, in view of the polities which we have collected, to consider the preservatives and destructives of states and of particular polities, and the reasons why some polities are good and others bad. For when we have considered these, it will perhaps be easier to see what kind of polity is best, and what is the best way of ordering it and what are its laws and customs.

The Nature of Politics

*Except for the fact that Aristotle was more systematic and, perhaps,
more prudent than Plato, there is very little difference between their
principles of political theory. Two interesting exceptions are their
opinions about slavery and about women. The following selection
comes from the first part of the* Politics *and includes Aristotle's
comments on slavery, which have been frequently misrepresented.*

Every state is a community of some kind, and every community is
established with a view to some good; for mankind always act in order
to obtain that which they think good. But, if all communities aim at
some good, the state or political community, which is the highest of all,
and which embraces all the rest, aims, and in a greater degree than any
other, at the highest good.

Now there is an erroneous opinion that a statesman, king, house-
holder, and master are the same, and that they differ, not in kind, but
only in the number of their subjects. For example, the ruler over a few
is called a master; over more, the manager of a household; over a still
larger number, a statesman or king, as if there were no difference
between a great household and a small state. The distinction which is
made between the king and the statesman is as follows: When the government is personal, the ruler is a king; when, according to the principles
of the political science, the citizens rule and are ruled in turn, then he
is called a statesman.

But all this is a mistake; for governments differ in kind, as will be
evident to any one who considers the matter according to the method
which has hitherto guided us. As in other departments of science, so in
politics, the compound should always be resolved into the simple elements or least parts of the whole. We must therefore look at the elements of which the state is composed, in order that we may see in what
they differ from one another, and whether any scientific distinction can
be drawn between the different kinds of rule.

He who thus considers things in their first growth and origin, whether
a state or anything else, will obtain the clearest view of them. In the
first place (1) there must be a union of those who cannot exist without
each other; for example, of male and female, that the race may continue;
and this is a union which is formed, not of deliberate purpose, but
because, in common with other animals and with plants, mankind have
a natural desire to leave behind them an image of themselves. And (2)
there must be a union of natural ruler and subject, that both may be
preserved. For he who can foresee with his mind is by nature intended
to be lord and master, and he who can work with his body is a subject,

SOURCE: "Politics," translated by B. Jowett, in *The Politics of Aristotle* (Oxford:
Clarendon Press, 1885), *7*, pp. 1–11.

and by nature a slave; hence master and slave have the same interest. Nature, however, has distinguished between the female and the slave. For she is not niggardly, like the smith who fashions the Delphian knife for many uses; she makes each thing for a single use, and every instrument is best made when intended for one and not for many uses. But among barbarians no distinction is made between women and slaves, because there is no natural ruler among them: they are a community of slaves, male and female. Wherefore the poets say,

It is meet that Hellenes should rule over barbarians;

as if they thought that the barbarian and the slave were by nature one.

Out of these two relationships between man and woman, master and slave, the family first arises, and Hesiod is right when he says—

First house and wife and an ox for the plough,

for the ox is the poor man's slave. The family is the association established by nature for the supply of men's everyday wants, and the members of it are called by Charondas "companions of the cupboard"..., and by Epimenides the Cretan, "companions of the manger".... But when several families are united, and the association aims at something more than the supply of daily needs, then comes into existence the village. And the most natural form of the village appears to be that of a colony from the family, composed of the children and grandchildren, who are said to be "suckled with the same milk." And this is the reason why Hellenic states were originally governed by kings; because the Hellenes were under royal rule before they came together, as the barbarians still are. Every family is ruled by the eldest, and therefore in the colonies of the family the kingly form of government prevailed because they were of the same blood. As Homer says [of the Cyclopes]:

Each one gives law to his children and to his wives.

For they lived dispersedly, as was the manner in ancient times. Wherefore men say that the Gods have a king, because they themselves either are or were in ancient times under the rule of a king. For they imagine, not only the forms of the Gods, but their ways of life to be like their own.

When several villages are united in a single community, perfect and large enough to be nearly or quite self-sufficing, the state comes into existence, originating in the bare needs of life, and continuing in existence for the sake of a good life. And therefore, if the earlier forms of society are natural, so is the state, for it is the end of them, and the [completed] nature is the end. For what each thing is when fully developed, we call its nature, whether we are speaking of a man, a horse, or a family. Besides, the final cause and end of a thing is the best, and to be self-sufficing is the end and the best.

Hence it is evident that the state is a creation of nature, and that man is by nature a political animal. And he who by nature and not by mere accident is without a state, is either above humanity, or below it; he is the

Tribeless, lawless, heartless one,

whom Homer denounces—the outcast who is a lover of war; he may be compared to a bird which flies alone.

Now the reason why man is more of a political animal than bees or any other gregarious animals is evident. Nature, as we often say, makes nothing in vain, and man is the only animal whom she has endowed with the gift of speech. And whereas mere sound is but an indication of pleasure or pain, and is therefore found in other animals (for their nature attains to the perception of pleasure and pain and the intimation of them to one another, and no further), the power of speech is intended to set forth the expedient and inexpedient, and likewise the just and the unjust. And it is a characteristic of man that he alone has any sense of good and evil, of just and unjust, and the association of living beings who have this sense makes a family and a state.

Thus the state is by nature clearly prior to the family and to the individual, since the whole is of necessity prior to the part; for example, if the whole body be destroyed, there will be no foot or hand, except in an equivocal sense, as we might speak of a stone hand; for when destroyed the hand will be no better. But things are defined by their working and power; and we ought not to say that they are the same when they are no longer the same, but only that they have the same name. The proof that the state is a creation of nature and prior to the individual is that the individual, when isolated, is not self-sufficing; and therefore he is like a part in relation to the whole. But he who is unable to live in society, or who has no need because he is sufficient for himself, must be either a beast or a god: he is no part of a state. A social instinct is implanted in all men by nature, and yet he who first founded the state was the greatest of benefactors. For man, when perfected, is the best of animals, but, when separated from law and justice, he is the worst of all; since armed injustice is the more dangerous, and he is equipped at birth with the arms of intelligence and with moral qualities which he may use for the worst ends. Wherefore, if he have not virtue, he is the most unholy and the most savage of animals, and the most full of lust and gluttony. But justice is the bond of men in states, and the administration of justice, which is the determination of what is just, is the principle of order in political society.

Seeing then that the state is made up of households, before speaking of the state, we must speak of the management of the household. The parts of the household are the persons who compose it, and a complete household consists of slaves and freemen. Now we should begin by examining everything in its least elements; and the first and least parts of a family are master and slave, husband and wife, father and children. We have therefore to consider what each of these three relations is and ought to be:—I mean the relation of master and servant, of husband and wife, and thirdly of parent and child. . . . And there is another element of a household, the so-called art of money-making, which, according to some, is identical with household management, according to others, a principal part of it; the nature of this art will also have to be considered by us.

Let us first speak of master and slave, looking to the needs of practical life and also seeking to attain some better theory of their relation than exists at present. For some are of opinion that the rule of a master is a science, and that the management of a household and the mastership of slaves, and the political and royal rule, as I was saying at the outset, are all the same. Others affirm that the rule of a master over slaves is contrary to nature, and that the distinction between slave and freeman exists by law only, and not by nature; and being an interference with nature is therefore unjust.

Property is a part of the household, and therefore the art of acquiring property is a part of the art of managing the household; for no man can live well, or indeed live at all, unless he be provided with necessaries. And as in the arts which have a definite sphere the workers must have their own proper instruments for the accomplishment of their work, so it is in the management of a household. Now, instruments are of various sorts; some are living, others lifeless; in the rudder, the pilot of a ship has a lifeless, in the look-out man, a living instrument; for in the arts the servant is a kind of instrument. Thus, too, a possession is an instrument for maintaining life. And so, in the arrangement of the family, a slave is a living possession, and property a number of such instruments; and the servant is himself an instrument, which takes precedence of all other instruments. For if every instrument could accomplish its own work, obeying or anticipating the will of others, like the statues of Daedalus, or the tripods of Hephaestus, which, says the poet,

> of their own accord entered the assembly of the Gods;

if, in like manner, the shuttle would weave and the plectrum touch the lyre without a hand to guide them, chief workmen would not want servants, nor masters slaves. Here, however, another distinction must be drawn: the instruments commonly so called are instruments of production, whilst a possession is an instrument of action. The shuttle, for example, is not only of use; but something else is made by it, whereas of a garment or of a bed there is only the use. Further, as production and action are different in kind, and both require instruments, the instruments which they employ must likewise differ in kind. But life is action and not production, and therefore the slave is the minister of action [for he ministers to his master's life]. Again, a possession is spoken of as a part is spoken of; for the part is not only a part of something else, but wholly belongs to it; and this is also true of a possession.

The master is only the master of the slave; he does not belong to him, whereas the slave is not only the slave of his maiter, but wholly belongs to him. Hence we see what is the nature and office of a slave; he who is by nature not his own but another's and yet a man, is by nature a slave; and he may be said to belong to another who, being a human being, is also a possession. And a possession may be defined as an instrument of action, separable from the possessor.

But is there any one thus intended by nature to be a slave, and for whom such a condition is expedient and right, or rather is not all slavery a violation of nature?

There is no difficulty in answering this question, on grounds both of reason and of fact. For that some should rule, and others be ruled is a thing, not only necessary, but expedient; from the hour of their birth, some are marked out for subjection, others for rule.

And whereas there are many kinds both of rulers and subjects, that rule is the better which is exercised over better subjects—for example, to rule over men is better than to rule over wild beasts. The work is better which is executed by better workmen; and where one man rules and another is ruled, they may be said to have a work. In all things which form a composite whole and which are made up of parts, whether continuous or discrete, a distinction between the ruling and the subject element comes to light. Such a duality exists in living creatures, but not in them only; it originates in the constitution of the universe; even in things which have no life, there is a ruling principle, as in musical harmony. But we are wandering from the subject. We will, therefore, restrict ourselves to the living creature which, in the first place, consists of soul and body: and of these two, the one is by nature the ruler, and the other the subject. But then we must look for the intentions of nature in things which retain their nature, and not in things which are corrupted. And therefore we must study the man who is in the most perfect state both of body and soul, for in him we shall see the true relation of the two; although in bad or corrupted natures the body will often appear to rule over the soul, because they are in an evil and unnatural condition. First then we may observe in living creatures both a despotical and a constitutional rule; for the soul rules the body with a despotical rule, whereas the intellect rules the appetites with a constitutional and royal rule. And it is clear that the rule of the soul over the body, and of the mind and the rational element over the passionate is natural and expedient; whereas the equality of the two or the rule of the inferior is always hurtful. The same holds good of animals as well as of men; for tame animals have a better nature than wild, and all tame animals are better off when they are ruled by man; for then they are preserved. Again, the male is by nature superior, and the female inferior; and the one rules, and the other is ruled; this principle, of necessity, extends to all mankind. Where then there is such a difference as that between soul and body, or between men and animals (as in the case of those whose business is to use their body, and who can do nothing better), the lower sort are by nature slaves, and it is better for them as for all inferiors that they should be under the rule of a master. For he who can be, and therefore is another's, and he who participates in reason enough to apprehend, but not to have, reason, is a slave by nature. Whereas the lower animals cannot even apprehend reason; they obey their instincts. And indeed the use made of slaves and of tame animals is not very different; for both with their bodies minister to the needs of life. Nature would like to distinguish between the bodies of freemen and slaves, making the one strong for servile labour, the other upright, and although useless for such services, useful for political life in the arts both of war and peace. But this does not hold universally: for some slaves have the souls and others have the bodies of freemen. And doubtless if men differed from one another in the mere forms of their bodies as much as the statues of the Gods do from men, all would acknowledge that the inferior class should be slaves of the superior. And if there is a difference in the body, how much more in the soul? but the beauty of the body is seen, whereas the beauty of the soul is not seen. It is clear, then, that some men are by nature free, and others slaves, and that for these latter slavery is both expedient and right.

But that those who take the opposite view have in a certain way right on their side, may be easily seen. For the words slavery and slave are used in two senses. There is a slave or slavery by law as well as by nature. The law of which I speak is a sort of convention, according to which whatever is taken in war is supposed to belong to the victors. But this right many jurists impeach, as they would an orator who brought forward an unconstitutional measure: they detest the notion that, because one man has the power of doing violence and is superior in brute strength, another shall be his slave and subject. Even among philosophers there is a difference of opinion. The origin of the dispute, and the reason why the arguments cross, is as follows: Virtue, when furnished with means, may be deemed to have the greatest power of doing violence: and as superior power is only found where there is superior excellence of some kind, power is thought to imply virtue. But does it likewise imply justice?—that is the question. And, in order to make a distinction between them, some assert that justice is benevolence: to which others reply that justice is nothing more than the rule of a superior. If the two views are regarded as antagonistic and exclusive [i.e. if the notion that justice is benevolence excludes the idea of a just rule of a superior], the alternative [viz. that no one should rule over others] has no force or plausibility, because it implies that not even the superior in virtue ought to rule, or be master. Some, clinging, as they think, to a principle of justice (for law and custom are a sort of justice), assume that slavery in war is justified by law, but they are not consistent. For what if the cause of the war be unjust? No one would ever say that he is a slave who is unworthy to be a slave. Were this the case, men of the highest rank would be slaves and the children of slaves if they or their parents chance to have been taken captive and sold. Wherefore Hellenes do not like to call themselves slaves, but confine the term to barbarians. Yet, in using this language, they really mean the natural slave of whom we spoke at first; for it must be admitted that some are slaves everywhere, others nowhere. The same principle applies to nobility. Hellenes regard themselves as noble everywhere, and not only in their own country, but they deem the barbarians noble only when at home, thereby implying that there are two sorts of nobility and freedom, the one absolute, the other relative. The Helen of Theodectes says:

> Who would presume to call me servant who am on both sides sprung from the stem of the Gods?

What does this mean but that they distinguish freedom and slavery, noble and humble birth, by the two principles of good and evil? They think that as men and animals beget men and animals, so from good men a good man springs. But this is what nature, though she may intend it, cannot always accomplish.

We see then that there is some foundation for this difference of opinion, and that all are not either slaves by nature or freemen by nature, and also that there is in some cases a marked distinction between the two classes, rendering it expedient and right for the one to be slaves and the others to be masters: the one practising obedience, the others exercising the authority which nature intended them to have. The abuse of this authority is injurious to both; for the interests of part and whole, of body and soul, are the same, and the slave is a part of the master, a living but separated part of his bodily frame. Where the relation between them is natural they are friends and have a common interest, but where it rests merely on law and force the reverse is true.

The Nature of Tragedy

Besides their countless other achievements, the Greeks also created tragedy. Thus, Aristotle had numerous excellent examples from which to draw his interpretation of the nature of tragedy and literary criticism.

Having thus distinguished the parts, let us now consider the proper construction of the Fable or Plot, as that is at once the first and the most important thing in Tragedy. We have laid it down that a tragedy is an

Source: "Poetics," translated by I. Bywater, in *Aristotle, On the Art of Poetry* (Oxford, England: The Clarendon Press, 1909), pp. 23–41.

imitation of an action that is complete in itself, as a whole of some magnitude; for a whole may be of no magnitude to speak of. Now a whole is that which has beginning, middle, and end. A beginning is that which is not itself necessarily after anything else, and which has naturally something else after it; an end is that which is naturally after something itself, either as its necessary or usual consequent, and with nothing else after it; and a middle, that which is by nature after one thing and has also another after it. A well-constructed Plot, therefore, cannot either begin or end at any point one likes; beginning and end in it must be of the forms just described. Again: to be beautiful, a living creature, and every whole made up of parts, must not only present a certain order in its arrangement of parts, but also be of a certain definite magnitude. Beauty is a matter of size and order, and therefore impossible either (1) in a very minute creature, since our perception becomes indistinct as it approaches instantaneity; or (2) in a creature of vast size—one, say, 1000 miles long—as in that case, instead of the object being seen all at once, the unity and wholeness of it is lost to the beholder. Just in the same way, then, as a beautiful whole made up of parts, or a beautiful living creature, must be of some size, a size to be taken in by the eye, so a story or Plot must be of some length, but of a length to be taken in by the memory. As for the limit of its length, so far as that is relative to public performances and spectators, it does not fall within the theory of poetry. If they had to perform a hundred tragedies, they would be timed by water-clocks, as they are said to have been at one period. The limit, however, set by the actual nature of the thing is this: the longer the story, consistently with its being comprehensible as a whole, the finer it is by reason of its magnitude. As a rough general formula, "a length which allows of the hero passing by a series of probable or necessary stages from misfortune to happiness, or from happiness to misfortune," may suffice as a limit for the magnitude of the story.

The Unity of a Plot does not consist, as some suppose, in its having one man as its subject. An infinity of things befall that one man, some of which it is impossible to reduce to unity; and in like manner there are many actions of one man which cannot be made to form one action. One sees, therefore, the mistake of all the poets who have written a *Heracleid*, a *Theseid*, or similar poems; they suppose that, because Heracles was one man, the story also of Heracles must be one story. Homer, however, evidently understood this point quite well, whether by art or instinct, just in the same way as he excels the rest in every other respect. In writing an *Odyssey*, he did not make the poem cover all that ever befell his hero—it befell him, for instance, to get wounded on Parnassus and also to feign madness at the time of the call to arms, but the two incidents had no probable or necessary connexion with one another—instead of doing that, he took an action with a Unity of the kind we are describing as the subject of the *Odyssey*, as also of the *Iliad*.

The truth is that, just as in the other imitative arts one imitation is always of one thing, so in poetry the story, as an imitation of action, must represent one action, a complete whole, with its several incidents so closely connected that the transposal or withdrawal of any one of them will disjoin and dislocate the whole. For that which makes no perceptible difference by its presence or absence is no real part of the whole.

From what we have said it will be seen that the poet's function is to describe, not the thing that has happened, but a kind of thing that might happen, i.e. what is possible as being probable or necessary. The distinction between historian and poet is not in the one writing prose and the other verse—you might put the work of Herodotus into verse, and it would still be a species of history; it consists really in this, that the one describes the thing that has been, and the other a kind of thing that might be. Hence poetry is something more philosophic and of graver import than history, since its statements are of the nature rather of universals, whereas those of history are singulars. By a universal statement I mean one as to what such or such a kind of man will probably or necessarily say or do—which is the aim of poetry, though it affixes proper names to the characters; by a singular statement, one as to what, say, Alcibiades did or had done to him. In Comedy this has become clear by this time; it is only when their plot is already made up of probable incidents that they give it a basis of proper names, choosing for the purpose any names that may occur to them, instead of writing like the old iambic poets about particular persons. In Tragedy, however, they still adhere to the historic names; and for this reason: what convinces is the possible; now whereas we are not yet sure as to the possibility of that which has not happened, that which has happened is manifestly possible, else it would not have come to pass. Nevertheless even in Tragedy there are some plays with but one or two known names in them, the rest being inventions; and there are some without a single known name, e. g. Agathon's *Antheus*, in which both incidents and names are of the poet's invention; and it is no less delightful on that account. So that one must not aim at a rigid adherence to the traditional stories on which tragedies are based. It would be absurd, in fact, to do so, as even the known stories are only known to a few, though they are a delight none the less to all.

It is evident from the above that the poet must be more the poet of his stories or Plots than of his verses, inasmuch as he is a poet by virtue of the imitative element in his work, and it is actions that he imitates. And if he should come to take a subject from actual history, he is none the less a poet for that; since some historic occurrences may very well be in the probable and possible order of things; and it is in that aspect of them that he is their poet.

Of simple Plots and actions the episodic are the worst. I call a Plot episodic when there is neither probability nor necessity in the sequence of its episodes. Actions of this sort bad poets construct through their own fault, and good ones on account of the players. His work being for public performance, a good poet often stretches out a Plot beyond its capabilities, and is thus obliged to twist the sequence of incident.

Tragedy, however, is an imitation not only of a complete action, but also of incidents arousing pity and fear. Such incidents have the very greatest effect on the mind when they occur unexpectedly and at the same time in consequence of one another; there is more of the marvellous in them then than if they happened of themselves or by mere chance. Even matters of chance seem most marvellous if there is an appearance of design as it were in them; as for instance the statue of Mitys at Argos killed the author of Mitys' death by falling down on him when a looker-on at a public spectacle; for incidents like that we think to be not without a meaning. A Plot, therefore, of this sort is necessarily finer than others.

Plots are either simple or complex, since the actions they represent are naturally of this twofold description. The action, proceeding in the way defined, as one continuous whole, I call simple, when the change in the hero's fortunes takes place without Peripety or Discovery; and complex, when it involves one or the other, or both. These should each of them arise out of the structure of the Plot itself, so as to be the consequence, necessary or probable, of the antecedents. There is a great difference between a thing happening *propter hoc* and *post hoc*.

A Peripety is the change from one state of things within the play to its opposite of the kind described, and that too in the way we are saying, in the probable or necessary sequence of events; as it is for instance in *Oedipus*: here the opposite state of things is produced by the Messenger, who, coming to gladden Oedipus and to remove his fears as to his mother, reveals the secret of his birth. And in *Lynceus*: just as he is being led off for execution, with Danaus at his side to put him to death, the incidents preceding this bring it about that he is saved and Danaus put to death. A Discovery is, as the very word implies, a change from ignorance to knowledge, and thus to either love or hate, in the personages marked for good or evil fortune. The finest form of Discovery is one attended by Peripeties, like that which goes with the Discovery in *Oedipus*. There are no doubt other forms of it; what we have said may happen in a way in reference to inanimate things, even things of a very casual kind; and it is also possible to discover whether some one has done or not done something. But the form most directly connected with the Plot and the action of the piece is the first-mentioned. This, with a Peripety, will arouse either pity or fear—actions of that nature being what Tragedy is assumed to represent; and it will also serve to bring about the happy or unhappy ending. The Discovery, then, being of persons, it may be that of one party only to the other, the latter being already known; or both the parties may have to discover themselves. Iphigenia, for instance, was discovered to Orestes by sending the letter; and another Discovery was required to reveal him to Iphigenia.

Two parts of the Plot, then, Peripety and Discovery, are on matters of this sort. A third part is Suffering; which we may define as an action of a destructive or painful nature, such as murders on the stage, tortures, woundings, and the like. The other two have been already explained.

The parts of Tragedy to be treated as formative elements in the whole were mentioned... (previously). From the point of view, however, of its quantity, i.e. the separate sections into which it is divided, a tragedy has the following parts: Prologue, Episode, Exode, and a choral portion, distinguished into Parode and Stasimon; these two are common to all tragedies, whereas songs from the stage and *Commoe* are only found in some. The Prologue is all that precedes the Parode of the chorus; an Episode all that comes in between two whole choral songs; the Exode all that follows after the last choral song. In the choral portion the Parode is the whole first statement of the chorus; a Stasimon, a song of the chorus without anapaests or trochees; a *Commos*, a lamentation sung by chorus and actor in concert. The parts of Tragedy to be used as formative elements in the whole we have already mentioned; the above are its parts from the point of view of its quantity, or the separate sections into which it is divided.

The next points after what we have said above will be these: (1) What is the poet to aim at, and what is he to avoid, in constructing his Plots? and (2) What are the conditions on which the tragic effect depends?

We assume that, for the finest form of Tragedy, the Plot must be not simple but complex; and further, that it must imitate actions arousing pity and fear, since that is the distinctive function of this kind of imitation. It follows, therefore, that there are three forms of Plot to be avoided. (1) A good man must not be seen passing from happiness to misery, or (2) a bad man from misery to happiness. The first situation is not fear-inspiring or piteous, but simply odious to us. The second is the most untragic that can be; it has no one of the requisites of Tragedy; it does not appeal either to the human feeling in us, or to our pity, or to our fears. Nor on the other hand should (3) an extremely bad man be seen falling from happiness into misery. Such a story may arouse the human feeling in us, but it will not move us to either pity or fear; pity is occasioned by undeserved misfortune, and fear by that of one like ourselves; so that there will be nothing either piteous or fear-inspiring in the situation. There remains, then, the intermediate kind of personage, a man not pre-eminently virtuous and just, whose misfortune, however, is brought upon him not by vice and depravity but by some error of judgement, of the number of those in the enjoyment of great reputation and prosperity; e.g. Oedipus, Thyestes, and the men of note of similar families. The perfect Plot, accordingly, must have a single, and not (as some tell us) a double issue; the change in the hero's fortunes must be not from misery to happiness, but on the contrary from happiness to misery; and the cause of it must lie not in any depravity, but in some great error on his part; the man himself being either such as we have described, or better, not worse, than that. Fact also confirms our theory. Though the poets began by accepting any tragic story that came to hand, in these days the finest tragedies are always on the story of some few houses, on that of Alcmeon, Oedipus, Orestes, Meleager, Thyestes, Telephus, or any others that may have been involved, as either agents or sufferers, in some deed of horror. The theoretically best tragedy, then, has a Plot of this description. The critics, therefore, are wrong, who blame Euripides for taking this line in his tragedies, and giving many of them an unhappy ending. It is, as we have said, the right line to take. The best proof is this: on the stage, and in the public performances, such plays, properly worked out, are seen to be the most truly tragic; and Euripides, even if his execution be faulty in every other point, is seen to be nevertheless the most tragic certainly of the dramatists. After this comes the construction of Plot which some rank first, one with a double story (like the *Odyssey*) and an opposite issue for the good and the bad personages. It is ranked as first only through the weakness of the audiences; the poets merely follow their public, writing as its wishes dictate. But the pleasure here is not that of Tragedy. It belongs rather to Comedy, where the bitterest enemies in the piece (e.g. Orestes and Aegisthus) walk off good friends at the end, with no slaying of any one by any one.

The tragic fear and pity may be aroused by the Spectacle; but they may also be aroused by the very structure and incidents of the play—which is the better way and shows the better poet. The Plot in fact should be so framed that, even without seeing the things take place, he who simply hears the account of them shall be filled with horror and pity at the incidents; which is just the effect that the mere recital of the story in *Oedipus* would have on one. To produce this same effect by means of the Spectacle is less artistic, and requires extraneous aid. Those, however, who make use of the Spectacle to put before us that which is merely monstrous and not productive of fear, are wholly out of touch with Tragedy; not every kind of pleasure should be required of a tragedy, but only its own proper pleasure.

The tragic pleasure is that of pity and fear, and the poet has to produce it by a work of imitation; it is clear, therefore, that the causes should be included in the incidents of his story. Let us see, then, what kinds of incident strike one as horrible, or rather as piteous. In a deed of this description the parties must necessarily be either friends, or enemies, or indifferent to one another. Now when enemy does it on enemy, there is nothing to move us to pity either in his doing or in his meditating the deed, except so far as the actual pain of the sufferer is concerned; and the same is true when the parties are indifferent to one another. Whenever the tragic deed, however, is done within the family —when murder or the like is done or meditated by brother on brother, by son on father, by mother on son, or son on mother—these are the situations the poet should seek after. The traditional stories, accordingly, must be kept as they are, e.g. the murder of Clytaemnestra by Orestes and of Eriphyle by Alcmeon. At the same time even with these there is something left to the poet himself; it is for him to devise the right way of treating them. Let us explain more clearly what we mean by "the right way." The deed of horror may be done by the doer knowingly and consciously, as in the old poets, and in Medea's murder of her children in Euripides. Or he may do it, but in ignorance of his relationship, and discover that afterwards, as does the Oedipus in Sophocles. Here the deed is outside the play; but it may be within it, like the act of the Alcmeon in Astydamas, or that of the Telegonus in *Ulysses Wounded*. A third possibility is for one meditating some deadly injury to another, in ignorance of his relationship, to make the discovery in time to draw back. These exhaust the possibilities, since the deed must necessarily be either done or not done, and either knowingly or unknowingly.

The worst situation is when the personage is with full knowledge on the point of doing the deed, and leaves it undone. It is odious and also (through the absence of suffering) untragic; hence it is that no one is made to act thus except in some few instances, e.g. Haemon and Creon in *Antigone*. Next after this comes the actual perpetration of the deed meditated. A better situation than that, however, is for the deed to be done in ignorance, and the relationship discovered afterwards, since there is nothing odious in it, and the Discovery will serve to astound us. But the best of all is the last; what we have in *Cresphontes*, for example, where Merope, on the point of slaying her son, recognizes him in time; in *Iphigenia*, where sister and brother are in a like position; and in *Helle*, where the son recognizes his mother, when on the point of giving her up to her enemy.

This will explain why our tragedies are restricted (as we said just now) to such a small number of families. It was accident rather than art that led the poets in quest of subjects to embody this kind of incident in their Plots. They are still obliged, accordingly, to have recourse to the families in which such horrors have occurred.

On the construction of the Plot, and the kind of Plot required for Tragedy, enough has now been said.

A STUDY GUIDE TO ARISTOTLE'S THOUGHT

1. What are the ten categories? According to what principle are the categories derived? What is the definition of substance? What is the difference between primary and secondary substance?

2. What are the equivocals and the univocals?

3. What is the difference between "being predicable of a subject and never present in a subject" and "being present in a subject but never predicable of a subject"?

4. What is the subject matter of Aristotelian physics? How does this differ from contemporary physics?

5. Can you define "science" in Aristotelian terms?

6. How does Aristotle define change? What is unqualified change? What does Aristotle mean by form? matter? privation?

7. Does Aristotle have any methodological reason for discussing the theories of his predecessors?

8. Is Aristotle's use of "substance" in the physics consistent with his treatment of it in the *Categories*?

9. How does the treatise *On Generation and Corruption* differ from the *Physics*?

10. What is the subject matter of *Metaphysics*? How does metaphysics relate to the other sciences?

11. What are some of the senses of "substance"? What is the primary sense of substance? If form—that is, the definition of a thing—is the primary instance of being, how does Aristotle differ from Plato?

12. What does Aristotle mean by "actuality"? How does actuality relate to "substance"?

13. What is Aristotle's definition of "soul"? What does Aristotle mean when he says the soul is "the first grade of actuality of a natural organized body" and that the soul is "the form of forms"?

14. What is happiness according to Aristotle? What does Aristotle mean when he says that happiness is activity in accordance with virtue?

15. What is the ideal life according to Aristotle? How does this ideal differ from Plato's?

16. What is the relationship between *Ethics* and *Politics*? What does Aristotle mean when he says "Man by nature is a political animal"? In what sense is the state prior to the family and to the individual? What is Aristotle's argument for slavery?

17. What is Aristotle's definition of tragedy? What are the essential components of tragedy? What does Aristotle mean by imitation? Can Aristotle's definition of tragedy be applied to Shakespeare? To contemporary works?

5
MODERN COMMENTARY ON PLATO

Alexandre Koyré

The dialogues . . . are dramatic works which could and even should be staged. Needless to say, a drama is not played in the abstract before empty benches. It necessarily pre-supposes a public to which it is addressed. In other words, the drama—or the comedy—implies a spectator, or more properly an auditor. That is not all: the spectator-auditor has a part, a very important part, to play in the ensemble of the acting. The drama is not a "spectacle," and the public witnessing it do not, or at least should not, conduct themselves purely as "spectators." They must collaborate with the author, understand his intentions, draw conclusions from the action that unfolds before their eyes; they must capture the meaning and become imbued with it. The more perfect and the more truly "dramatic" the work, the more important and the greater is this collaboration of the auditor or of the public. How sorry, indeed, would be the theatrical piece in which the author should place himself in some way upon the stage, there to comment on and to explain himself. Or, conversely, how pitiful would be the public for which such an explanation, such an authorized commentary, would be necessary.

But again, dialogue, at least true dialogue, like Plato's, dialogue in the literary tradition, not a simple expository artifice such as that of Malebranche or Valéry, is a dramatic piece. Whence it follows that in every dialogue there exists besides the two obvious personages—the two interlocutors who discuss—a third, invisible, but present and quite as important, the reader-auditor. Now Plato's reader-auditor, the public for which his work was written, was a singularly well-informed person, aware of many things which we, unfortunately, do not know and doubtless never shall know; he was also singularly intelligent and

SOURCE: Alexandre Koyré, *Discovering Plato*, translated by Leonora C. Rosenfield (New York: Columbia University Press, 1945), pp. 4–7. Reprinted with permission of the publishers.

penetrating. Hence he understood much better than we the allusions strewn throughout the dialogues, and he was not deceived as to the value of elements that so often appear to us as subordinate. Thus, he comprehended the importance of the dramatis personae, of the actors who were the protagonists of the work in dialogue form. He knew also how to discover for himself the Socratic or Platonic solution for the problems that the dialogue apparently left unsolved.

Apparently—for from our very simple and in fact banal considerations on the dialogue's structure and meaning, one must conclude, it seems to me, that every dialogue carries with it a conclusion. Certainly not a conclusion formulated by Socrates; but one that the reader-auditor is in duty bound and is in a position to formulate.

I fear that the modern reader may not be entirely satisfied. Why, he may ask, all these complications? If Socrates possessed a doctrine, a doctrine with which Plato was perfectly acquainted, to judge by all the evidence, why does he let us flounder about instead of explaining it clearly and simply? And if one were to object that the absence of an explicit conclusion pertains to the very essence of the dialogue, the answer would doubtless be that no one forced Plato to choose this very special mode of exposition and that he could well have written books like everybody else's and so explained Socratic doctrines that all his readers could understand and even learn them.

Once again, the modern reader is simultaneously right and wrong. He is right in judging that the mode of exposition Plato chose did not render Socratic doctrine readily accessible. On the other hand, he is wrong in thinking that Plato ever wished to so present it. Quite the contrary; for Plato this was not feasible or even desirable.

As a matter of fact, for Plato real science, the only kind worthy of the name, is not learned from books, is not imposed upon the soul from without; it is attained, discovered, invented by the soul in solitary travail. The questions formulated by Socrates, that is to say, by the one who knows, stimulate, fecundate, and guide the soul (the celebrated Socratic maieutic consists in just that); the soul itself, however, must furnish the response to the questions.

As for those who are incapable of such effort and therefore do not grasp the meaning implicit in the dialogue, so much the worse for them. Plato, in fact, never asserts that science and, of course, philosophy are accessible to all or that everyone is capable of dealing with these subjects. He always taught the contrary. That is precisely why the difficulty inherent in the dialogue, incompleteness, the need for a personal effort on the part of the reader-auditor, is not a defect in Plato's eyes, but quite the reverse, an advantage, even a great advantage, in this type of exposition. It constitutes a test and allows for differentiation between those who understand and those, doubtless the majority, who do not.

W. K. C. Guthrie

Socrates and Plato are an inseparable unity. To understand Plato therefore we must first ask what it was in these conversations of Socrates that so filled the younger man's mind that he cast Socrates for the chief role in most of his own writings. Here I must briefly remind you of what I said last time about the class of people known as Sophists, the impact of whose popular teaching was a major influence in the Athens of Socrates's maturity and Plato's youth. Athens was then a democracy far more extreme than any that we know today. Every full citizen had the right of speaking and voting in the assembly, and the community was small enough to make this a practical possibility. More than that, any citizen might find himself called to high office, not through wealth, rank or ability, but by lot. No regular schools or colleges existed to meet the need of education for leadership to which this state of things gave rise, and to satisfy it there emerged this series of free-lance teachers who made their living travelling from city to city and claiming to provide the particular mental culture needed as a training for public life. Some taught special subjects also like music, mathematics and astronomy, but the emphasis was on political action and public speaking. I also mentioned that although they had nothing which could be called a common philosophy, these fifth-century Sophists shared a certain scepticism characteristic of the period, which arose in part from an apparent deadlock in more strictly philosophical spheres. . . .

We saw in my last lecture how Socrates reacted to these current trends of thought. He made it his life-work to combat them, and Plato made it *his* life-work to defend and elaborate the teaching of Socrates. Socrates had insisted that knowledge, though difficult of attainment, was not impossible, and that only on a foundation of knowledge could states be well governed or individuals lead morally sound and worth-while lives. The kind of knowledge that he had in mind was that which expressed itself in the definition of universal concepts, particularly ethical concepts like justice or courage. I remarked also on Socrates's belief—rather a naive one as it seems to us—that this knowledge of the principles of right action would inevitably have its outcome in the actual performance of right action. By explaining today a little more of the contemporary background of thought I have tried to show more clearly how it was possible and natural for him to link together in this way the ideas of intellectual

SOURCE: W. K. C. Guthrie, *Socrates and Plato* (St. Lucia, Brisbane, Australia: University of Queensland Press, 1958), pp. 18–22. Reprinted with permission of the publishers.

ignorance or scepticism on the one hand and laxity of moral standards on the other. If people understood the true nature of what is good—which involves, of course, no less than understanding the true end and aim of human life—they would inevitably pursue it. In other words "virtue is knowledge" and "no-one does wrong willingly".

That is Socrates's contribution. He did not think that he had himself attained this knowledge, but he was convinced that right and wrong and similar notions were not just a matter of the expediency of the moment, changing with the changing needs of individual or state. They were the same at all times and everywhere, and if others would admit, as he did, that they had not yet understood their real meaning, then together they might start the search for it with some hope of success.

The genius of Plato was much more universal than that of Socrates. His mind was always ready to take flight from the market-place where Socrates sat (like the modern Greek on his hard wooden chair at the café table) arguing out the problems of practical life with anyone who was willing to talk, and to lose itself in the metaphysical problems of the nature of reality and its relation to appearances. The intellectualism of Parmenides impressed him deeply, and another current of influence flowed strongly in his thought since, shortly before he founded the Academy, he paid his first visit to South Italy and made personal contact with members of the Pythagorean school. These new friends greatly encouraged, if they did not originate, two further sides of his own philosophy: its mathematical bias and its interest in the fate of the human soul after death.

Nevertheless the personal impact of Socrates, strengthened by his tragic death and the imperturbable calm with which he met it, remained paramount, and it is not hard to see how his own doctrines took their origin from the Socratic conversation and its untiring search for definitions. Parmenides, the Pythagoreans, and his own intellectual powers were brought in rather as powerful aids to the consolidation and preservation of the Socratic heritage.

Socrates's insistence on the definition of abstract terms—his reiterated questions: "Yes but what exactly *is* justice? What *is* virtue?" (or freedom or whatever it might be) had in fact, though he himself was almost certainly not aware of it, raised for the first time what was to be a central question of philosophy for many centuries to come. They seemed to imply that justice or courage or virtue is a *thing* which *exists*—for what would be the point of trying to define something which had no existence? But is there in fact such a thing as absolute justice or virtue, apart from the individual actions which we call just or good? No one would claim that any of these actions is "justice itself"; they are all thought of as only imperfect instances of, or approximations to, it. Where then, or what, is this justice or virtue? So we are faced with the question of what would now be called the ontological status of universals or abstractions.

Philosophy up to Plato's time had seemed to show that everything in this world of experience is mutable, unstable and therefore unknowable: Parmenides had made men believe that what can be known must be eternal and changeless. Being then, under Socrates's influence, determined to deny the relativism of Sophistic morality, Plato adopted what seemed at the time to be the only alternative. He declared that these absolutes did exist, indeed they alone had full existence, in a world beyond time and change. They are "models laid up in Heaven", the forms or patterns of earthly things, and men's actions deserve the name of just or good in so far as they share fleetingly and imperfectly in the nature of these unchanging norms.

In this way Plato's characteristic doctrine of Forms (or Theory of Ideas as it is commonly but somewhat misleadingly called) arose out of the philosophical demands of Socrates's simple ethical teaching. Human laws and institutions cannot be "real" in Plato's sense, but will have merit in so far as they approximate to the real. We might say "to the ideal", but that only shows the difference between us and Plato. For him the changeless Forms are highest not only in the scale of value but also in that of being; indeed (though to most modern philosophers this is a serious stumbling-block) the two scales are the same.

I have suggested that the doctrine of Forms arose primarily out of the need to give theoretical support to the practical aims of Socrates, which seemed to demand that a concept like justice or freedom should stand for something real and permanent. This I believe to be true, but it is difficult to know exactly how these ideas took shape in Plato's mind, and even if this gave the first impulse, there is no doubt that in formulating his views he was greatly helped by his familiarity with, and sympathy for, the outlook of the Pythagoreans. As his philosophy developed, the doctrine took on a significance far beyond the moral field, and proved to contain all sorts of difficulties whose solution had to be sought elsewhere.

. . . .

W. K. C. Guthrie

As a student of scientific method, Professor Popper is entirely on Plato's side when he adopts a geometrical theory of the world.

SOURCE: W. K. C. Guthrie, "Twentieth Century Approaches to Plato," pp. 242–245, in *Lectures in Memory of Louise Taft Semple: First Series, 1961–1965*, Vol. I in the University of Cincinnati Classical Studies, edited by D. W. Bradeen, et al. (Princeton University Press, 1967) for the University of Cincinnati. Reprinted with permission of Princeton University Press and the University of Cincinnati.

But he parts company with him when he transfers this theory from macrocosm to microcosm, arguing in favour of geometrical relationships in the structure not only of the universe but of human society. This he does explicitly in the *Gorgias*, where his Socrates, rebuking an opponent who upholds a life of unbridled greed and ambition, attributes his fault to ignorance of the "great power exercised by geometrical equality both among gods and among men."

Geometrical equality is not numerical equality: it is a matter of preserving a relationship of due proportion or ratio. Its introduction as a principle of social or political organization is not favourable to democracy in the sense of a simple counting of heads. To say that all men were created equal was for Plato not a self-evident truth, but a manifest falsehood. They differed in many respects, but for the purposes of living together in a state might be grouped in three classes: the wise and philosophic, the combative and ambitious, and the materially minded whose interest was in wealth and comfort. In a well-ordered country the first should rule, the second should be entrusted with defence, and the third with the production and exchange of material commodities.

What shocks the modern reader is that Plato when he wrote the *Republic* felt it necessary for the welfare and safety of his community to freeze and perpetuate these distinctions in a rigid system of social classes. Should an artisan or merchant—or a body of these relying on their numbers—try to break into the sphere of defence, or one of the military caste usurp the functions of a ruler, this would be fatal to the community and must be counted criminal. He does, it is true, allow that a man with the qualities proper to one class might accidentally be born into another, and proposes that there should be machinery for official transfer in such cases; but in his opinion they would be rare, for he was a firm believer in eugenics, and breeding is to be confined within each class, and at least in the higher classes, only to the best within that class.

The modern attacks on Plato go back to the days of the Fascist and Nazi regimes, and have intensified since their defeat in the Second World War. In the *Journal of Education* for 1945 two Germans cited passages from the *Republic* to prove that, in Plato's view, "the main purpose of the state (i.e. the legal and civic administration) is to preserve the purity of the race and to organize the people for war". It was certainly frightening to read in this article that the officially declared aim of the Nazi Party had been "to govern as Guardians in the highest Platonic sense". Plato was quoted as saying that a nation must inevitably expand at the expense of others, that non-Greeks are natural enemies to the Greek, that fighting-men should be bred like horses or dogs, inferior children inhumanly-disposed of, and the people governed by lies.

Others were not slow to leap to the defence. Texts were met with counter-texts as in old-fashioned religious controversies. Did not Plato say at *Republic* 373 e: "We have discovered the origin of war in desires which are the most fruitful source of evils both to individuals and states"? The fate of inferior children was not to be exposure (though this was current practice in Greece), but only relegation to a lower class. If Plato "despised democratic ideals", this refers to contemporary democracy, a system in which offices were filled by lot without regard to capability. Modern democracy, it was claimed, embodies "a thoroughly Platonic notion", in favouring the *carrière ouverte aux talents*. Joad agreed that Plato's system resembles Fascism in taking a pessimistic view of human nature, and in advocating an authoritarian state in which the best make the laws and the many achieve the happiness and virtue of which they are capable by obeying. But it differs, he said, in two respects. The criterion for choice of the best is knowledge or wisdom. Goodness and beauty exist, and a few men may by education be brought to apprehend them. In Fascism the self-elected rulers treat power itself as a good. Secondly, the end of government is the well-being of the community as a whole. Justice is defined as the discovery and contented performance by each man of the work for which he is most naturally fitted. Only a few are capable of wisdom: the others will be both more happily and more properly employed in other pursuits. It is not true, said Joad, that Plato regards the ordinary man as a means: his welfare is an end, though an end of inferior value.

The controversy shows no signs of abating. Plato's attackers do not always agree among themselves, particularly in their attitudes to Socrates. To some, Socrates is the hero of democracy and freedom of thought, whose ideals Plato betrayed. To others Socrates himself led the intellectual assault on the democratic way of life. Professor Popper's main indictment of Plato is that he tried to arrest political development at a theoretically perfect stage which was essentially that of the closed, early tribal society. To this the best answer possible has probably been made by Hackforth in a review. It "fails", he says, "to appreciate the seriousness of Plato's conviction, inherited from Socrates, that government is a science, and a science which can only be mastered by a few persons of exceptional powers. . . . It is surely this conviction that dominates the *Republic*, not any hankering after a tribal society. . . . To say that 'Platonic wisdom is acquired largely for the sake of establishing a permanent political class rule' seems to me a precise inversion of the truth: rule is placed in the hands of one class (or rather set of persons, for 'class' is a misleading word) because only a few were capable of Platonic wisdom."

Plato's aim is certainly not the aggrandisement or wealth or happiness of his ruling class in any accepted sense. They are chosen in the first place for their lack of acquisitive and ambitious instincts. After an ordinary education up to the age of 18, followed by two years of military service, they study mathematics and astronomy for 10 years as a preparation for 5 years of philosophy. This gives unity and coherence to their knowledge, and enables them to judge all earthly existence and value in the light of the perfect Forms. They are then sent back into the world and tested by fifteen years of subordinate office. Those who survive all this must from the age of 50 take their turn to govern, though their taste will be all for philosophic pursuits. Their life is one of extreme austerity, in communal barracks on rations provided by the State, debarred from family life, personal property and the use of money. Whatever the Nazi Party may have said, Hermann Goering would hardly have qualified for rulership in the Platonic State.

Paul Friedlander

Painful progressing in stages, from darkness to the beholding of the divine light—if we reconsider this picture imbued with the awe of the Eleusinian mysteries, must we not, to see Plato clearly, ask the question: Is Plato a mystic? The question is the more justified because, while all mysticism expresses a timeless striving of the human soul, the historical forms in which this eternal dimension has manifested itself in Christian, Islamic, and cabalistic mysticism were primarily influenced by Plotinos and thus, at least to a high degree, by Plato.

Plato's "dialectical journey," his rise from the darkness of the cave to the light of the sun, the ascent of the soul's chariot to the realm beyond the heavens—all these elements have their equivalents in any form of mysticism. Dante's pilgrimage through the three realms is the highest poetic expression of this theme. But the same thing is envisaged in the *Itinerarium mentis ad Deum* of St. Bonaventura, which outlines "the ascent from the lowest to the highest, from the external to the innermost, from the temporal to the eternal"; and in the "ladder to heaven" and the "stairway to perfection" found in the writings of mystic monks. Mystical pilgrimages are made in Protestant England as well as in the Islamic Orient. The Sufi is a voyager upon a road; he must pass through seven valleys or climb seven steps, from "remorse" to "union," each station bringing him closer to God. In India, the Buddha taught the "noble eightfold

SOURCE: Paul Friedlander, *Plato, An Introduction*, translated by Hans Meyerhoff, Bollingen Series LIX (Princeton, N. J.: Princeton University Press), pp. 72–78. Copyright © 1958 by the Bollingen Foundation, New York. Reprinted with permission of Princeton University Press and Routledge & Kegan Paul, Ltd.

path." Beginning with right faith and ending with right contemplation, it leads to release from suffering. The religion of Vishnu also
knows the "path of knowledge" and the "path of divine love" whose
common goal is union with the godhead.

Darkness and light, prison and freedom. To the Indian worshiper
of Shiva, man is an animal enchained in matter. Only by breaking
these chains can the soul get to Shiva. For the Sufi the soul is im-
prisoned, separated by seventy thousand veils from the godhead from
which it has sprung. "The body, you know, is a prison," says Goethe
in the *Westöstlicher Diwan*, in the Sufi spirit. Above all, there is the
broad stream of the "metaphysics of illumination" flowing through
late antiquity and the Middle Ages; originating in a deep human
impulse, it has several historical sources besides Plato's *Republic*,
primarily the Fourth Gospel ("and the light shineth in darkness"), and
the circle of Hellenistic mystery worship to which this "mystical"
gospel belongs. Platonic elements are present in the Hermetic writings
and in Philo, though Oriental sources must not be overlooked. Running through Plotinos, Dionysius the Areopagite, and St. Augustine,
this stream continues into the Middle Ages. Henry Suso "stares into
the glorious reflected light"; Mechthild of Magdeburg sees the "flowing
light of the godhead." Dante's point of departure is the "dark forest,"
his goal is "To fix upon the eternal light my gaze," and his union
with the highest reality he describes thus: "That what I speak of is
one simple flame."

Like Plato's dialectical way, the path of the mystic begins with a
release and reversal, severance of the bonds with the sensual world,
and turning of the soul to God. Again, the intellectual structure—
though not the historical movement itself—comes from Plato. Following Plato, the Neoplatonists envisaged the soul's destiny as a "descent"
from . . . and an "ascent" to . . . God, adding the act of "turning" . . .
between these two movements. Augustine combined the latter with
the call of the new teaching, "change your minds," and with the
turning around . . . which, in the New Testament, meant the "conversion of the pagan to the true God, and which, as such, became part of
the permanent structure of Western life and thought. But even this
experience is much more general; there is no mystical way of life
whose beginning is not marked by such a radical turn. Often it is
experienced as a sudden act: "As lightning flashes in the dark of
night, so it comes to pass that by the grace of the Buddha man's
thought of a sudden turns to the good." . . .

The highest good to which love elevates the seeker is, according to
Plato, "not being, but beyond being." This paradoxical form of
expression is another trait characteristic of mysticism in general. The
Neoplatonists are constantly engaged in asserting that the highest

One is beyond all form of predication, sometimes by echoing and enlarging upon the Platonic concept of the "beyond," sometimes by heaping contradictory predicates upon the same One. To mention only one such statement: "The One has no being and all being—no being because being comes later; all being because it comes from the One" (Plotinos VI 7 32). The Christian Neoplatonist Dionysius the Areopagite, in an effort "to name the many names of the godhead, nameless and unreachable," expressed the same idea in an almost theoretical formulation: "With regard to God, we must assert and affirm all forms of being; for He is the cause of all—and, at the same time, negate the predications, for He is beyond all being. And we must not think that the negations contradict the affirmations; rather, that He is beyond negations— He from whom nothing can be taken away, or to whom nothing can be added." This apophatic theology re-echoes in Eckhart's "It is His nature to be without nature," in Scotus Erigena's "*Deus propter excellentiam non immerito nihil vocatur*," in Suso's "not-being," in Angelus Silesius' "God is a pure Nothingness," and likewise in the cabala's names for the unlimited. But aside from this development Indian thinkers have, on their own, said strikingly similar things. In the *Upanishads* we find the same contradictory assertions: "The One moves and does not move; it is remote and near; it is within and beyond all things." We find the same abundance of negations: "The imperishable is neither crude nor fine, neither short nor long; it is without taste or smell, vision or hearing, speech or reason, without life or breath, without mouth or measure, without inside or outside. Consumed by nothing, it consumes nothing." And we know that it is the double negation, the "not-not," which, to many of the old Indian sages, most truly characterizes the nature of the Brahman.

The structure of mystical consciousness, and especially of mystic thought, shows a great similarity with the structure of Plato's view of the world. This is due to the fact of Plato's historical influence upon many systems of mysticism on the one hand, and of common roots in both owing to a basic human orientation on the other. We have now reached the point, however, where we must say that Plato, after all, is not a mystic, and show how he differs from genuine mysticism.

Plato's highest idea does not extinguish being, but is, as it were, within the chain of being; only it is so far above everything else that paradoxically it may be called *beyond* being, though still beyond *being*. It is reached, not through lonely introspection, violent leaps, and submergence in darkness, but through a path by which knowledge grasps the nature of being. Without arithmetic, geometry, astronomy, musical theory, without the discipline of philosophical dialectics, the goal cannot be approached—although, once in view, words and concepts are no longer adequate. Mysticism, on the other hand, even when it is most concerned with knowledge, remains within the realm of theology, conscious, moreover, that the object of its quest cannot be discovered through ratio, but only through a descent "to a depth that is unfathomable." Usually it is even more emphatic in its rejection of knowledge. The "gnosis" prevailing in the Hermetic writings, to be sure, uses Platonic patches to weave a glittering garb for its ecstasies; but we must not be deceived. "To make oneself like God," "to become eternity" . . . , "to consider oneself as immortal and capable of knowing everything, all art, all science, the nature of all living beings, to be everywhere and everything, to know everything simultaneously, times, places, objects, qualities, quantities"—this excited collection is symptomatic of a new spirit. The same spirit is apparent when, instead of the knowledge of everything, the silence of knowledge is proclaimed. Thus, according to Philo, to cite but one voice among many, the divine light dawns only when human reason has perished and darkness, surrounding man, produces ecstasy and God-inspired madness. Nothing could be more foreign to Plato than such ecstatic exaggeration, using Platonic phrases, yet denying man's highest power. If a step further is taken, the life of the mystic is subject to the compulsion of magic: the Christian mystic's castigations; the wild dance of the dervishes and the endless repetition of the name Allah in Islam; and, in India, regulation of the breath, rigid contemplation of the tip of the nose, the magic of the sacred syllable *om.* There is a world of difference between these ritualistic acts and Plato's severe scientific attitude and discipline. Plato not only avoided any form of magic; from the point of view of mysticism, he must even be regarded as a rationalist. To him, no God made folly of this world's wisdom. He would not understand the contradiction so moving in Pascal's exclamation: *"Dieu d'Abraham, Dieu d'Isaac, Dieu de Jacob, non des philosophes et des savants!"* In Plato, both divine inspiration and mathematical science lead man upward—geometry leads to God. His world is one, unbroken in its dynamic tension.

G. M. A. Grube

We have now seen the Ideas slowly emerge from the Socratic definition, as Aristotle said they did, and then blaze forth in all their glory in the dialogues of the middle period. We have seen them remain, until the very end of Plato's life, the fundamental hypothesis upon which he based the rest of his philosophy, in spite of the fact that he was well aware of the difficulties which the theory implied. To make

SOURCE: G. M. A. Grube, *Plato's Thought* (Boston: Beacon Press, 1935), pp. 49–50. Reprinted with permission of Methuen & Company, Ltd., London.

completely valid knowledge possible it was essential that there be some such universal realities not subject to change and decay, and that these should be apprehended by the human intelligence. And, since some such realities were necessary, Plato was satisfied to assert that there existed such a reality corresponding to what we are more apt to call every abstract concept. But to look upon the Ideas as concepts in any shape or form is a mistake, for a concept cannot by definition exist until the mind has conceived it, and this Plato quite deliberately refused to admit of his Ideas. They are rather the objective reality to which the concept corresponds, and they exist whether we know them or not. If the whole human race were senseless savages, the eternal Form of justice would exist as fully in any case, though it would be even less perfectly realized in the world. So that in the intelligible world there is no place for progress or evolution: the pattern is the same though the copy—the world of sense—may reflect it more or less closely at different times. That it progresses in this direction in a sure and certain manner is not definite; if we are to trust the *Politicus* myth, the old belief in cycles of alternate advance and relapse had its attraction for Plato.

The Ideas are spaceless and immaterial. That is perfectly clear from the *Phaedo* on, and to press poetical expressions used in certain myths which would seem to assert the contrary, is childish and ridiculous. Ideas are quite independent of particulars: men may come and men may die, they may even all die, but the Idea of man, like that of beauty, goodness and all the rest, would still exist. In fact humanity does not die, and the problem of extinct species probably did not occur to Plato.

Considered as truth, the Ideas are the objective realities that general terms connote. It is from this aspect that Plato thought of them as mathematical formulae which governed the physical world and brought order out of chaos, laws that governed every human action as well as the movements of the stars and planets, the one right way of doing things in the moral sphere. For as a mathematician he dreamed of introducing mathematical accuracy even there. And as they make for harmony they are beautiful and are the objects of our passionate longing to see, to know and understand beauty and, by means of this understanding, to create further beauty. Again as the source of order, bringing harmony where chaos reigned, they are good, for harmony is the essence of goodness and usefulness (almost synonymous terms to a Greek) whereas what is discordant is not only ugly, but useless and self-destructive. They are also the truths of logic, for it is from them that both subject and predicate derive their meaning. But to regard them merely as logical entities and rules of thought is to deprive Platonism of all its inspiration and emotional appeal.

Julius Stenzel

My first aim in the present work is to secure an historically accurate
view of the meaning of the doctrine of Ideas, which modern scholarship has only succeeded in rendering more and more doubtful. To
this end, it seems absolutely necessary to discover, by a systematic
analysis which does not go beyond the horizon of Plato's doctrines,
what form of Universal it is, and how constituted, that he names an
Idea. The most important result of such an inquiry will be that
Plato's discovery of the concept comes at the end rather than at the
beginning of his evolution. The view which finds in the theory of
Ideas a consistent and comprehensive doctrine of the Concept must
be rejected as a survival of the obsolete treatment of Plato as a systematic philosopher in the modern sense of the word—equally whether
the concepts are held to have been *substantialized*, or are interpreted
as "rules of method". There is, no doubt, equally little justification for
speaking of a continuous development traceable from one Dialogue
to the next. The truth here is best described in a phrase of Goethe's,
"the form impressed by Nature, which develops because it lives". In
Plato's work there is both unity and development—unity, because he
has a sharply defined manner of viewing things and securing an
intellectual grasp of them, and this manner *is* the Platonic Idea or
"vision"; and development, because there is a change in the kind of
objects on which his main interest rests at different times. Being objective, his thought necessarily takes on the shape of its favourite objects.
Upon these principles I shall here attempt to define more precisely
the change of interest which (so much has never been disputed) led
Plato to relinquish Socrates and his primarily ethical problems, and to
aspire to a wider knowledge of reality; and I shall also try to trace the
influence of this change upon the logical function ascribed to the Idea.
That being done, it becomes possible to assign the Dialogues of Plato
to two periods, according as his predominant interest is in morals and
practice, or in theory and natural philosophy. By analysing the
central Idea of the Good, we find that in the earlier period the Ideas
have the characteristic transcendent existence of an Aretê, in the
specifically Greek sense—each Idea is a cause . . . in the double sense
of explanation and end; whereas in the later period, Ideas are the
substantial reality implied by the "permanence of kinds", the classes
defined by natural science; and . . . division, is a method whose
purpose it is to determine them in order to bring individual reality

SOURCE: Julius Stenzel, *Plato's Method of Dialectic*, translated by D. Allan (New York:
Russell and Russell, 1924), pp. 23–24. Reprinted with permission of The Clarendon
Press, Oxford.

within the grasp of science. The evidence of outward form points to the same general division of Plato's work; I may refer to my essay on the literary form and philosophical content of the Dialogues. A significant point here is the retirement of Socrates from the centre of the stage; although Plato treats the historical Socrates with the greatest independence, it remains his artistic purpose to preserve the Socratic type of inquiry, wherein some practical problem of ethics is explained, and the "maieutic" method, *i.e.* instruction through hints at the positive truth, is employed. This view of the outward form will assist us in our detailed interpretation of the *Theaetetus* and *Sophist;* we shall find that the problems *solved* in the latter of these Dialogues are *stated* in the former; the artistic device is one which Plato had freely and consciously chosen; and the *Theaetetus* is a genuine Socratic Dialogue. We shall offer a similar interpretation of the *Phaedrus,* in which old and new are so mysteriously blended. Plato was consciously employing a form of presentation which would show the continuity between the two periods. More general considerations will lead us from this to a survey of Plato's relationship to Democritus and Aristotle.

The mere announcement of the purpose of my work in these historical and philological terms shows that it will diverge from the "philosophical" exposition practised by the Marburg school; my only purpose is to restore Plato's views, if possible, in his own sense and in that of his time. Even where I have argued philosophically, it is with the purpose of interpretation. Hence my frequent disagreement with Natorp's study of the Theory of Ideas, a work which is indispensable for any inquiry which pretends to go deeply into Plato's thought. For just this reason, however, the author feels that he must strongly endorse a remark often made by his teacher Wendland, that "at no time are Platonic problems so clear as when one engages in careful study of Natorp".

Thomas Gould

What shall we say about Plato's notion of beauty, the idea that beauty is a sudden, unexplained glimpse of what we are really always after in our pursuit of happiness? If Plato is right, it would mean that aesthetic theory as it is often explored today, divorced, that is, from all attempts at constructing a metaphysical system, must be doomed. If Plato is right, we shall never have anything very illuminating to say about

SOURCE: Thomas Gould, *Platonic Love* (London, Routledge & Kegan Paul, Ltd., 1963), pp. 184–186. Reprinted with permission of Routledge & Kegan Paul, Ltd. and The Macmillan Company (© The Free Press, A Corporation).

beauty until we try to connect it with our understanding of what makes a thing good and what we want when we want to be happy. Are we so satisfied, after all, with our talk about tone or metaphor, our talk about the ordinary uses of words like "dainty" and "dumpy," or our talk of disguised audio-visual sexuality?

And Plato's general tendency to hang on always to the rare, the special, and the valuable in humanity might be just the thing we need to put in opposition to the Freudian approach and so raise the discussion to a more intelligent level. Is it perhaps only our Romantic prejudice—a prejudice in favor of that within our submerged imagination which links us with the vicious tendencies of detestable people, with the uncompromising appetites of our own childhood, and with the thoughtless savagery of nature—which has led us to this startling new picture of ourselves: the depressing conclusion that we are all really after organ pleasure and nothing more, and that our concern for others is but an anxiety to hang on to a "love object"? Why should we not start rather with the observation that we sometimes do in fact manage—as animals never begin to do—to transform our infantile instincts into far more satisfying pursuits, and that the naturalness and excellence of the usual transformations of our energies are more basic facts than are the details of the history of our energies as they were manifested in childhood? The Freudian hypothesis is at least not proved to be true beyond all shadow of doubt.

Since the Platonic theory of love is really a theory about life, it is an idea with almost endless ramifications. Everybody will have his favorites. I could have mentioned the ideal of teaching, the call to base government on a high standard of friendship, the insistence that the way to greater sureness in life lies in the restriction of our greatest tenderness to the finest things only, the warning that the way we have been taught to look at things and to talk about them may be far more crude and misleading than we have suspected, or the ideal of philosophy as nothing less than life itself when it is lived most bravely and most wonderfully.

But the last word, perhaps, should be reserved for that most characteristic of all of Plato's suggestions, the idea which is the link between the paradoxes of Socrates and the metaphysics of Aristotle, that calculation is not the interesting thing about rationality at all, that perception of goals which are genuine goods is what we really value intelligence for. For one thing, this suggestion might offer an interesting solution to the strange mystery of the disappearing *ego*. What would happen if we took more seriously than we usually do the assumption that what embraced and employed the *id* and the *super-ego* in the healthy man was his correct grasp of the world as a fine and happy place? More important, Plato's suggestion might offer a way to rehabilitate the notion of intelligence in an honorific sense in our never ending battle against stupidity, violence, and vulgarity. Intelligence in the Socratic sense would include, notice, even the simple, slow, uneducated people who nevertheless somehow come to understand the important things, and it would exclude the fast, accurate calculators who nevertheless fail in all the major tests in life. Might it not have a salutary effect in some ways if we could just persuade people to withhold the attribution of intelligence from anyone who failed to see what he ought to be doing for his own happiness? You and I, here and now, trying to do the best for ourselves, cannot sit back and hope that we are among those rare people who do the right thing without ever having thought things out; we had better calculate. On the other hand, correct calculation carried out in pursuit of the desires we are now experiencing will be valuable only if we are experiencing desires for the most desirable things. On this interpretation of intelligence and rationality, philosophy, love, and the art of living itself really do become one and the same thing.

Plato's assertion that the pursuit of happiness is the pursuit of one goal, a single good, should not put us off, I think. To be sure, it does seem more likely that good is the same in different experiences only insofar as various experiences are in fact rewarding, that life presents us with many possible goals, indeed that we would be better off to assume that we must divide our energies and look for no single description of success. Once we have said this, however, we have not said very much. Listing and mulling over the plurality of activities which might or might not be worth trying, or throwing up our hands in weariness at the discovery that it is precisely the biggest questions which are the hardest to answer, will certainly not get us very far. We might still listen to Plato's call to wake up—to see that our desires may in fact be ill-conceived, that the exercise of intelligence can change desires, and that there may be experiences which, if we could but taste them, would make our present goals lose all desirability.

A STUDY GUIDE

1. What is Platonic dialogue according to Koyré? What is the implication of his statement that, "for Plato real science . . . is attained, discovered, invented by the soul in solitary travail"?

2. How does Guthrie interpret the relationship between Plato and Socrates? Do you agree?

3. What is a strong argument for viewing Plato as a totalitarian? Is Guthrie's argument sufficient to reject this interpretation?

4. What are the arguments in favor of the mystical interpretation of

Platonic thought? What are Friedlander's arguments against the mystical interpretation? If Plato were a mystic, how would you interpret his statement at the end of the *Parable of the Cave*, that the philosopher must turn away from the light of the sun and descend back into the cave?

5. Is it necessary to agree with Grube that the theory of forms is the central part of Plato's philosophy?

6. What assumptions underlie the argument that Plato's philosophy underwent a process of development? What are the arguments against the developmental position?

7. Compare the Freudian and the Platonic treatment of love. What is Gould's recommendation for the modern world and its treatment of love?

6
MODERN COMMENTARY ON ARISTOTLE

T. Chase

... Platonism is the doctrine that the individuals we call things only become, but a thing is always one universal form beyond many individuals, *e.g.* one good beyond seeming goods; and that without supernatural forms, which are models of individuals, there is nothing, no being, no knowing, no good. Aristotelianism is the contrary doctrine: a thing is always a separate individual, a *substance* (...), natural such as earth or supernatural such as God; and without these individual substances, which have attributes and universals belonging to them, there is nothing, to be, to know, to be good. Philosophic differences are best felt by their practical effects: philosophically, Platonism is a philosophy of universal forms, Aristotelianism a philosophy of individual substances: practically, Plato makes us think first of the supernatural and the kingdom of heaven, Aristotle of the natural and the whole world.

So diametrical a difference could not have arisen at once. For, though Aristotle was different from Plato, and brought with him from Stagira a Greek and Ionic but colonial origin, a medical descent and tendency, and a matter-of-fact worldly kind of character, nevertheless on coming to Athens as pupil of Plato he must have begun with his master's philosophy. What then in more detail was the philosophy which the pupil learnt from the master? When Aristotle at the age of eighteen came to Athens, Plato, at the age of sixty-two, had probably written all his dialogues except the *Laws*; and in the course of the remaining twenty years of his life and teaching, he expounded "the so-called unwritten dogmas" in his lectures on the Good. There was therefore a written Platonism for Aristotle to read, and an unwritten Platonism which he actually heard.

Source: T. Chase, "Aristotle," *Encyclopaedia Britannica* (1911), *2*, pp. 502–503, 519–522.

To begin with the written philosophy of the Dialogues. Individual so-called things neither are nor are not, but become: the real thing is always one universal form beyond the many individuals, *e.g.* the one beautiful beyond all beautiful individuals; and each form (. . .) is a model which causes individuals by participation to become like, but not the same as, itself. Above all forms stands the form of the good, which is the cause of all other forms being, and through them of all individuals becoming. The creator, or the divine intellect, with a view to the form of the good, and taking all forms as models, creates in a receptacle . . . individual impressions which are called things but really change and become without attaining the permanence of being. Knowledge resides not in sense but in reason, which, on the suggestion of sensations of changing individuals, apprehends, or (to be precise) is reminded of, real universal forms, and, by first ascending from less to more general until it arrives at the form of good and then descending from this unconditional principle to the less general, becomes science and philosophy, using as its method the dialectic which gives and receives questions and answers between man and man. Happiness in this world consists proximately in virtue as a harmony between the three parts, rational, spirited and appetitive, of our souls, and ultimately in living according to the form of the good; but there is a far higher happiness, when the immortal soul, divesting itself of body and passions and senses, rises from earth to heaven and contemplates pure forms by pure reason. Such in brief is the Platonism of the written dialogues; where the main doctrine of forms is confessedly advanced never as a dogma but always as a hypothesis, in which there are difficulties, but without which Plato can explain neither being, nor truth nor goodness, because throughout he denies the being of individual things. In the unwritten lectures of his old age, he developed this formal into a mathematical metaphysics. In order to explain the unity and variety of the world, the one universal form and the many individuals, and how the one good is the main cause of everything, he placed as it were at the back of his own doctrine of forms a Pythagorean mathematical philosophy. He supposed that the one and the two, which is indeterminate, and is the great and little, are opposite principles or causes. Identifying the form of the good with the one, he supposed that the one, by combining with the indeterminate two, causes a plurality of forms, which like every combination of one and two are numbers but peculiar in being incommensurate with one another, so that each form is not a mathematical number, . . . but a formal number. . . . Further he supposed that in its turn each form, or formal number, is a limited one which, by combining again with the indeterminate two, causes a plurality of individuals. Hence finally he concluded that the good as the one combining with the indeterminate two is directly the cause of all forms as formal numbers, and indirectly through them all of the multitude of individuals in the world.

Aristotle knew Plato, was present at his lectures on the Good, wrote a report of them . . . , and described this latter philosophy of Plato in his *Metaphysics*. Modern critics, who were not present and knew neither, often accuse Aristotle of misrepresenting Plato. But Heracleides and Hestiacus, Speusippus and Xenocrates were also present and wrote similar reports. What is more, both Speusippus and Xenocrates founded their own philosophies on this very Pythagoreanism of Plato. Speusippus as president of the Academy from 347 to 339 taught that the one and the many are principles, while abolishing forms and reducing the good from cause to effect. Xenocrates as president from 339 onwards taught that the one and many are principles, only without distinguishing mathematical from formal numbers. Aristotle's critics hardly realize that for the rest of his life he had to live and to struggle with a formal and a mathematical Platonism, which exaggerated first universals and attributes and afterwards the quantitative attributes, one and many, into substantial things and real causes.

Aristotle had no sympathy with the unwritten dogmas of Plato. But with the written dialogues of Plato he always continued to agree almost as much as he disagreed. Like Plato, he believed in real universals, real essences, real causes, he believed in the unity of the universal, and in the immateriality of essences; he believed in the good, and that there is a good of the universe; he believed that God is a living being, eternal and best, who is a supernatural cause of the motions and changes of the natural world, and that essences and matter are also necessary causes; he believed in the divine intelligence and in the immortality of our intelligent souls; he believed in knowledge going from sense to reason, that science requires ascent to principles and is descent from principles, and that dialectic is useful to science; he believed in happiness involving virtue, and in moral virtue being a control of passions by reason, while the highest happiness is speculative wisdom. All these inspiring metaphysical and moral doctrines the pupil accepted from his master's dialogues, and throughout his life adhered to the general spirit of realism without materialism pervading the Platonic philosophy. But what he refused to believe with Plato was that reality is not here, but only above; and what he maintained against Plato was that it is both, and that universals and forms, one and many, the good, are real but not separate realities. This deep metaphysical divergence was the prime cause of the transition from Platonism to Aristotelianism. . . .

The Aristotelian Philosophy

. . . It remains to answer the final question: What is the Aristotelian philosophy, which its author gradually formed with so much labour?

Here we have only room for its spirit, which we shall try to give as if he were himself speaking to us, as head of the Peripatetic school at Athens, and holding no longer the early views of his dialogues, or the immature views of such treatises as the *Categories*, but only his mature views, such as he expresses in the *Metaphysics*. Aristotle was primarily a metaphysician, a philosopher of things, who uses the objective method of proceeding from being to thinking. We shall begin therefore with that primary philosophy which is the real basis of his philosophy, and proceed in the order of his classification of science to give his chief doctrines on:

(1) Speculative philosophy, metaphysical and physical, including his psychology, and with it his logic.
(2) Practical philosophy, ethics and politics.
(3) Productive science, or art.

Things are substances . . . , each of which is a separate individual . . . and is variously affected as quantified, qualified, related, active, passive and so forth, in categories of things which are attributes . . . , different from the category of substance, but real only as predicates belonging to some substance, and are in fact only the substance itself affected. . . . The essence of each substance, being what it is . . . , is that substance; *e.g.* this rational animal, Socrates. Substances are so similar that the individuals of a species are even the same in essence or substance, *e.g.* Callias and Socrates differ in matter but are the same in essence, as rational animals. The universal . . . is real only as one predicate belonging to many individual substances: it is therefore not a substance. There are then no separate universal forms, as Plato supposed. There are attributes and universals, real as belonging to individual substances, whose being is their being. The mind, especially in mathematics, abstracts numbers, motions, relations, causes, essences, ends, kinds; and it over-abstracts things mentally separate into things really separate. But reality consists only of individual substances, numerous, moving, related, active as efficient causes, passive as material causes, essences as formal causes, ends as final causes, and in classes which are real universals only as real predicates of individual substances. Such is Aristotle's realism of individuals and universals, contained in his primary philosophy, as expressed in the *Metaphysics*, especially in Book Z, his authoritative pronouncement on being and substance.

The individual substances, of which the universe is composed, fall into three great irreducible kinds: nature, God, man.

I. Nature—The obvious substances are natural substances or bodies . . . , *e.g.* animals, plants, water, earth, moon, sun, stars. Each natural substance is a compound . . . of essence and matter; its essence . . .

being its actual substance, its matter . . . not; its essence being determinate, its matter not; its essence being immateriate, its matter conjoined with the essence; its essence being one in all individuals of a species, its matter different in each individual; its essence being cause of uniformity, its matter cause of accident. At the same time, matter is not nothing, but something, which, though not substance, is potentially substance; and it is either proximate to the substance, or primary; proximate, as a substance which is potentially different, *e.g.* wood potentially a table; primary, as an indeterminate something which is a substratum capable of becoming natural substances, of which it is always one; and it is primarily the matter of earth, water, air, fire, the four simple bodies . . . with natural rectilineal motions in the terrestrial world . . . ; while aether . . . is a fifth simple body, with natural circular motion, being the element of the stars . . . in the celestial world. Each natural substance is a formal cause, as being what it is; a material cause, as having passive power to be changed; an efficient cause, as having active power to change, by communicating the selfsame essence into different matter so as to produce therein a homogeneous effect in the same species; and a final cause, as an end to be realized. Moreover, though each natural substance is corruptible . . . , species is eternal . . . , because there was always some individual of it to continue its original essence . . . in which is ungenerated and incorruptible; the natural world therefore is eternal; and nature is for ever aiming at an eternal propagation, by efficient acting on matter, of essence as end. For even nature does nothing in vain, but aims at final causes, which she uniformly realizes, except so far as matter by its spontaneity . . . causes accidental effects; and the ends of nature are no form of good, nor even the good of man, but the essences of natural substances themselves, and, above them all, the good God Himself. Such is Aristotle's natural realism, pervading his metaphysical and physical writings.

II. God—Nature is but one kind of being . . . . Above all natural substances, the objects of natural science, there stands a supernatural substance, the object of metaphysics as theology. Nature's boundary is the outer sphere of the fixed stars, which is eternally moved day after day in a uniform circle round the earth. Now, an actual cause is required for an actual effect. Therefore, there must be a prime mover of that prime movable, and equally eternal and uniform. That prime mover is God, who is not the creator, but the mover directly of the heavens, and indirectly through the planets of sublunary substances. But God is no mechanical mover. He moves as motive . . . ; He is the efficient only as the final cause of nature. For God is a living being, eternal, very good . . . . While nature aims at Him as design, as an end, a motive, a final cause, God's occupation . . . is intelligence . . . and since essence, not indeed in all being, but in being understood, becomes identical with intelligence, God in understanding essence is understanding Himself; and in short, God's intelligence is at once intelligence of Himself, of essence and of intelligence . . . . But at the same time the essence of good exists not only in God and God's intelligence on the one hand, but also on the other hand on a declining scale in nature, as both in a general and in his army; but rather in God, and more in some parts of nature than in others. Thus even God is a substance, a separate individual, whose differentiating essence is to be a living being, eternal and very good; He is however the only substance whose essence is entirely without matter and unconjoined with matter; and therefore He is a substance, not because He has or is a substratum beneath attributes, but wholly because He is a separate individual, different both from nature and men, yet the final good of the whole universe. Such is Aristotle's theological realism without materialism and the origin of all spiritualistic realism, contained in his *Metaphysics*. . . .

III. Man—There is a third kind of substance, combining something both of the natural and of the divine: we men are that privileged species. Each man is a substance, like any other, only because he is a separate individual. Like any natural substance, he is composed of matter and immateriate essence. But natural substances are inorganic and organic; and a man is an organic substance composed of an organic body . . . as matter, and a soul . . . as essence, which is the primary actuality of an organic body capable of life . . . . Still a man is not the only organism; and every organism has a soul, whose immediate organ is the spirit . . . , a body which—analogous to a body diviner than the four so-called elements, namely the aether, the element of the stars— gives to the organism its nonterrestrial vital heat, whether it be a plant or an animal. In an ascending scale, a plant is an organism with a nutritive soul; an animal is a higher organism with a nutritive, sensitive, orectic and locomotive soul; a man is the highest organism with a nutritive, sensitive, orectic, locomotive and rational soul. What differentiates man from other natural and organic substances, and approximates him to a supernatural substance, God, is reason . . . or intellect . . . . Now, though only one of the powers of the soul, intellect alone of these powers has no bodily organ; it alone is immortal: it alone is divine. While the soul is propagated, like any other essence, by the efficient, which is the seed, to the matter, which is the germ, of the embryo man, intellect alone enters from without . . . , and is alone divine . . . , because its activity communicates with no bodily activity . . . . A man then is a third kind of substance, like a natural substance in bodily matter, like a supernatural substance in divine reason or intellect. Such is Aristotle's dual, or rather triple, realism. . . .

G. R. G. Mure

So far we have looked on the universe through Aristotle's eyes as a scale on which consciousness appears only midway. We treated the emerging stages of consciousness as essentially characterising the ascending grades of conscious substance, and we ignored at first the fact that we can in the end say nothing of the whole ordered universe, the whole *Scala Universi*, save as the object of knowledge . . . . But we learned at last that in God—and perhaps at moments in man—knowledge is completely one with its object. And the problem of efficient reason should at least have warned us that if we are to maintain this ultimate identity of subject and object without embracing the relativism of Protagoras, we cannot continue to treat knowledge as no more than the adjective of an individual thinker.

Aristotle, as we saw, does not develop these results, nor reach beyond the conception of a single hierarchy of beings. But he does supplement this conception by reflecting explicitly from two points of view upon the universe as the object of thought. In Met. VII and VIII he discusses the nature of substance as such, laying emphasis on the object. In the *Organon*—the name afterwards given to the group of logical works—he treats of thought itself, not as the function of an individual subject, but in terms of truth and falsehood and with special reference to its form. This systematic separation of aspects conspicuously differentiates him from Plato, but he is held by his view of the relation between, and the ultimate identify of, mind and its object from pursuing methodological distinction so far towards divorce of form from content as did some of his successors. In the doctrine of the categories, which gives its title to the first book of the *Organon*, the two points of view are somewhat ambiguously combined.

The Categories

A doctrine of categories is fundamental in Aristotle's philosophy, but its origin and development are so obscure that the *Categories*, where alone it is formulated in detail, has been attributed both to the beginning and to the end of Aristotle's career. Moreover, at least its latter half is probably not Aristotle's work.

Source: G. R. G. Mure, *Aristotle* (London: Oxford University Press, 1932), pp. 177–189. Reprinted with permission of the publishers.

In a phrase which aptly links the Socratic conversation with his own philosophic dialectic, Plato speaks of thought as "the soul's conversation with herself" (*Theaetetus* . . .). The implied view of language, developed in the *Cratylus*, reappears in Aristotle as a rather crude correspondence theory of word and thought: "Spoken words are the symbols of experiences in the soul, written words the symbols of spoken words. As all men have not the same script, so not all have the same speech sounds, but the experiences, which these primarily symbolise, are the same for all, and so are the things of which our experiences are the likenesses". *Prima facie*, at any rate, Aristotle deduces the categories from an analysis of linguistic forms. He proceeds roughly thus:—(*a*) He divides language into "things said without combination" and "things said in combination," *i.e.* simple terms (nouns and verbs) and prepositions; (*b*) he classifies the senses in which ordinary usage predicates one term of another—hence the name "categories," which means "predications"; thereby (*c*) he reaches a classification of being.

(*a*) All terms will be found to fall under one of ten categories:

Substance (*e.g.* "Socrates," "man").
Of a certain quantity (*e.g.* "two cubits long").
Of a certain quality (*e.g.* "white").
In a relation (*e.g.* "double," "greater").
Somewhere (*e.g.* "in the Lyceum").
At some time (*e.g.* "yesterday").
Being in a position (*e.g.* "reclines").
Being in a state (*e.g.* "is shod").
Doing (*e.g.* "cuts").
Suffering (*e.g.* "is cut").

(*b*) The singular individual—. . . "this somewhat," as Aristotle calls it—is primarily entitled to the name of substance. It is *par excellence* the subject of predication, and itself neither predicable "of" a subject (*i.e.* as a universal of a particular), nor predicable as "inherent in" (*i.e.* as an accident which cannot exist apart from) a subject. Species and genus are "secondary substances," predicable only "of" a subject—genus of both species and singular, species only of singular. All other terms fall under the remaining categories, and are accidents predicable only as inherent in substance.

(*c*) But the subject of a proposition need not be a substance, and the categories are not only the main heads of predication: they also classify all nameable things in respect to the precise character of their reality. If we take any definitory judgment, and ask what kind of essential being is predicated of the subject, the answer is bound to be one of the categories. Thus, for example, if we define Socrates as essentially a man a cubit as essentially a measure, white as essentially a colour, four as essentially twice two, we are predicating respectively of these four subjects as their essential being, substance, quantity, quality, and relation.

The list of categories seems somewhat arbitrary. Aristotle apparently assumes that the accidental categories, which, because substance alone is self-dependent, are all logically posterior to substance, themselves too form some sort of logically developing series in which each succeeding term presupposes and depends on its predecessor . . . . But he never works out such a series, and the efforts of his commentators to do so do not convince. In the *Categories* only substance is treated with any care, and in the lists given outside that work position and state only once appear. At best the categories constitute a system, surprisingly comprehensive if one tries to apply it, despite its empirical character.

Before we consider difficulties arising from Aristotle's formulation of the doctrine, it may help us to ask what are its probable antecedents. As a theory of how the real is reflected in the forms of judgment, it seems to presuppose Plato's *Sophist* . . . but the list bears no obvious relation to the common characters of the *Theaetetus* and *Parmenides*, or to the inter-participant forms of the *Sophist*. Nor are the categories put forward as all-pervasive characters of the real such as we seemed to detect when we followed Plato's more dialectical line of thought . . . . On the other hand, Plato's distinction of self-subsistent from dependent being is possibly the source of Aristotle's conception of substance and accident, and in shaping it he may be following Plato's second line of thought in the *Sophist* . . . . Yet, if he is doing so, he takes as his cornerstone what Plato seems merely to suggest in passing. We found that in the *Sophist* the introduction of this distinction increased a tendency to confuse being as the minimal characterisation of all that is, with being in the sense of the real as a complete whole . . . . Aristotle, as we might expect . . . , makes no attempt to work in logic with the notion of an absolute whole, and reduces the four terms of Plato's antitheses to three: substance, accidental being, and being as a minimal character of all that is. Minimal being is not a kind, or genus, of which the categories are the subgenera. For, according to Aristotle, classification by genus and species implies division into co-ordinate groups. Strictly speaking, it classifies only substances, and at all events it can apply only within each several category. But the categories are not co-ordinate; they exhibit a logical order. Hence there is only being as substance, being as *quantum*, *quale*, etc. The categories are highest genera, and minimal being is analogous to a grammatical stem present in, but not apart from, the inflected forms in which it is conjugated or declined.

On the whole, then, Aristotle seems to follow Plato's second line of thought. He does not offer the categories as a dialectical system in which the real as a whole develops and grows concrete through an ascending series of partial definitions. On the other hand, the categories do not directly reflect the stages of that ordered universe of which we have watched the gradual construction in Aristotle's thought. So far as they classify real things, those real things are not precisely the members of the *Scala Universi* as such. God and the other perfect beings are pure substance, but *quanta* and *qualia* are not, as such, things of a lower grade on the scale. For all the members of the *Scala Universi* are, as such, substances, albeit less and less perfect—more deeply immersed in matter—as the scale descends; and they are classified, where classification is possible, by genus and species. The *Scala Universi* and the categories are two systems which coincide at their summits inasmuch as God is perfect substance, but do not coincide elsewhere. Rather the various categories serve to order and determine that diversity of accidental characters whereby imperfect things reveal their changing natures, their various degrees of failure to be divine.

But the position thus reached is an ambiguous compromise; for Plato's first line of thought—or something like it—is not altogether without its influence, since the earlier categories, at all events, might, with modification, take their place in a philosophical dialectic as partial definitions of the real as a whole. What happens is perhaps this: Aristotle discovers certain all-pervasive characters of the real, but he cannot set them out as a series of partial definitions of reality as a whole, because of reality as a whole he has no genuinely operative conception beyond the *Scala Universi*, which he has reached empirically. He aims at Monism, and his central doctrine of causation demands it; but he fails to rise above a more or less pluralistic system. The scheme of things entire is to him a hierarchy of substances and not a whole of dialectical moments. Hence the categories have to classify characters which belong to a plurality of substances already empirically systematised, and, so far as they constitute a developing series, they order and determine, not reality as a whole, but the degrees of imperfection in those substances. Thus, because Aristotle regards the complete and perfect as that which is finite and limited . . . ; because he does not equate perfect being with being that is all-comprehensive, the two systems in the main diverge. But because the highest members of the *Scala Universi* are perfect beings, they coincide at the summit.

The categories are the highest universals of a pluralist system, and the universals of a pluralist system are inevitably empirical. They tend to become mere abstract common characters which classify externally. Universal and particular make claims that pluralism cannot reconcile. The universal cannot genuinely characterise its particulars, nor they afford the universal its proper articulate content. Pluralism refuses to recognise that all judgment has ultimately a single subject—that the very claim of the universal to *be* universal is a claim to characterise reality as a whole and a criticism of the pluralist universe. Lastly pluralism tends gradually to treat the universal as a mere mental concept, and to oppose it to "external" real things.

Though Aristotle reaches the categories through the reflexion of the real in words, the symbols of thoughts, yet on the whole he refrains from this final step. The real and the intelligible remain for him ultimately one. He does not embrace that realism which a pluralist metaphysic in the end involves. Yet, when the theory of substance as singular individual breaks down . . . , he is forced to seek an alternative within the limits set by Plato's second line of thought, and his field is further narrowed by his resolute rejection of the Platonic Forms as he conceives them. The universal must be individualised in what it characterises, not divorced from that and then given a fresh individuality in a new world of its own.

Substance

In the *Categories* the essential characteristics assigned to substance are three. It is always a subject and never a predicate. It has no contrary, and admits of no degree: there is no contrary of Socrates or man, and a man cannot be less or more man. It persists identical, while accidents vary between contrary poles: the same man is now hot, now cold, etc. As the ultimate subjects of predication, which "underlie everything else" . . . , singular individuals fulfil these conditions more adequately than species, species than genera. Hence in the first book of the *Organon* the categories are chiefly considered as a means of classifying all the predicates applicable to an individual subject: *e.g.* Socrates *qua* substance is a man, *qua* quantified is tall, *qua* qualified snub-nosed, *qua* related a husband, etc. They thus exhibit the varying degrees of intimacy with which its various possible predicates attach to a subject. But the main distinction is between substance and the accidental categories. Accidents may change—even, if they qualify superficially, disappear—whereas substance abides, unvarying in degree. But if any substantial character be removed, the individual itself disappears.

Nevertheless Aristotle's formulation of the theory leads to contradiction. (1) Since the categories classify being exhaustively, the category of substance will contain not only the substantial characters such as animal, man, etc.—the secondary substances—but also the singular sensible substances of which these are predicated. And this Aristotle maintains. Yet (2) if the categories classify universal predicates, the singular substances to which they apply—those at all events which are sensible—must remain outside all the categories. But (3) if the singular substance is isolated from the substantial predicates which define its essential nature, it becomes simply nothing. Hence (4) all its essence, all that you can say of it in defining it, does turn out to be contained in the category of substance—except its individuality, its unique "thisness." But (5) even if the singular *qua* a unique particular is apprehended by sense and not by thought, yet a substance must be individual.

Another route leads to the same difficulty, but also to a possible solution. The substantial characters predicable of the sensible singular are the genus and differentia which together constitute its definable form. The genus is conceived by Aristotle as a universal which by itself is abstract and potential, no more really existent than is minimal being apart from the categories. This mere potentiality begins to actualise in the first subgenera into which the genus is divisible; but actualisation continues until the genus receives its final logical differentiation into infimae species. Genus and differentia are thus the termini of a process of logical actualisation. Together they sum up a group of substantial characters, which form an indissoluble unity, just because they are the stages of a development and are only significant as actualised in the culmination of that development . . . . So Aristotle appears to follow that second line of thought contained in the *Sophist* which led Plato from true dialectic towards division. For though the genus, like minimal being apart from the categories, is abstract and potential, yet the subgenera through which, and the infimae species in which, it actualises, are regarded by Aristotle as sets of co-ordinates, and not as presenting a developing series. The *Scala Universi is* a developing series, but within its lower stages development is apparently superseded by a scheme of co-ordinate groups: "An individual man is no more truly substance than an individual ox" . . . .

In Met. VII, where Aristotle debates with masterly penetration how to meet the claim of substance to be at once universal, intelligible, and definable, and at the same time unique and individual, the singular is at length superseded on the throne of substance by the infima species. That is to say the genus is taken to be fully actualised in its infimae species, and its further differentiation into singulars is treated as irrelevant. Singulars—so runs the thread of Aristotle's thought—are not intelligible, but the infima species *is* intelligible; and is also, in contrast to the genus, individual—it is, in fact, the nearest approximation to a true individual which thought can grasp in the lower stages of the *Scala Universi*. In the light of this change not only the superficial peculiarities but all the accidents inherent in sensible singulars are treated as differences due to the material element which is the principle of their plurality.

If this solution is intended by Aristotle as metaphysical we must regard the *Scala Universi* somewhat as follows. God, the astral intelligences, and efficient reason will not be affected. In them the clash of universal and particular does not arise; for they are individuals, not as units of a plurality actual or possible, but as each utterly unique in its kind, because a pure and not a materiate form. In them essence and existence are one. But in the sphere of sensible substance thought can distinguish as fully real only genera as articulate in systems of co-ordinate infimae species. Plurality and superficial differentiation must be ascribed to an indeterminacy, which is real, but real with a reality not as such intelligible. . . . Between the two, however, there are certain accidents, which inhere necessarily in a genus or a species, characterising in some degree all its singulars. . . . And though the indissoluble unity of substantial characters which constitutes the infima species is that which is primarily real and intelligible in this sphere, yet these accidents too, because they attach necessarily, are permeable to thought. But they inhere dependently in substance, and this dependence is their essence. Their *esse* is *inhaerere*, because this is the essential nature of all that is classified by the accidental categories. They all express capacities of variation, and are marked as belonging to the world of change. They attach only to infimae species, or materiate forms, for in perfect substance no accident inheres, superficial or necessary.

Joseph Owens

The . . . survey undertaken in the . . . present study centered the problem in the relations of the universal and the real, and still more fundamentally in the relation of form to individual thing. The initial passage of Book *A* explained universality as a conception of singular things according to one form. Form seemed to be the reason for universality and to involve the cause that scientific knowledge attained. [Book] *ZH* has shown that the form is the cause of Being and the principle according to which things different in number are one in species. The form should therefore explain Being. It should be the cause sought by the science of Beings according as they are Beings. It should be the basis of universality in that science. Yet the form in itself is not a universal. It is a "this," without being a singular. It is the *actual* expression of the singular composite, and so enters into a *per se* unity with the individual thing. In this way the most fundamental aspect of the problem is solved. The relation of form and individual thing has been made clear. If the English word "individual" may be used to render both senses of a "this," it will allow the solution to be stated in a

SOURCE: Joseph Owens, *The Doctrine of Being in the Aristotelian Metaphysics* (Toronto: Pontifical Institute of Mediaeval Studies, 1963), pp. 398–399. Reprinted with permission of the publishers.

more modern fashion. The Aristotelian form is individual in itself, and is the cause of the individuality in the singular thing of which it is the act. In this two-fold way form and individual coincide. Form and singular thing are respectively the primary and secondary senses of a "this."

After so long and tedious an investigation of the text, the basis for finally solving the problem of Being in the *Metaphysics* seems at last to have been reached. It lies in the doctrine implied by the Aristotelian notion of a "this." The relation of form to individual thing has been determined. The doctrine of a "this" shows that the form is individual and is identified *per se* with the singular thing as its act. But the consequences of this doctrine upon the relations of Being and universality have still to be explored.

Because it is a "this," form cannot be a universal. Yet even in the context of ZH it is associated with universality. It is the reason why singular things are one in species. The same Aristotelian term εἶδος is used for both form and species, and the species is one of the universals. Is this another case of equivocals? Has εἶδος two equivocal meanings, one the individual form, the other the universal species? Are these two senses purely equivocal, or is there some reason for the equivocity? If there is some reason for it, what type of equivocity is present?

In the section of Z in which form was associated with universality, *universal* cognition seemed contrasted with *actual* knowledge. Does this indicate a solution in terms of act and potency? Is εἶδος applied equivocally to form and species according to the type of equivocity that is based on potency and act? The sensible form has seemed to be identified with act. As an act it is a "this," and so is something individual. While *actually* individual, can it be *potentially* universal?

The ensuing study of act and potency should be watched for indications along these lines. The presentation of form as the act of the composite singular seems to have solved the most fundamental problem of form and individual. Will the Aristotelian doctrine of act ultimately confirm this solution, and at the same time show satisfactorily that the individual non-singular form is also the basis of universality? If universal and individual are ultimately identified in terms of potency and act, they should provide the solution to Book A's equation of universal and form, and so point to the final identification of universal and Being.

S. H. Butcher

We are here brought back to Aristotle's theory of poetry as a representation of the universal. Tragedy exemplifies with concentrated power

SOURCE: S. H. Butcher, *Aristotle's Theory of Poetry and Fine Art* (London: Macmillan & Co., 1898), pp. 261–268.

this highest function of the poetic art. The characters it depicts, the actions and fortunes of the persons with whom it acquaints us, possess a typical and universal value. The artistic unity of plot, binding together the several parts of the play in close inward coherence, reveals the law of human destiny, the causes and effects of suffering. The incidents which thrill us are intensified in their effect, when to the shock of surprise is added the discovery that each thing as it has happened could not be otherwise; it stands in organic relation to what has gone before. Pity and fear awakened in connexion with these larger aspects of human suffering, and kept in close alliance with one another, become universalised emotions. What is purely personal and self-regarding drops away. The spectator who is brought face to face with grander sufferings than his own experiences a sympathetic ecstasy, or lifting out of himself. It is precisely in this transport of feeling, which carries a man outside his individual self, that the distinctive tragic pleasure resides. Pity and fear are purged of the impure element which clings to them in life. In the glow of tragic excitement these feelings are so transformed that the net result is a noble emotional satisfaction.

The *katharsis*, viewed as a refining process, may have primarily implied no more to Aristotle than the expulsion of the disturbing element, namely, the pain, which enters into pity and fear when aroused by real objects. The mere fact of such an expulsion would have supplied him with a point of argument against Plato, in addition to the main line of reply above indicated. In the *Philebus* Plato had described the mixed ... or impure ... pleasures as those which have in them an alloy of pain; and the pleasure of tragedy was stated to be of the mixed order. The Aristotelian theory asserts that the emotions on which tragedy works do indeed in real life contain a large admixture of pain, but that by artistic treatment the painful element is expelled or overpowered.

In the foregoing pages, however, we have carried the analysis a step farther, and shown how and why the pain gives way to pleasure. The sting of the pain, the disquiet and unrest, arise from the selfish element which in the world of reality clings to these emotions. The pain is expelled when the taint of egoism is removed. If it is objected that the notion of universalising the emotions and ridding them of an intrusive element that belongs to the sphere of the accidental and individual, is a modern conception, which we have no warrant for attributing to Aristotle, we may reply that if this is not what Aristotle meant, it is at least the natural outcome of his doctrine; to this conclusion his general theory of poetry points.

Let us assume, then, that the tragic *katharsis* involves not only the idea of an emotional relief, but the further idea of the purifying of the emotions so relieved. In accepting this interpretation we do not ascribe to tragedy a direct moral purpose and influence. Tragedy, according to the definition, acts on the feelings, not on the will. It does not make men better, but removes certain hindrances to virtue. The refinement of feeling under temporary and artificial excitement is still far removed from moral improvement. Aristotle would probably admit that indirectly the drama has a moral influence, in enabling the emotional system to throw off some perilous stuff, certain elements of feeling, which, if left to themselves, might develop dangerous energy, and impede the free play of those vital functions on which the exercise of virtue depends. The excitation of noble emotions will probably in time exert an influence on the will. But whatever may be the indirect effect of the repeated operation of the *katharsis*, we may confidently say that Aristotle in his definition of tragedy is thinking, not of any such remote result, but of the immediate end of the art, of the aesthetic function it fulfils.

It is only under certain conditions of art that the homoeopathic cure of pity and fear by similar emotions is possible. Fear cannot be combined with the proper measure of pity, unless the subject matter admits of being universalised. The dramatic action must be so significant, and its meaning capable of such extension, that through it we can discern the higher laws which rule the world. The private life of an individual, tragic as it may be in its inner quality, has never been made the subject of the highest tragedy. Its consequences are not of far-reaching importance; it does not move the imagination with sufficient power. Within the narrow circle of a *bourgeois* existence a great action is hardly capable of being unfolded. The keenest feeling of pity may be elicited by the conditions of such a life; the action may even be represented with much dramatic force: but it is open to question whether it will not of necessity retain some traces of littleness, which hinder the awakening of tragic fear,—still more of that solemnity and awe which is the final feeling left by genuine tragedy. Some quality of greatness in the situation as well as in the characters appears to be all but indispensable, if we are to be raised above the individual suffering, and experience a calming instead of a disquieting feeling at the close. The tragic *katharsis* requires that suffering shall be exhibited in one of its comprehensive aspects; that the deeds and fortunes of the actors shall attach themselves to larger issues, and the spectator himself be lifted above the special case, and brought face to face with universal law and the divine plan of the world.

In order that an emotion may be not only excited but also allayed,— that the tumult of the mind may be resolved into a pleasurable calm,— the emotion, stirred by a fictitious representation, must divest itself of its purely selfish and material elements, and become part of a new order of things. It is perhaps for this reason that love in itself is hardly a tragic motive. The more exclusive and self-absorbed a passion is, the more does it resist *kathartic* treatment. The feelings excited must have their basis in the permanent and objective realities of life, and be independent of individual caprice or sentiment. In the ordinary novel the passion of love in its egoistic and self-centred interest does not admit of being generalised, or its story enlarged into a typical and independent action. The rare cases where a love story is truly tragic go to prove the point which is here enforced. In *Romeo and Juliet* the tragedy does not lie merely in the unhappy ending of a tale of true love. Certain other conditions, beyond those which contribute to give a dramatic interest, are required to produce the tragic effect. There is the feud of the two houses, whose high place in the commonwealth makes their enmity an affair of public concern. The lovers in their new-found rapture act in defiance of all external obligations. The elemental force and depth of their passion bring them into collision with the fabric of the society to which they belong. Their tragic doom quickly closes in upon them. Yet even in death the consequences of their act extend beyond the sphere of the individual. Over the grave of their love the two houses are reconciled.

Tragedy, as it has been here explained, satisfies a universal human need. The fear and pity on and through which it operates are not, as some have maintained, rare and abnormal emotions. All men, as Aristotle says, are susceptible to them, some persons in an overpowering measure. For the modern, as for the ancient world, they are still among the primary instincts; always present, if below the surface, and ready to be called into activity. The Greeks, from temperament, circumstances, and religious beliefs, may have been more sensitive to their influence than we are, and more likely to suffer from them in a morbid form. Greek tragedy, indeed, in its beginnings was but a wild religious excitement, a bacchic ecstasy. This aimless ecstasy was brought under artistic law. It was ennobled by objects worthy of an ideal emotion. The poets found out how the transport of human pity and human fear might, under the excitation of art, be dissolved in joy, and the pain escape in the purified tide of human sympathy.

George Santayana

AVICENNA My benefactor had entitled his profound work *The Wheel of Ignorance and the Lamp of Knowledge*; because, he said, the Philosopher having distinguished four principles in the understanding of nature, the ignorant conceive these principles as if they were the four quadrants of

SOURCE: George Santayana, "The Secret of Aristotle," in *Dialogues in Limbo* (New York: Charles Scribner's Sons, 1948), pp. 229–248. Copyright © 1948 by Daniel M. Cory. Reprinted with permission of the publishers.

a wheel, on any one of which in turn the revolving edifice of nature may be supported; whereas wisdom would rather have likened those principles to the four rays of a lamp suspended in the midst of the universe from the finger of Allah, and turning on its chain now to the right and now to the left; whereby its four rays, which are of divers colours, lend to all things first one hue and then another without confusing or displacing anything. The ignorant, on the contrary, pushing their wheel like the blind Samson, imagine that the four principles (which they call causes) are all equally forces producing change, and co-operative sources of natural things. Thus if a chicken is hatched, they say the efficient cause is the warmth of the brooding hen; yet this heat would not have hatched a chicken from a stone; so that a second condition, which they call the formal cause, must be invoked as well, namely, the nature of an egg; the essence of eggness being precisely a capacity to be hatched when warmed gently—because, as they wisely observe, boiling would drive away all potentiality of hatching. Yet, as they further remark, gentle heat-in-general joined with the essence-of-eggness would produce only hatching-as-such, and not the hatching of a chicken; so that a third influence, which they call the final cause, or the end in view, must operate as well; and this guiding influence is the divine idea of a perfect cock or of a perfect hen, presiding over the hatching, and causing the mere eggness in that egg to assume the likeness of the animals from which it came. Nor, finally, do they find these three influences sufficient to produce here and now this particular chicken, but are compelled to add a fourth, the material cause; namely, a particular yolk and a particular shell and a particular farmyard, on which and in which the other three causes may work, and laboriously hatch an individual chicken, probably lame and ridiculous despite so many sponsors. Thus these learned babblers would put nature together out of words, and would regard the four principles of interpretation as forces mutually supplementary, combining to produce natural things; as if perfection could be one of the sources of imperfection, or as if the form which things happen to have could be one of the causes of their having it.

Far differently do these four principles clarify the world when discretion conceives them as four rays shed by the light of an observing spirit. One ray which, as the lamp revolves, sweeps space in a spiral fan, like the tail of a comet, is able to illuminate the receding past, and bears the name of memory. Memory only can observe change or disclose when and where and under what auspices one thing has been transformed into another, whether in nature or in the spirit's dream; and memory only, if its ray could spread to the depths of the infinite, would reveal the entire efficient principle, the only proper *cause*, in the world; namely, the radical instability in existence by which everything is compelled to produce something else without respite. The other three principles, made visible by the three other rays, have nothing to do with genesis or change, but distinguish various properties of accomplished being; namely, existence, essence, and harmony. The rays by which these are revealed also have separate names. Thus the faculty that discerns existence is called sense, since it is sense that brings instant assurance of material things and of our own actuality in the midst of them. The faculty that discerns essence is called logic or contemplation, which notes and defines the characters found in existence and (in so far as may be opportune or possible) the innumerable characters also which are not found there. The faculty which discerns harmony is called pleasure or desire or (when chastened by experience and made explicit in words) moral philosophy. In themselves things are always harmonious, since they exist together, and always discordant, since they are always lapsing inwardly and destroying one another; but the poignant desire to be and to be happy, which burns in the heart of every living creature, turns these simple co-existences and changes into the travail of creation, in one juxtaposition of things finding life, happiness, and beauty, and in another juxtaposition, no less unstable, finding ugliness, misery, and death. Thus as the Lamp of Knowledge revolves, the red ray of sense and the white ray of contemplation and the blue ray of memory and the green ray of love (for green, as the Prophet teaches, is the colour of the beautiful) slowly sweep the whole heaven; and the wise heart, glowing in silence, is consumed with wonder and joy at the greatness of Allah.

THE STRANGER   Allegory has its charm when we know the facts it symbolizes, but as a guide to unknown facts it is perplexing; and I am rather lost in your beautiful imagery. Am I to understand that matter alone is substantial, and that the other three principles are merely aspects which matter presents when viewed in one light or another?

AVICENNA   Matter? If by that word you understand an essence, the essence of materiality, matter would be something incapable of existing by itself, much less could it be the ground of its own form or of its own impulses or transformations: like pure Being it would be everywhere the same, and could neither contain nor produce any distinctions. But the matter which exists and works is matter formed and unequally distributed, the body of nature in all its variety and motion. So taken, matter is alive, since it has bred every living thing and our own spirit; and the soul which animates this matter is spontaneous there; it is simply the native plasticity by which matter continually changes its forms. This impulse in matter now towards one form and now towards another is what common superstition calls the attraction or power of the ideal. But why did not a different ideal attract this matter, and turn this hen's egg into a duckling, save that here and now matter was predisposed to express the first idea and not the second? And why was either idea powerful over the fresh-laid egg, but powerless over the same egg boiled, except that boiling had modified the arrangement of its matter? Therefore my benefactor boldly concluded that this habit in matter, which is the soul of the world, is the only principle of genesis anywhere and the one true cause.

THE STRANGER   I see: 'Tis love that makes the world go round, and not, as idolatrous people imagine, the object of love. The object of love is passive and perhaps imaginary; it is whatever love happens to choose, prompted by an inner disposition in its organ. You are a believer in automatism, and not in magic.

AVICENNA   Excellent. If the final cause, or the object of love, bears by courtesy the title of the good, believe me when I tell you that the efficient cause, the native impulse in matter, by moving towards that object, bestows that title upon it. Who that has any self-knowledge has not discovered by experience in his own bosom, as well as by observation of the heavens, and of animals and men, that the native impulse in each of us chooses its goal, and changes it as we change, and that nothing is pursued by us or sensible to us save what we have the organ to discern, or the innate compulsion and the fatal will to love?

THE STRANGER   There indeed you touch the heart-strings of nature; and I well conceive your enthusiasm at finding at last a philosophy that vibrates with so much truth. But as for Aristotle, does not such an interpretation entirely reverse his doctrine? Did he not blame his predecessors for having regarded living matter as the only principle of the world?

AVICENNA   And most justly. Wisdom is not confined to the knowledge of origins or of this living body of nature—things important only for the sake of the good or evil which they involve. The forms of things are nobler than their substance, and worthier of study; and the types which discourse or estimation distinguishes in things are more important than the things themselves. A philosopher is a man, and his first and last care should be the ordering of his soul: from that centre only can he survey the world. Naturalists are often betrayed by their understanding of origins into a sort of inhumanity; conscious of necessity, they grow callous to good and evil. Moreover, those early naturalists were at fault in their own science, because they identified matter with some single kind of matter, like water or air, and made that substance the sole principle of genesis; whereas the distribution, movement, habits, and fertility of all sorts of matter must be taken into account if nature and the soul of nature are to be described rightly. But the Philosopher never blamed the naturalists for being naturalists in season, and he was the greatest of naturalists himself. Doubtless in his popular works he accommodated himself to the exigences of current piety and of human conceit, seeming to make nature a product of morals, which is absurd; and the converse is evidently the truth.

THE STRANGER I agree that the converse is the truth; but is this truth to be found in Aristotle?

AVICENNA If it is the truth, it must have been his doctrine. Do you imagine that the wisest of men, living at the place and hour when human reason reached its noon, could be blind to so great a truth, when it is obvious to me and even to you?

THE STRANGER Admirable principle of exegesis, which assigns all truth to Aristotle and absolves us from consulting his works!

AVICENNA On the contrary, for that very reason, we need to consult and to ponder them unceasingly. Why else read a philosopher? To count the places where his pen has slipped? To note his inconsistencies? To haggle over his words and make his name a synonym for his limitations? Even if with some fleck or some crack, he is a mirror reflecting nature and truth, and for their sake only do we look into him; because without this mirror, in the dungeon in which we lie, we might be cut off from all sight of the heavens.

THE STRANGER Was it a slip of the pen or a limitation to assert that the divine life has no material principle? Must we not be wrong, then, in asserting that matter is the one principle of existence?

AVICENNA Not at all. When the plectrum, in the hand of an imperfect player, strikes the strings of the lute, the hard dull blow is sometimes heard, as well as the pure music. In this way the material principle, when not fully vivified and harmonized, can disturb and alloy the spirit, in a life that is not divine. In the mind of God no such material accident intrudes, and all is pure music. But would this music have been purer, or could it have sounded at all, if there had been no plectrum, no player, no strings, and no lute? You have studied the Philosopher to little purpose, if you suppose that it is by accident only that the deity is the final cause of the world, and that without any revolution of the spheres the divine intellect would contemplate itself no less blissfully than it now does. That is but a sickly fancy, utterly divorced from science. The divine intellect is the perfect music which the world makes, the perfect music which it hears. Hermes and Pan and Orpheus drew from reeds or conches, or from their own throats such music as these instruments were competent to make; all other sorts of harmony, musically no less melodious, they suffered to remain engulfed in primeval silence. So the soul of this world draws from its vast body the harmonies it can yield, and no others. For it was not the essence of the sounds which conches and throats and reeds might produce that created these reeds and throats and conches, but contrariwise. These sources of sound, having arisen spontaneously, the sounds they naturally make were chosen out of all other sounds to be the music of that particular Arcadia: even so the divine intellect is the music of this particular world. It contemplates such forms as nature embodies. The Philosopher would never have so much as mentioned a divine intellect—the inevitable note, eternally sustained, emitted by all nature and the rolling heavens—if the rolling heaven and nature had not existed.

THE STRANGER   I admit that such is the heart of his doctrine, and if he was never false to it, he was a much purer naturalist than his disciples have suspected. The eternity he attributed to the world, and its fixed constitution, support this interpretation: nature was the organ of deity, and deity was the spirit of nature. Yet this confirmation creates a difficulty for you in another quarter, since a Moslem must deny the eternity of the world.

AVICENNA   Not if we distinguish, as we should eternity from endless time. The world is eternal, under the form of truth, as the divine intellect apprehends it; but, measured by its own measure of days and years, the world had a beginning and will have an end. So revelation teaches, and it is not by a feigned conformity that I accept this dogma. My own time is over; I have passed into the eternal world; and something within me tells me that universal nature also is growing weary of its cycles, and will expire at last.

THE STRANGER   And when nature is no more, will God have ceased to be?

AVICENNA   Have you read the Philosopher and do you ask such a question? The vulgar imagine that when change ceases, empty time will continue after; or, that before change began empty time had preceded; and it is a marvel to them who one moment of that vacant infinity could have been chosen rather than another for the dawn of creation. All this is but childish fancy and the false speech of poets. Eternity is not empty or tedious, nor does time occupy one part of it, leaving the rest blank. Eternity is but the synthesis of all changes, be they few or many; and truth, can neither arise nor lapse. They are immutable, though the flux they tell of is fugitive, and themselves not anchored in time, though the first and the last syllable of time are graven on them as on a monument.

THE STRANGER   Is eternity the tomb of time, and does intellect resemble those Egyptian monarchs who went to dwell in their sepulchres before they died? Ah, we Christians and artists have a secret hidden from the children of this world, the secret of a happy death. Sometimes life, by a rapturous suicide, likes to embalm itself in a work of art, or in a silent sacrifice. The breathlessness of thought also is a kind of death, the happiest death of all, for spirit is never keener than in the unflickering intellect of God, or in that of a philosopher like you or even like me, who can raise the whole or a part of the flux of nature into the vision of truth.

AVICENNA   Tombs, indeed, and visions, and death, and eternity—why harp on them now, when you are still alive? Leave us while yet you may. We have no need of you here, or you of us there. Soon enough you must join us, whether you will or no. Hasten, before it is too late, to your thriftless brothers in the earth; or if they will not listen, admonish your own heart, and be not deceived by the language which philosophers must needs borrow from the poets, since the poets are the fathers of speech. When they tell you that Allah made the world, and that its life and love are an emanation from him, and that quitting this life you may still live more joyfully elsewhere, they speak in inevitable parables; for in truth it is the pulse of nature that creates the spirit and chooses a few thoughts (among many thoughts unchosen) and a few perfections (among all the perfections unsought) to which it shall aspire; and the special harmony which this vast instrument, the revolving world, makes as it spins is the joy and the life of God. Dishonour not then the transitive virtue within you, be it feeble or great; for it is a portion of that yearning which fills the world with thought and with deity, as with a hum of bees. Love peoples even these regions with us melancholy phantoms; and had my body not moved and worked mightily on earth, you would never have found among the Shades even this wraith of my wisdom.

A STUDY GUIDE

1. In his development of Aristotle's philosophy, how does Chase view the relationship between Plato and Aristotle? If you were Aristotle how would you criticize Plato's philosophy? If you were Plato how would you criticize Aristotle's philosophy?   In general what are the major points of Chase's interpretation of Aristotle? Do you agree?

2. What role does Mure think the categories play in Aristotle's thought? How are they derived?

3. How does Owen's interpret Aristotle's notion of "entity" or "substance"?

4. According to Butcher, what is the nature of the tragic *katharsis* in Aristotelian theory?

5. Although Santayana does not profess to be writing history, how does he view Aristotle's philosophy? Compare his interpretation with Chase's. If you wanted to solve the disagreement, what would be some of the central questions you would have to answer?

A B C D E F G H I J   5 4 3 2 1 7 0 6 9